Visual Evidence and the
Gaza Flotilla Raid

Visual Evidence and the Gaza Flotilla Raid

Extraterritoriality and the Image

Maayan Amir

I.B. TAURIS

LONDON • NEW YORK • OXFORD • NEW DELHI • SYDNEY

I.B. TAURIS
Bloomsbury Publishing Plc
50 Bedford Square, London, WC1B 3DP, UK
1385 Broadway, New York, NY 10018, USA
29 Earlsfort Terrace, Dublin 2, Ireland

BLOOMSBURY, I.B. TAURIS and the I.B. Tauris logo are
trademarks of Bloomsbury Publishing Plc

First published in Great Britain 2022
This paperback edition published 2023

Series design by Adriana Brioso
Cover image © MENAHEM KAHANA/AFP/Getty Images

A catalogue record for this book is available from the British Library.

A catalog record for this book is available from the Library of Congress.

ISBN: HB: 978-0-7556-2727-1
       PB: 978-0-7556-4678-4
       ePDF: 978-0-7556-2728-8
       eBook: 978-0-7556-2729-5

Typeset by Integra Software Services Pvt. Ltd.

To find out more about our authors and books visit www.bloomsbury.com
and sign up for our newsletters.

Contents

Figures

Acknowledgments

The following research was conducted in the framework of a collaborative art project which, together with artist Ruti Sela, we have been pursuing over the past decade. Springing from the wish to offer an image that transcends arbitrary discriminating border regimes, and galvanized by the breadth and currency of extraterritorial practices in shaping contemporary political orders, we set ourselves to study and provoke the concept's interdisciplinary understanding.

As part of the project, we attempted not only to articulate the ways in which violence exercised in the name of law is maintained through a regime of images or a set of restrictions imposed over the representation of such images, but also to confront the political, conceptual, and representational limits that sustain this regime and equip it with legal protection. The paths this research took often branched off from the extraterritorial journey we have embarked upon together. An uncompromising, brilliant artist unrelentingly committed to challenging the shortcomings of dominant political perceptions, Ruti Sela continues to provide inspiration, and I am forever grateful for the opportunity to collaborate with her.

In the course of my research, I conducted a series of interviews with some of the key figures who shaped the Gaza flotilla incident and its legal aftermath, including the flotilla's organizers, those involved in the military operation to stop it, and those concerned with the ensuing legal actions.

For their willingness to be interviewed, I particularly thank former Knesset member Haneen Zoabi, who participated in the flotilla; Gülden Sönmez, a senior executive board member in the IHH *İnsan Hak ve Hürriyetleri ve İnsani Yardım Vakfı* (Turkish Foundation for Human Rights and Freedoms and Humanitarian Relief—the main Turkish organization behind the flotilla), who was a testifying witness and also one of the lawyers representing the victims at the trial held in Istanbul against the former commanders from the Israeli military; retired General Tal Russo, the direct commander of the takeover operation; Colonel (in reserve) Oded Hershkovitz, who commanded the operation on behalf of the IDF Spokesperson's Unit, and S. E. Bourhane Hamidou, President of the Assembly of the African Muslim Republic of the Union of Comoros, the country on whose behalf charges against the Israeli military commanders were brought to the ICC (International Criminal Court).

I would like to express my deep gratitude for the inspirational guidance I received at the Centre for Research Architecture at Goldsmiths University of London, where the bulk of this research was first developed, especially Professor Eyal Weizman, whose work constitutes a prodigious intellectual resource and model for rigorous standards of investigation of both the past and present regarding the spatial-political presentation of events. I wish to offer my great appreciation to Dr. Susan Schuppli, the current director of the Centre at Goldsmiths for her insightful observations and invigorating comments. I am also very grateful to have had the opportunity to conduct parts of this research as a team member in the Forensic Architecture project along with my colleagues at the Centre for Research Architecture at Goldsmiths University of London, and thank them for the stimulating discussions. Tracing the Freedom Flotilla's aftermath impelled me to explore aspects related to the Turkish legal system. I am greatly indebted to the help I received in translation from historian Gennady Kurin in Turkey. For her kindness and further assistance in translation, I am grateful also to Y. Can Gümüş; whereas for the legal proofreading of the related research, I am much obliged to advocates Fatma Arda Bicaz and Yunus Arican as well as to Andrew Ellis for his editing services.

Special thanks go also to my brother Micheal Amir and my friend Tal Yahas for their valuable comments and unflagging encouragement. Moreover, I am indebted to the enormous generosity of Vivian Ostrovsky and the Ostrovsky Family Fund, which helped to finance this research. Bravely supporting experimental projects, the Ostrovky's foundation represents a rare type of philanthropy that is not dictated by mainstream ideas. I also extend heartfelt thanks to Carolina Ben Shemesh for her additional support and close friendship. Last but most certainly not least, my sincere appreciation goes out to all my colleagues at the Exterritory project and to all those who have contributed to the project over the years.

Another special debt of gratitude will remain only virtual. In my private life, the tragedy of the *Marmara* is inseparable from that of my father Ohad Amir, who furiously fought cancer for several years and passed away right after the incident. The *Marmara* raid outcome and the Exterritory project objective were the topics of our last unfinished conversation, and therefore to a degree in this book, I continue this exchange with him, the publication becoming also a living reminder of his painful absence. My gratitude to him here is for impressing upon me the commitment to follow up and try to fill the gaps or at least better understand the mechanisms behind them.

Introduction

This book engages with pivotal examples of extraterritoriality—from Antiquity and into the twenty-first century—in order to broaden the original judicial and geographical definition and thereby include physical and digitized information, and visual data in particular. By focusing on a critical incident of recent Middle Eastern history—namely, the much-debated and polarizing Gaza Freedom Flotilla of 2010—it shows how the device of extraterritoriality not only shapes the political situation in Gaza, the legal status of the maritime environment in which the flotilla incident took place, and the judicial actions taken in response, but also reveals how the concept of extraterritoriality is key to explaining the State's subsequent efforts to confiscate and monopolize all visual evidence of its alleged violations of international statutes.

In the small hours of May 31, 2010, in the extraterritorial waters of the southeastern Mediterranean, large forces of Israeli military commandos were preparing to swoop upon a group of six civilian vessels sailing together under the banner of the "Gaza Freedom Flotilla." Carrying medical supplies and other essential equipment, along with scores of activists from a wide range of countries, the convoy had been organized by the Foundation for Human Rights and Freedoms and Humanitarian Relief (*İnsan Hak ve Hürriyetleri ve İnsani Yardım Vakfı* (IHH)) based in Turkey, in collaboration with the Free Gaza Movement and other non-governmental organizations (NGOs) and activist networks.[1] The organizers' declared aims included bringing humanitarian aid to the people of Gaza who, because of Israel's blockade, were suffering from a severe rationing of food and medical products, and countless other basic necessities. No less important than the physical conveyance of desperately needed supplies, however, was the goal of raising international awareness of the plight of the Gazans, and to protest the violation of their basic human and civil rights, while campaigning for the broader Palestinian cause.[2] It should be noted that the two professed intentions were to some degree at odds with each other, inasmuch as providing aid might be seen as a sign of compromise and quiet diplomacy, whereas as a rule protest and agitation encourages open confrontation and ensures a high media profile.[3] Indeed, once Israel had decided to overrun the flotilla, a clash between the activists and the military was all but inevitable. Few expected, however, that the ensuing skirmish onboard the *Mavi Marmara*, the flotilla's largest vessel, would devolve into a lethal confrontation that would leave ten Turkish activists dead, and many more on both sides wounded, among them nine soldiers from the Israeli forces.

Though the commandos stormed the flotilla boats around 5 a.m. on May 31, the takeover effort had already begun the preceding evening, when the Israeli forces effectively jammed all communication to and from the vessels by implementing electronic warfare. In pursuit of taking control over the information spectrum on the high seas, the operation began with attempts to block their signals by blasting their satellite transmissions, creating a frequency blackout in advance.[4] By this means, the first effective battle between the activists and the Israeli forces was this implementation of technological means to command communications, thereby wrestling for complete control over all the digital evidence, and thwarting one of the principal aims of the flotilla itself, which was to ensure the confrontation was mediated globally.

Indeed, from the outset, the campaign had focused on raising the visibility of the Israeli blockade and the plight of the Gazan population, and so Israel's primary tactic was to forestall it. Despite their furious opposition on political fronts, both sides were equally aware of the critical primacy of visual evidence; each side strove to be first to release material that would incriminate the other via images that would fashion both legal and public opinion. However, while the activists advocated a free flow of information, the Israeli military realized its chance to exploit the unique legal ambiguities offered by this encounter in extraterritorial waters to take absolute control over all the coverage of the offshore exchange.

Eager to make their protest visible, the flotilla organizers had meticulously planned for securing their ability to propagate images throughout the journey, especially at the prospected climax point of documenting the military response. A high-end "first of its kind"[5] infrastructure to allow live broadcasting across the open sea was installed on the most manned vessel, the *Mavi Marmara*, including an alternative classified frequency known only to a few associates. Foreseeing the need to protect information flow in case of attack, this additional channel would provide a hidden backup system. A large pressroom commanded by employees appointed by the organizers was set up to accommodate the many journalists and broadcasters invited onboard.[6] The vessel was duly kitted out with closed-circuit cameras, positioned in advance to monitor strategic areas.[7] Most prominently, the numerous media professionals all brought their own photography gear, and a significant amount of the individual's activists also had video equipment with them, ready to document the event.

While the declared aim of the military was to prevent entry to Gaza without any direct use of force,[8] it was ready and willing to take out the flotilla's surveillance and media appliances should any other scenario occur. To this end, the military executed a large-scale information operation combining complementary forces (navy, air, and special forces) to affect a series of coordinated measures, weaponized in order to gain maximum documentation of the interaction under its total control. For the military, therefore, the decisive element of the battle was to secure its role as the exclusive source of visual evidence, both for release to the media and for possible future demands arising from any legal inquest.

In order to achieve this aim, the army engaged a unit specializing in electronic warfare to block all communication to and from the vessels.[9] Meanwhile, so as to provide comprehensive coverage of the action mid-sea, a broad array of manned and unmanned surveillance cameras were put into operation. Once the boats had been brought to a halt, a second unit of commandos skilled in penetrating prison cells[10] was sent in to search those aboard and confiscate the memory cards from the hundreds of cameras and filming devices, and to seize any image storage equipment onboard the ship.[11] For the first time in Israeli military history, special helicopters were assigned solely to fly this valuable booty out of the media blackout zone and back to shore, where it would be selectively edited by the Spokesperson's Unit for state advocacy.[12] In addition, the navy designated one of its warships for a group of commissioned news reporters to escort the forces, providing them with a pressroom equipped with on-sea editing units to support its communication.[13]

Despite the asymmetrical reciprocity, as soon as the violence erupted, the activists broke through the electronic barricade, and managed to transmit a number of images of the ongoing confrontation in real time, which reached various platforms around the world, thereby scuttling the army's strategy of preempting the media coverage. In many ways, the battle over image control more than merely symbolized the underlying reasons of the confrontation: it actually impacted the course of events, with deadly consequences. Since the flotilla's organizers had planned the event as a live performance of sorts, part of the violence arose through their attempt to defend the communications and transmission gadgetry on board the vessels. The military meanwhile exploited its state-of-the-art assets to thwart the flotilla's attempts to document events as they unfolded, and, to ensure their success, employed brutal means that turned lethal. The bitter irony was that the efforts to stream images live led to death, including that of some of the photographers.[14] Moreover, the measures taken by Israeli troops raiding the *Mavi Marmara* in their effort to locate and seize any footage were in many cases as forceful as their apprehension of the activists themselves. The numbers are astonishing: an estimated 2,600 media storage devices were confiscated that night, with the result that control over the activists' co-authored documentation of the violence onboard passed directly to the Israeli military and government.

This war over the evidence was not limited to image production, however. It also involved their circulation and subsequent interpretation, as the military trimmed several hours of material taken from multiple points of view down to a handful of sporadic sequences which, when made publicly available, ensured a one-sided view of the exchange that confirmed the State's official line. Notably, although the military operation to prevent the boats from crossing through the Gaza blockade spiraled out of control, the meticulously planned operation to take command of all the visual documentation was completed. The event was captured, though its historic visual record has ever since remained out of sight.

The conditions for achieving this appropriation are particularly significant: Israel strategically planned to shift this information war out to the neutral space of extraterritorial waters so that it could enforce its own legal system and thereby seize and control the visual evidence, without the risk of being challenged by a stronger power. The further I delved into the *Mavi Marmara* case, the more I realized that the lab-like conditions in which the event took place provide a broader perspective on extraterritoriality itself, as both category and practice.

The complex logic behind the event's missing visual evidence can be analyzed through the lens of *extraterritoriality*—in this case not only geographical, legal, and political, but also visual. Furthermore, the factor of extraterritoriality remains central to the flotilla event and its aftermath in several distinct ways, some more obvious than others. The flotilla was launched to protest against Israel's forcible extraterritorial control over the Gaza Strip, which it has been tightening since 2007, creating a regional lockdown that poses severe restrictions on the movement of people and goods. Perhaps more obviously, the extraterritorial factor applies to the stretch of sea in which the confrontation between the Israeli military and the activists took place. According to international law, the high seas are beyond the limits of national jurisdiction, and are defined as a shared space of passage.[15] Israel chose to intercept the flotilla in the extraterritorial waters, insisting that such action was necessary in order to defend its blockade of Gaza and thus its own sovereignty, but by doing this, it expanded the ongoing occupation into the open sea.

The extraterritorial logic of the flotilla episode seems to have extended to the legal proceedings and tactics assumed by the flotilla organizers both before and after the Israeli takeover of the boats. In search for justice beyond the limits of territorial laws, the activists artfully deployed an abundance of spatial-legal codes, evidencing how diverse extraterritorial practices have come to offer devices at the service of conflicting ends. The *Mavi Marmara* case illustrates the nexus of diverse extraterritorial effects that come into play, such as Israel's isolation of Gaza, the vulnerability of a floating media effort and its destroyed satellite connection, and the lack of judicial resolution for international crimes, to name only a few. In what follows, I will examine the unseen affinities of the different effects and provide insights on the underlying visual apparatus.

Taking extraterritoriality as an umbrella concept defining a flexible phenomenon applied variously down through history, we can see it has been implemented both legally and illegally as a form of logistical "trapdoor," an escape route for any number of international arrangements over time. Arising from the point or seam of contact between separate legal systems or technologies of governance, and from the convergence of permitted spaces of circulation, extraterritoriality as a practice denotes certain elusive statuses of representation. At its core a relational category, extraterritoriality pivots on how we determine where points meet and margins chafe or overlap, and hence where legal responsibilities lie. By presenting the practice of extraterritoriality in diverse and even contradictory instances—not only historically and philosophically, but also within the present case study—I show how its spectrum ranges from a unilateral act of appropriation to a mode of full cooperation between sovereignties and nations, and as such it offers a method of navigating spheres of legal representation, while providing a useful lens through which to calibrate how disparate jurisdictions may interweave or conflict.[16]

This exploration of the extraterritorial logic of representation will cover the spectrum of implementations from loose abstraction to its most concrete utilizations. This feat involves shuttling between the legalities of geographical entities, whereby laws are employed to protect the most powerful, but appear side by side, and sometimes even overlap, with claims to deploy laws that safeguard the most vulnerable. Here we encounter regulations devised in the national interest that even claim to advance the cause of human rights, whereby legal codes at the service of war share mutual (extraterritorial) ground with those tailored for peace. Although discussions of extraterritoriality have involved a fairly wide range of fields, the interdisciplinary applications remain largely underexplored. My analysis will draw on several disciplines to examine a variety of phenomenons that correspond to some of its more conventional legal-geographical definitions, and reveal how extraterritoriality abets and in certain cases even endorses legal loopholes in the system, with significant consequences.

Central to the issue under discussion here is the capacity of extraterritoriality to usurp the accountability of a given local/geographical/territorial entity and subject it to outside laws, effecting a sort of include out clause that is traditionally brought to bear on people and spaces physically comprised within a certain territory. In such cases, the said element is alienated from the custody of its embedded system of laws, and placed under the auspices of a different legal authority that operates by being present while enjoying a form of legal exemption. Through the lens of the missing visual evidence characterizing the *Mavi Marmara* incident after-effects, extraterritoriality offers a tool for explaining how images are legally excluded from the public sphere and even judicial investigation—visual evidence that might challenge the legitimacy of the legal system itself, especially when involving a conflict between competing legal systems, be they domestic or international.

My line of reasoning is fairly straightforward: just as the role of extraterritoriality involves the mechanisms regulating the circulation of people and commodities beyond borders, whereby they transition to a different legal system, so is extraterritoriality key to explaining certain aspects of how visual evidence concerning sensitive international affairs is regulated and placed beyond visibility. The faculty by which extraterritoriality effectively bypasses regular legal responsibilities in favor of extraneous legal codes sheds light on the practice of rendering certain evidence out of reach. In the case discussed here, despite the event in question unfolding outside of its sovereign jurisdiction, the State of Israel employed its own national laws to impound the visual evidence and prohibit its circulation by storing it out of reach in the State's archives, precluding any inquiry by those it involves and impacts. In this way, extraterritoriality has produced not only a legal void but also a visual one. Put simply, the evidence itself is now trapped in an extraterritorial limbo.

By this means, the lethal attack that took place in international waters has undergone the further violence of being "disappeared" by the State, and whatever visual material remains publicly available is largely propaganda, demonstrating how extraterritoriality can also generate a legal-visual culture of its own inasmuch as the offshore images produced here are denied their testimonial value. Removed thus from public view and, most importantly, from the scrutiny of the court as a means of preempting a proper inquest into the event, the sequestered images are open to speculation and even misrepresentation.

Nevertheless, the flotilla has been the subject of various national and international judicial inquiries. In Israel, the conclusions were detailed in the Eiland Report,[17] the Turkel Commission Report,[18] and the Israel State Comptroller's Report.[19] The State also opened investigations against Israeli citizens who were onboard the *Marmara*, notably the then-member of the Israeli parliament, Haneen Zoabi and Sheikh Raed Salah; however, these were eventually closed due to "evidential and legal difficulties."[20] An unprecedented indictment was reported in Israel when in 2014, one of the commandos injured on board the *Marmara* pressed charges against the Israeli military, claiming it was negligence on the part of the Israeli Defense Forces (IDF) that enabled his photos from the ship to be distributed abroad.[21] Internationally, the United Nations Human Rights Council (UNHRC) launched a fact-finding mission,[22] and the UN Secretary-General commissioned a Panel of Inquiry (headed by Sir Geoffrey Palmer).[23] The International Bureau of Humanitarian NGOs and the Friends of Charities Association conducted their own investigation.[24] In addition, following a request submitted in May 2013 by the Istanbul-based law firm Elmadag on behalf of the African archipelago Union of Comoros (whose flag the ship was flying), the International Criminal Court (ICC) conducted a preliminary examination of the incident "in order to establish whether the criteria for opening an investigation are met."[25] On November 6, 2014, the ICC prosecutor announced it concluded the procedure "since the legal requirements under the Rome Statute have not been met."[26] After a pre-trial request submitted on November 15, 2018, it reinstated the decision not to proceed with pressing charges, and published its detailed conclusions on December 2, 2019.[27] An investigation was also carried out by the US Congress.[28]

In Turkey, investigations were pursued not only at the governmental level (e.g., the Turkish National Inquiry Committee), but also in response to pleas initiated by plaintiffs in local courts. For example, a civil trial to obtain compensation for the Turkish victims was held in city of Kayseri in central Turkey.[29] Most prominently, criminal charges were pressed against the four senior Israeli officers allegedly in command of the interception. The latter were tried *in absentia* at İstanbul's Seventh Aggravated Criminal Court for over a quarter of a decade before the proceedings' cancelation (by many considered arbitrary), when the Turkish government made an agreement with the State of Israel to order all charges dismissed (2012–16). In fact, the judicial procedure was supplanted by an ex-gratia compensation from Israel in exchange for a new

Turkish amnesty law, retroactively exempting the Israeli commandos from any future allegations over crimes that took place in extraterritorial waters, as well as preempting other possible civil lawsuits against individual Israeli soldiers who participated in the raid.[30] Court proceedings were also reportedly launched in the Republic of South Africa, Spain, Belgium, Sweden, and the UK, to mention only a few.[31]

Removed from national and international public scrutiny, all these investigations—except the ones conducted by the State of Israel—have taken place in the absence of the extant visual documentation of the event, and in particular of the lethal attack. Consequently, despite the presence of many eyewitnesses, what actually unfolded onboard the *Mavi Marmara* that night remains prone to conflicting accounts, and many on both sides believe that, regardless of the mass of investigations, not one had reached an appropriate judicial outcome. Since then, the flotilla has garnered extensive attention in the international media, becoming the subject of books, essays, movies, YouTube clips, exhibitions, and even a theatrical play.[32] Last but not least, to compensate for the lack of available visuals, the authors of some of these reports created various reenactments of what purportedly happened, including an alternative computer-graphic illustration prepared by the military itself.[33]

My purpose here is not to offer yet another reconstruction of the events based on the available evidence. Instead, I will examine the ways in which the fallout from the deadly assault has been shaped and impacted by the very absence of visual evidence that is known to exist but is being withheld, with the emphasis on extraterritoriality's fundamental role in fashioning our current legal and political orders. In **Chapter 1: Extraterritoriality: A Historical and Conceptual Overview**, I provide a brief survey of legal formulas historically recognized as "extraterritorial," beginning with an overview of the concept's history starting from the "pre-territorial" era, that is, before the world was carved up almost entirely into sovereign territorial jurisdictions.[34] The review does not attempt to be comprehensive; instead it evaluates several key instances of the two predominant categories of extraterritoriality in the pre-modern, pre-territorial age: (1) as a *personal legal status* applicable to persons or individuals within a juridical system; and (2) as *the assignment of separate geographical locations within which people are allocated with such status.* Early instances of such extraterritorial practices can be traced back to ancient Egypt, Greece, and imperial Rome, only to reemerge in the form of Ottoman "capitulations." Subsequently, I discuss modern colonial implementations of the phenomenon.

The chapter concludes with particular emphasis on contemporary perceptions and precedents of its application, addressing the current tendency of critical thought to analyze extraterritoriality mostly in relation to the work of Italian philosopher Giorgio Agamben, especially his critique of sovereign power's ability to suspend the law as manifested in the "state of exception," the internment camp, and the figure of the refugee. I argue that this framework is limited, owing to its focus on a model of suspension of laws dominated by a single sovereign: a model that is adequate in capturing certain contemporary manifestations of extraterritorialities, but not others. I then examine the complexities of this approach, which risks obscuring certain features that are unique to extraterritoriality. Inasmuch as extraterritoriality is often the result of the encounter between legal systems and different politics that enables their co-existence while producing complex regimes of representation, it can be understood only partially through Agamben's "state of exception," which he conceptualizes within Western politics and which emerges as a zone in which "violence without any juridical form acts."[35] In fact, in his analysis of Jerusalem and the Israeli–Palestinian conflict, Agamben's own discussion indicates that he himself made a distinction between these two phenomena: extraterritoriality and the "state of exception."[36]

Chapter 2: Extraterritorial Impasses: Background to the Gaza Freedom Flotilla begins with an introduction to the Israeli–Palestinian conflict from the perspective of the extraterritorial phenomenon that generates it, highlighting its presence in the very foundations of its designated legal geography. Although the flotilla incident marks a unique case of contemporary activists' resistance to the Israeli occupation, it is historic that the tenor of Israel's hold over Palestine has been increasingly gravitating toward extraterritorial activities. The struggle over territory is perceived predominantly in terms of land (holy, promised, sacred, not to mention the seizure of estate and/or revocation of rightful property deeds, etc.), however—and no less drastically—national boundaries and frontiers have meanwhile been shaped and consolidated through diverse exercises of extraterritoriality and forcible appropriation. At its root, the Israeli–Palestinian conflict sprawls chaotically over unrecognized borders and unacknowledged sovereignties. Using extraterritoriality as my compass to review a ruinous century-long history, I pinpoint some of the more recognizable landmarks of the extraterritorial processes under way.

On the ground, the fight over the exclusive claim of land gave rise to a variety of extraterritorial arenas, even within the separate communities. Furthermore, the limits of these manifestations of extraterritoriality were not pre-set but deftly fabricated, tailored, and adjusted according to the shifting political needs. I then narrow the lens of observation to focus on Gaza. Previously occupied for nearly two decades by its neighbor Egypt, the Gaza coastal strip was subsequently conquered in the June 1967 War by Israel, which imposed its own military rule in the area. In 2005, Israeli forces withdrew from Gaza and the various Israeli settlements were evacuated. In the democratic legislative elections held in Gaza the following year, Hamas rose to power, replacing the secular Fatah. In real terms, however, Gaza continues to remain under Israeli control: with the collusion of Egypt, Israel holds control over all the land, naval and aerial pathways to and from Gaza. Invoking security concerns, in 2007, Israel tightened its stranglehold by imposing a harsh closure on the Gaza Strip that severely limits the transit of goods in and out of the region.

Since then, territorial restrictions have continued to intensify. In 2007, the Israeli authorities declared Gaza a "hostile zone," the following year a "combat zone," and during Operation Cast Lead in 2009, it became a "military enclosure" and "exclusion zone." In this way, Gaza has come to be defined by a series of Israeli actions and proclamations devised to isolate it from its immediate geographical environment, as well as from the other Palestinian territories in the West Bank.[37] This chapter introduces the evaluation of these processes, and is particularly attuned to the diverse legal language employed to describe it—"embargo," "siege," "blockade"[38]—with each of these territorial practices being perceived differently by Israel and by the activists. We also find that the extension of the territorial conflict into extraterritorial waters produced both the violent confrontation, and its convoluted judicial-legal aftermath.

Chapter 3: Extraterritorial Images in Action: The Gaza Freedom Flotilla calls attention to a central feature of the military interception of the Gaza Freedom Flotilla, namely the Israeli military's seizure of all visual documentation of the event. I reconstruct the complex logic of the event from the hundreds of testimonies provided in various legal reports and elsewhere, and contend that the battle over the visual material was not only virtual, but actually shaped the deadly encounter. Despite the intentionally large presence of camera equipment to ensure maximum coverage, accessible video evidence of the confrontation remains limited to less than five minutes, all of which has been carefully edited to serve Israel's propaganda purposes.[39] Owing to the paucity of media released to the public, the void has been filled with interpretations and speculation, leaving the door wide open for misinformation. Despite this, the few publicly available images have served both as visual evidence in official inquiries, and as the basis for rival attempts to expose the truth.

I then move to unravel the emerging extraterritorial geography of vision generated by the State's suppression of vital visual evidence. One of the notable features of this archive of material, however, is that it is *co-authored*, inasmuch as it involved the military on one side acting in the name of the law, and the activists on the other who staged a spectacle to challenge the authority, only to see their efforts rescripted according to terms defined by the very authority they intended to expose. The upshot is a digital archive of conflict co-authored by both sides, but which remains entirely in the hands of the forces of aggression. Having the knife by the handle, so to speak, it is precisely from amongst the critical footage that might reveal possible violations of human rights that the State hand-picks what to show and caption with its own interpretation, suppressing the rest in the name of national security. The upshot is a confluence of physical embargo on Gaza and visual embargo on critical coverage of the event.

Chapter 4: The *Mavi Marmara* Trial: From Absent Images to Absent Defendants reveals a further stage in the logic of extraterritorial representation, by which the court case brought against the four senior Israeli commanders was held before İstanbul's Seventh Aggravated Criminal Court in Turkey, without the presence of the defendants.[40] Before the trial had even commenced, it was announced that, contrary to usual juridical procedures in Turkey, the proceedings would be videotaped but not broadcast.[41] The Turkish court has reserved exclusive filming and distribution rights, refusing to release the footage publicly. It becomes clear how the logic of absence and representation that characterized the visual documentation of the flotilla incident escalates to include both the absentee defendants and the inaccessible court footage. Notably, from the very onset of the trial, the missing visual documentation actively framed the legal proceedings. First, the absence of the confiscated visual footage was cited by the plaintiffs' lawyers as the reason for swiftly initiating the trial *in absentia*, claiming that the trial would occasion the production of new media in the form of eye-witness accounts—material that would then "substitute" the inaccessible footage.

The absence of the defendants was mirrored by the absence of the images, invoking them as images *in absentia*. The trial sessions would entail filmed oral testimony: an audio-visually documented verbal description of the original visuals. However, the relentless logic of concealment escalated still further, and all the new material thus created was yet again excluded from the public sphere. Having personally attended the trial, it occurred to me that the court cameras were in a sense documenting the divide between the court's actual conduct and the new EU judicial regulations, given that the cameras used in court were installed with EU funding as part of Turkey's long process of accession to the European Union, and were supposed to monitor the court's proceedings.[42] As part of its ongoing bid for membership, Turkey is officially committed to effect a string of legal reforms, yet the court's performance made it clear that in practice, the Turkish system has by no means assimilated the European standards.

Chapter 5: Images as Court Evidence provides a historical survey of the omission and exemption of images as legal evidence mostly in the context of Western common law systems. From the invention of the camera in the early decades of the nineteenth century, courts and legislators debated the reliability of photographic images' testimonial value, and consequently their status as evidentiary tools. Initially conceptualized as mere "evidentiary aid" or "demonstrative evidence," a form of illustration on a par with drawings and diagrams, the section appraises the technological development process that eventually gained images the legal status of "self-authenticating."[43] The chapter also outlines some of the history of courts as the producers, creators, and archivists of audio-visual criminal records. I suggest that the genre of court-made recordings of trials was motivated from the onset by the desire to create images of fair trials—to validate and legitimate the court's actions in juridically controversial or sensitive cases. There follows a survey of the production of court records, from the pre-electronic era to the introduction of film cameras into the courtroom, showing how such recordings were given the legal status of official court records in order to certify the court's conduct. I also raise questions about the authorship and ownership of such records. Examples discussed include some of the most visible international trials in which images have played a significant part. Different cases from different times and places are presented, each with its own diverse circumstances, scale, and nature of crimes. They are similar, however, in the kind of hierarchy that is likely to have shaped and regulated their regime of image production and circulation and thus reflects a characteristic of their ethics of representation. By this I mean that while these tribunals claimed adherence to standards of fairness and universal justice, their role as the exclusive creators and distributors of court records left ample margin for the prioritizing of national interests over universal impartiality.

In the **Epilogue**, I close with a glimpse into an unprecedented civil lawsuit against the Israeli army filed by the commando who was first to rappel down from the helicopter to board the *Marmara*. The indictment was the military's visual negligence, and its failure to protect his image from exposure, resulting from the ineffectiveness of the military's electronic screening in the early stages of the operation.[44]

The military mastery of visual evidence, the ability of combatants to operate with confidence that visual evidence will be kept under army control, is perceived by the fighter as no less than a binding legal contract requiring formal and public acknowledgment in the civic judicial sphere. For future applications of this model, we shift to another focal point the classification of the visual documentation of the American-led execution of Osama bin Laden, who was reportedly assassinated along with some of his family members and two other individuals, in Abbottabad, Pakistan, on May 1, 2011, in response to his involvement in the September 11 attacks on the United States.[45] This case study was chosen to demonstrate a potential implication in which the authorities are withholding visual evidence from the judicial system, while selectively diverging partial evidence asserting the creation of a preferred image through cinematic fiction.

Before moving forward, I would like to briefly reflect on the moment that instigated this research endeavor. In 2009, together with artist Ruti Sela, I conceived the art project "Exterritory" as a response to the enduring Israeli-Palestinian conflict. We aspired to create an image of art exhibited in a neutral space beholden to no national constraints of any kind. We decided to project a compilation of video works by Middle Eastern artists onto the sails of boats navigating in the extraterritorial waters of the Mediterranean. Originally, the naval limits of sovereign territories were demarcated in order to establish trade relations between nations. The extent of a given state's territorial waters was at first defined by the range covered by a cannon shot fired from the state's territory out to sea. In the ensuing centuries, the range of territorial waters was altered according to different strategic circumstances, and mainly stands today at twelve nautical miles from the shoreline.[46] For us, the extraterritorial waters—those lying outside the established range—represented a free domain out of reach of oppressive national regimes. Wishing to bring together artists and thinkers from various conflict areas around the world where such gatherings are forbidden, we organized an encounter in the extraterritorial waters. We launched an appeal for people from diverse disciplines to offer their interpretation of the concept of extraterritoriality, and to project their artwork onto the sails of the participating boats. Our project set out with the goal of freeing images from the control of national sovereignty, and exploring the potential of extraterritorial maritime space to achieve this aim.

After long months of intense research and production, a few days before our planned departure date to assemble in extraterritorial waters, the Israeli military intercepted the Gaza Freedom Flotilla. That tragic incident glaringly revealed how the armed forces of a state can use that very same space—an un-regulated and therefore relatively unprotected space—to expand its sovereign power, which in this case included gaining absolute control over the production and distribution of visual documentation of any kind. The unforeseen concurrence of the two flotillas in time and space, both politically motivated, with image production at their center, and marked by the crucial role of extraterritoriality, urged me to look further into the complex politics of extraterritoriality.

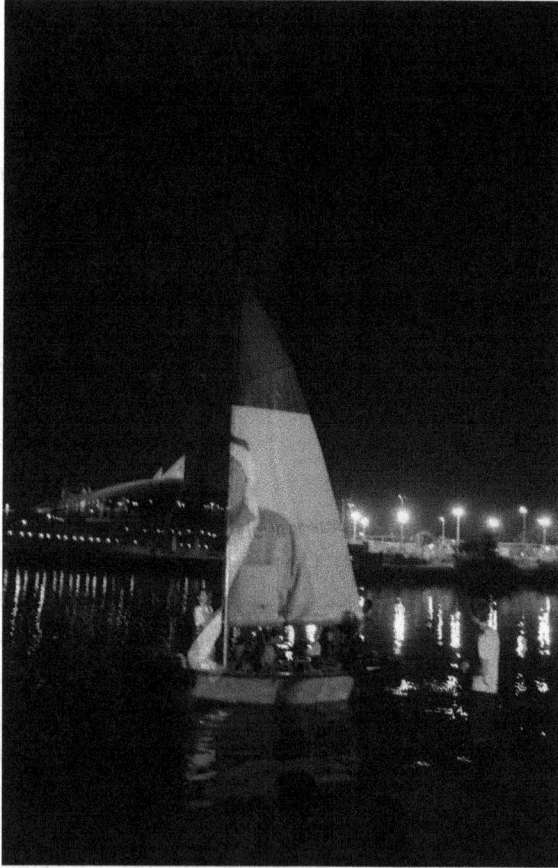

Figure 1 Ruti Sela and Maayan Amir, Exterritory Project, 2010.

1

Extraterritoriality: A Historical and Conceptual Overview

As with all legal and political concepts, the concept of extraterritoriality has carried different meanings according to each historical context, and is applied in myriad ways. Etymologically, the term "extraterritoriality" derives from the Latin *extra territorium*—meaning literally, "outside the territory." An examination of the different definitions of extraterritoriality, both historical and contemporary, not only reveals a complex dynamic between the term's various early meanings ("being outside of one's territory," "having no territory," etc.), but also shows how new extraterritorial phenomena helped redefine these terms over time, imbuing them with new meanings.[1]

In ancient Rome, the term was used to designate officials acting beyond their proper jurisdiction, as in the legal dictum *Extra territorium jus dicenti impune non paretur* (one who administers justice outside his territory is not obeyed with impunity).[2] According to early twentieth-century scholarship, the practice's origins may lie even further back in time, in Antiquity. However, in that era, non-community members were not fully subjected to the laws of the state in which they lived, and furthermore, absolute territorial sovereignty was not yet endorsed. At that time, extraterritoriality functioned as a form of legal tolerance—a way to resolve conflicts between different juridical systems.[3] Practices of extraterritoriality enabled foreigners to be exempt from local laws (to some degree, at least) and to retain their allegiance to the legislation of their place of origin. Such arrangements were crucial for ancient communities, which needed to establish stable relationships with their surroundings; they were probably encouraged by trade, conquests, and migrations, which helped decrease fear of foreigners and curbed practices of strict in-group exclusivity.[4]

Early practices of extraterritoriality can be divided into two categories. The first consisted simply in the ascription to foreigners of a distinct legal status, whereas, in addition to such ascription, the second involved the allocation of special physical spaces to such people. Examples of the first type include the *proxenoi* in ancient Greece (citizens of one state were appointed to serve the interests of another, and in return were awarded various honors and privileges—an early prototype of the modern consul),[5] and the Roman magistrates known as *praetor peregrinus* who applied the *Jus Genitum* (Law of the Nations) to decide legal cases between non-Roman foreigners.[6] In addition to the allocation of a special legal status to foreigners, extraterritorial practices of the second type included the designation of specific districts for them to inhabit. Scholar and later-official in the Chinese government, Shih-Shun Liu, and other academics have shown that "[u]nder the reign of King Proteus of Egypt in the thirteenth century BCE, Phoenician merchants from the city of Tyre were allowed to dwell around a special precinct in Memphis known as the 'camp of the Tyrians' and to have a temple for their own worship."[7] In other cases, foreigners remained subject to their own laws or were placed under special jurisdiction, as in the case of Jews and other tribes who were allowed to settle in Goshen under the eighteenth Egyptian dynasty (1580–1350 BCE).[8]

According to some, these early models of extraterritoriality existed in a pre-Westphalian world that was not carved up into sovereign territories, each under the exclusive authority of a sovereign political power and a unified system of laws.[9] According to this view, extraterritoriality developed as the rejection of the uniformity of law: as a system of governance that resisted territorially based laws.[10] It seems, however, that at least in some cases, extraterritorial practices did develop within a territorial legal-political system in which defined geographical regions were under exclusive sovereign control. In such cases, extraterritoriality was not a matter of certain *geographical regions* exempted from law, but of specific *ethnic groups* enjoying special legal status.

Extraterritorial practices of both types seem to have developed in different times and places. In his early study of the history of extraterritoriality published in 1969, Liu claimed that extraterritoriality, while traceable "to the absence of absolute territorial sovereignty" in Antiquity, was also rooted in the "tradition of the personality of laws."[11] The latter tradition was that of the personal jurisdiction system of medieval Europe—the system in which the law sought the person and not the territory.[12] Under this system, foreign subjects were governed by the laws of their place of origin, not by those of their place of residence.[13]

The literature discusses many other historical instances of extraterritoriality. Liu notes that in the times of Theodosius the Great (379–395) and Honorius (395–423), special magistrates, later known as Judge Consuls, were appointed to decide in cases of accidents at sea. According to Liu, the practice further evolved between the tenth and thirteenth centuries, when special courts were authorized to judge in commercial disputes with foreigner merchants.[14]

Similar practices developed later in the Levant, where extraterritorial control took the form of the so-called capitulations[15]—different sets of privileges and immunities given to Christians by Muslim rulers. (As was pointed out, the word "capitulations" is a translation of *sulh*—Arabic for truce, a condition in which an outsider or an enemy is allowed a degree of autonomy.)[16] Some scholars trace the regime of capitulations back to the Caliph Omar Ibn-Khattab, who in the year 636 CE granted special legal status to Christian churches in Syria.[17] In a letter from Christians to the caliph, a legal document now known as the "Pact of Umar," certain requirements from non-Muslims living under the rule of Islam appear, in exchange for their protection.[18] The contract safeguarded the rights of "People of the Book," the majority of whom are Jews, Christians, and Zoroastrians, who agree to pay a special *jizya* tax and acknowledge "the domination of Islam," exempting them from military service, while ensuring their protection.[19] These capitulations were also granted to Christians living in Egypt: in a letter sent to Pisa in 1154, an Egyptian official guaranteed to Pisans residing in Egypt legal and administrative autonomy on the condition that they live in special quarters in the cities.[20] Other Italian republics whose citizens enjoyed extraterritorial privileges in Egypt at that time were Venice, Genoa, and Florence, and similar arrangements were instated in later centuries throughout the Ottoman Empire.[21]

Certain degrees of exemption of non-Muslims from Sharia laws were also found in the East, for instance, during the reign of Jalaluddin Muhammad Akbar, the third emperor (r. 1556–1605) in India under the Mughal Empire.[22] For example, while some legal disputes such as marriage or social status were to be resolved on the local level, others could have been referred to the Sharia court. In her study of Mughal law, historian Nandini Chatterjee identifies a complex inclusive legal dynamic that could have had a role in the transformation of Shari'a into "Mohammedan Law"—or personal status legislation for Muslims in British-ruled India.[23]

More recently, scholars have taken a far more critical view of extraterritorial arrangements, especially those of the nineteenth century, which are viewed as related to Western colonialist and imperialist expansion.[24] In many cases, extraterritorial practices were an instrument of legal inequality, allowing Westerners to abuse their exemption from local laws, either for personal gain or in the service of their respective national interests.[25] Thus, for example, in her account of capitulations in the Ottoman Empire, Eliana Augusti writes:

Facing the raising of territorial sovereignty, the old principle of personality seemed to transmit in a principle of extraterritoriality ... first, foreigners enjoyed extraterritoriality in the sense that even if they were on the Ottoman territory, they were by *fictio* out of it, i.e., *extra territorium*; second, they were considered as in their country, even if in fact they were not.[26]

As a form of simultaneous representation and non-representation, extraterritoriality was an instrument of Western superiority and privilege. In theory, extraterritorial arrangements ostensibly promoted a rational regime of international law—a "regulative ideal of an inclusive political pluralism of the international society"[27]; in practice, however, these measures endorsed a hierarchical order, which privileged Western interests. Such unequal legal arrangements were often justified by designating the localities in which they were instituted as "uncivilized": Western imperial powers "legitimiz[ed] special agreements on jurisdiction in countries where institutions were 'inferior' or 'different' from the civilization of most European and American States."[28]

While some aspects of the capitulatory regime were subsequently replaced with the passport regime in early twentieth century,[29] other capitulatory manifestation prominent nineteenth- and twentieth-century extraterritorial arrangements for Westerners have been criticized as imperialist devices not only in the Ottoman Empire but also in China, Japan, and Siam, to name some famous examples. Under binding agreements, Westerners were exempted from the workings of the local justice systems, and special extraterritorial courts for foreigners were set up to circumvent local law and sovereignty.[30] According to Turan Kayaoğlu, extraterritorial courts were used to extend Western authority in non-Western countries, overriding the authority of the indigenous legal systems and turning these countries into semi-colonies.[31] Extraterritoriality functioned, then, as a form of Western privilege in non-Western regions. In Kayaoğlu's view, extraterritoriality in these countries thus served as a way to consolidate territorial (in this case legal) norms. In support of this view, Kayaoğlu points out that it was only *after* territorial norms were consolidated that extraterritorial privileges were abolished.[32] Some scholars believe, however, that the various models of extraterritoriality deployed during the era of Western imperialism cannot be reduced to simple power relations. In their view, extraterritoriality had a more benign role, and to varying degrees even contributed positively to the development of the societies in which it was exercised.[33]

As already noted, colonial extraterritoriality—for example in China—took the form not only of privileges accorded to foreigners but also of spatial divisions. "Exterritorial enclaves"[34] under the control of foreigners could be as small as a neighborhood or district within a city, or encompass an entire municipal region. Shanghai, for example, was designated as a place where "foreigners or natives shall be exempt from the interference of the Chinese Government."[35] Other extraterritorial regions include the so-called concessions, namely *de jure* colonies situated outside the jurisdiction and effective control of the Chinese government, in which complete political and administrative authority was given to foreign governments (e.g., in Shanghai, Tientsin, and Canton).[36]

Interestingly, it was in the aftermath of the Second World War, as Anglo-American extraterritoriality in China was being abolished,[37] that a discourse of extraterritorial human rights began to develop as a response to wartime atrocities. This new discourse found expression in the European Convention on Human Rights, ratified in 1953.[38] Since then, human rights have become an integral part of international law. Unlike the system of reciprocal rights and liabilities between states, the human rights regime prescribes unilateral obligations of the state toward individuals.[39] The principle of human rights aims to protect individuals from the package of territorial state laws that display a potential to betray even their own citizens. Alternatively, the need to draw up legislative measures that would ensure the safeguard of humanity at large—regardless of territorial affiliation—prompted a universal perception of law, and called for adherence to extraterritorial norms of justice, consequently giving rise to the idea of international human rights and international criminal law that prevails today, albeit always evolving.[40] It should be noted that despite its universal claim, international law itself originated in Europe, specifically by states involved in overseas colonization. Legal scholar Noura Erakat notes that "[t]hese sordid origins continue to characterize international law. It has never been rewritten by an international community of the present. Instead, former colonial powers, newly independent states, and also movements and peoples have incrementally developed international law based on its first articulation."[41]

International law itself distinguishes between two types of extraterritoriality whereby a given state is obliged to respect its duties under global human rights treaties: (1) "control over foreign territory as a result of occupation or otherwise," in which the occupier is required to guarantee human rights in the occupied territory; and (2) "control over persons [in which] individuals may be brought within the 'jurisdiction' of a state as a consequence of a … link between the individual and the state whose acts produce effects outside its territory."[42] Situations of the first type include, for example, the Israeli-Palestinian conflict.[43] Situations of the second type involve such diverse issues as the "war on terror"; legal black holes; drone warfare and targeted killings in Pakistan, Afghanistan, and Yemen under the post-9/11 American administration; and the status of refugees. These manifestations of extraterritoriality give rise to a variety of legal and ethical problems, especially in light of the eagerness of many governments to resort to extraterritorial measures in order to increase their power or deploy "strategies of 'extraterritorialisation'" to circumvent human rights obligations.[44] Scholars from various disciplines have tried to conceptualize and discuss critically the ethical implications of such measures.

In the latter half of the twentieth century, as the Westphalian system of territorial sovereignty became universal, the entire globe became "a fully occupied world": a world almost entirely divided into the sovereign territories of nation-states.[45] Various forms of extraterritoriality nevertheless survived; some were readapted from earlier forms while others were newly constituted. Together, forms of territoriality and extraterritoriality shape the current spatial-legal landscape worldwide, sometimes complementing each other, at other times conflicting and contradicting each other. According to contemporary writers, extraterritoriality not only continues to co-exist alongside territorial sovereignty as yet another spatial-juridical order; it is also deeply involved in preserving and shaping national borders. At the same time, extraterritoriality poses a challenge to the system of territorial sovereignty as a sole principle of the political ordering of spaces and subjects. In some cases, it is applied as a device for enhancing territoriality; in others, it is a way of keeping certain forms of personal jurisdiction alive. Furthermore, extraterritoriality can also be used to rethink current political concepts.

Contemporary thinking about extraterritoriality owes much to the writings of Giorgio Agamben, especially his critique of sovereign power and its manifestations in the "state of exception," the camp, and the figure of the refugee. All these, Agamben claims, are core features of the modern political order. Several contemporary scholars have also begun to discuss them in relation to the concept of extraterritoriality.[46]

Agamben's notion of the "state of exception" hinges on jurist and philosopher Carl Schmitt's concept of the "state of emergency."[47] According to Schmitt, sovereign power is to be understood as the right to claim special powers in times of "emergency" and suspend the law; in Schmitt's words, the sovereign is "he who decides on exceptions."[48] This power, he adds, is the ultimate foundation of modern political power. For Agamben, this same power defines the limits of politics. To this Agamben adds cultural theorist, Walter Benjamin's claim that the state of emergency is no longer an exception, but the rule. In doing so, Agamben seems to heed Benjamin's call for an effective critique of "legal violence"—the kind of violence that simultaneously "makes" (or "posits") and "preserves" the law.[49] At the same time, Agamben challenges Benjamin's notion of "pure violence"—violence for its own sake, or violence as a means without an end—and it is on this criticism that he bases his own notion of the "state of exception." Agamben thus writes, "[t]he violence exercised in the state of exception clearly neither preserves nor simply posits law, but rather conserves it in suspending it and posits it in excepting itself from it."[50]

According to Agamben, the state of exception which becomes a fundamental political structure appears as the legal form of that which can have no form—a form of emptiness of laws, a juridical void. At the same time, it is the very place where the law becomes valid—the threshold between what is outside and what is inside the law, and the source of the law's validity. It is thus a form of inclusive exclusion. For Agamben, the state of exception, the suspension of juridical order itself, "defines the law's thresholds or limit concepts"; it is the place where "facts and law fade into each other. ... On the one hand the norm is in force but is not applied; and on the other hand, acts that do not have the value of law acquire its force"; it is "an anomic space in which what is at stake is a force of law without law ... where logic and praxis blur with each other and pure violence without logos claims to realize an enunciation without real reference."[51]

In the opinion of Agamben, the state of exception materializes in the camp, a territory placed outside the normal juridical order of state law, allowing the suspension or elimination of the subjects' political value.[52] The camp is justified by its creators on grounds of security as a way to avert danger or ensure state security. In the camp, the state of exception becomes the rule. It is a hybrid of law and fact in which the two terms become indistinguishable, as do the notions of inside and outside.[53] Agamben thus describes the camp as "a dislocating localization" or a "localization without order."[54]

The state of exception is also embodied in the figure of the refugee, a political category that according to Agamben became a mass phenomenon after the First World War. For Agamben, the refugee is a modern incarnation of the ancient Roman *homo sacer*.[55] By declaring a person a *homo sacer*, Roman law stripped the person of all political rights, reducing his existence to that of "bare life." The person was thus positioned outside the law but under its effective control. This, Agamben claims, is precisely the condition of the modern refugee vis-à-vis state power.[56] It is for the refugee, he writes, that the identity between man and citizen breaks down, exposing the fiction of sovereignty based on nationality.[57]

My focus on Agamben stems from the fact that many significant recent scholars have linked the notion of extraterritoriality with Agamben's notion of the "state of exception," sometimes using the terms almost interchangeably. Like the phenomenon of extraterritoriality, Agamben's "state of exception" has its origins in conflicts of laws,[58] generating complex arrays of representation and non-representation which involve an effect of suspension, a dialect of inclusion and exclusion, and manifestations of the "irreducible difference between state and law."[59] Thus, as the following examples will demonstrate, extraterritorial phenomena such as the refugee camp are characterized by a state of exception: an ordering of space and legal status which makes possible the creation of, and infliction of pure violence upon, "bare life."[60]

Sociologist Sari Hanafi has outlined the emergence of the Palestinian refugee camps in Lebanon as extraterritorial sites, beginning with the burgeoning Palestinian nationalism in the mid-1960s and the rise of the Palestinian Liberation Organization (PLO),[61] and leading to the Cairo Agreement of 1969, which, while recognizing Lebanese sovereignty, gave the PLO direct control over the camps. As a result, the camps "virtually became a state within a state."[62] Hanafi notes that even after the expulsion of the PLO from Lebanon in 1982 and the subsequent handing over of the camps to UNRWA and to various NGOs, "to this day the camps make up enclaves out of reach of some Lebanese laws."[63]

Following Agamben, Hanafi describes these camps operating under extra-territorial jurisdiction as "spaces of exception." They exist, he writes, in a "state of void" in which laws are suspended. The result is chaos, discrimination, and deprivation. The camps have become a place of refuge for outlaws, while the refugees themselves are "often stripped of their political existence and identities and reduced to their status as individuals ... as bare life."[64] Writing, for example, about the camp Nahr el-Bared in northern Lebanon, Hanafi claims that the Lebanese authorities "turned [the camp] into a place where other extraterritorial elements like al-Qaeda can come to establish their microcosm."[65]

The camp thus brings together different manifestations of extraterritoriality into one territory. According to Hanafi, it is the camp's very extraterritorial status that allows the authorities to further marginalize the camp by denying its physical infrastructures and thus exacerbate its separation from nearby urban centers. Hanafi further argues that this strategy extends beyond the camps themselves and is now utilized "against the whole Palestinian refugee community in Lebanon."[66] That is, extraterritorial jurisdiction is imposed not only within the physical borders of the camp, but becomes a legal status applied to its denizens on a personal basis. In another discussion of policy and governance in the Palestinian refugee camps, Hanafi addresses the camp's exterritorial status not only in Lebanon but also in the Palestinian territories occupied by Israel,[67] pointing to the link between extraterritoriality and the exclusion of camp inhabitants from local elections. The camps, he writes, do "not truly belong to the place"; they "subsist 'in', but [are] not ... part 'of' the space that they physically occupy."[68]

The application of extraterritorial measures to refugees is also discussed by anthropologist and ethnologist Michel Agier in his studies of the efforts made by European governments to control migrant flow and decrease the number of asylum seekers in their respective countries. In late twentieth-century Europe, Agier writes, extraterritoriality had emerged not only as a "jurisdiction of exception," as in the camp, but also as a way to define the contemporary figure of the "stranger": "if he is physically present, he is administratively held over and beyond the national territory."[69]

Agier points in particular to two French laws, from 2003 and 2010, which imposed extraterritorial status on foreigners entering France's borders. Here, in contrast to the former example, it is not the camp's extraterritorial jurisdiction that follows the individual refugee: extraterritoriality is no longer constrained to the geographical location of the camp. Instead, the relationship between extraterritoriality and space is much more elastic, since it is now applied to the individuals on a *personal* basis. In effect, these laws utilize extraterritoriality to enable the state to circumvent the foreigner's right of asylum. International law demands that states respect all requests by asylum seekers from the moment the person sets foot on the state's national territory. Under the new laws, Agier writes, "everything that surrounds [the asylum seeker] becomes like an aura, extraterritorial, and therefore outside the Law."[70] Extraterritoriality is no longer a geographical status of exclusion applied, for example, to camps located within the state's boundaries or under its administration; rather, extraterritorial jurisdiction is now used as a device for blocking access to the state's territory.[71] Instead of constraining state power, these new extraterritorial measures serve states as means to elude their legal obligation to honor human rights within their national borders.

Increasingly and ever more regularly in recent years, extraterritorial devices have also enabled states to use their military forces to assert prescriptive jurisdiction beyond their territorial boundaries.[72] A well-known example is the so-called Camp X-Ray at Guantánamo Bay in Cuba, which served the United States in its "war on terror"—the international military campaign launched by the then residing President George W. Bush after the 9/11 terror attack on the World Trade Center and the Pentagon. Located on Cuban soil, the detention camp is under the control of the United States despite the fact that it is located outside that country's formal jurisdiction.[73] The camp is known for its implementation of the imprisonment, without trial, of hundreds of foreign nationals suspected of involvement with terrorist organizations. As a means of evading the national legal requirements and international human rights standards normally applied on US soil, the United States have argued that the prison's location is "extraterritorial" and therefore exempt.

In their essay, "The Geography of Extraterritoriality," Eyal Weizman, Ines Geisler, and Anselm Franke describe the Guantánamo Camp X-Ray as a legal loophole in which varied forms of inclusions and exclusions intersect:

> The political void in which the prisoners are held is mirrored by a sensual one—photographs of the camp show prisoners, their eyes, mouths and ears folded, incommunicado, prevented from sensing and comprehending their surroundings. Thus, without access to neither lawyers nor visitors, in the base on Guantánamo Bay as well as in American bases such as those in Bagram, Afghanistan and on the island of Diego Garcia, British Indian Ocean Territory, that operate according to similar juridical principles, prisoners may go on floating in indefinite detention. The absence of law has created a new type of space, one in which a person may be reduced to the level of biological life, a body without political or legal rights, a living dead.[74]

Though the writers do not themselves say this, the notion of "extraterritoriality" seems to be applicable here not only to the US government's attempt to evade its legal obligations, but also to the physical and bodily conditions imposed on the prisoners themselves, for example the state of sensory isolation imposed on detainees.[75]

Pointing to the foundations of the Guantánamo camp in nineteenth-century colonialism, as well as its current existence as a site of exception,[76] geographer Derek Gregory seems to draw similar conclusions. Comparing the aggression and torture carried out in the camp with the violence habitually inflicted by colonial regimes, he describes Guantánamo as a zone in which "the legalized and the extralegal cross over into one another."[77] Writing about the interrogative torture technics employed against the detainees, Gregory draws on the work of historian Alfred W. McCoy:

> These "no-touch" techniques leave no marks, but they create "a synergy of physical and psychological trauma whose sum is a hammer-blow to the fundamentals of personal identity": they deliberately ravage the body in order to "un-house" the mind.[78]

In Gregory's account, as in Weizman, Geisler, and Franke's, the camp's extraterritorial status becomes manifested in the prisoners' very bodies as well.

The use of extraterritorial measures in cases such as Guantánamo is also discussed by sociologist Boaventura de Sousa Santos, as part of his critique of Western epistemology. Santos conceives modern Western thought as embedded in what he calls "abyssal thinking." In his view, modern law and knowledge, dominated by Western science, form an "abyssal" legal and epistemological cartography, which imposes a hegemonic regime of visibility and invisibility in order to support the colonial order.[79] Santos's intellectual enterprise can be seen as an attempt to cross, in order to dismantle, what Schmitt terms the zone "beyond the line," the zone on which the state of exception is based. At the same time, as if echoing Benjamin's invocation (which Agamben also invokes), Santos believes that in order to confront the state of exception, one must reconceptualize the way we perceive oppressed populations as the current order renders them "non-existent" and invisible.[80]

A central characteristic of the abyssal paradigm is its non-dialectical rejection of the co-presence of forms of existence, instead holding the view Western Modernity's existence is conditioned solely by its absence, thus negating epistemological diversity or any other form of knowledge except for the scientific.[81] Similarly, abyssal thinking involves classifications of legal and non-legal forms, which are presented as the only relevant forms of existence before the law. Consequently, this dichotomy negates an entire social terrain of:

> the lawless, the a-legal, the non-legal and even the legal or illegal according to non-officially recognized laws. ... [This] other side of the line comprises a vast set of discarded experiences made invisible ... and with no fixed territorial location.[82]

According to Santos, what exists beyond the legal territory of modern law is the colonial zone: "in its modern constitution, the colonial represents not the legal or illegal, but rather the lawless."[83] In his view, abyssal thinking is most clearly manifested in Guantánamo: "the creation of the other side of the line as a non-area in legal and political terms, an unthinkable ground for the rule of law, human rights, and democracy."[84] It is not only the extraterritoriality of the camp that Santos has in mind, however, but an entire range of performances of lawlessness in everyday life. According to Santos, modern humanity is not conceivable without the production of a modern sub-humanity characterized by radical exclusion and legal nonexistence: "There are millions of Guantánamos," he writes, "in the sexual and racial discriminations ... in the savage zones of mega-cities ... in the black market of human organs."[85]

In order to overcome the determinism inscribed in the abyssal model, Santos suggests replacing it with a model characterized by an ecology that comprises a multiplicity of co-existences: "It is an ecology, because it is based on the recognition of the plurality of heterogeneous knowledges ... and on sustained and dynamic interactions between them without comprising their autonomy."[86] Santos's "abyssal" view of extraterritoriality as a representation of the "lawless" seems to echo Agamben's "state of exception." His emphasis on the co-existence of multiple knowledges meanwhile sheds light on the shortcomings of viewing extraterritoriality solely through the Agambenian lens, namely, as the action of a dominant sovereign exploiting its powers of inclusion and exclusion. Such an approach risks overlooking or rejecting extraterritoriality as the insidious (even inevitable) outcome of co-existing, overlapping, competing, and mutually negotiating legal systems. Even if these sometimes replicate the prevalent power structures and endorse discrimination and oppression, a full understanding of current applications of extraterritoriality requires that we view extraterritoriality from a perspective other than the dialectical models discussed above, which largely focus on the practices of inclusion and exclusion of a single dominant sovereign. The reality is far more subtle and layered. Similarly, viewing extraterritoriality only in terms of the dialectic of law and its absence, producing either a sovereign or naked life, likewise risks blurring the complex legal apparatus involved in the creation of extraterritoriality, and also overlooking the fact that extraterritoriality is a legal fiction which often allows the simultaneous operation of overlapping and mutually interacting legal systems. In this sense, our understanding of extraterritoriality should not be limited to the concept's ties to the "state of exception," nor to the preservation and validation of the laws of a single sovereign entity. Rather, it should recognize that there are many extraterritorial forms established as part of encounters between sovereigns or other politically organized communities. Moreover, while Agamben's "state of exception" is conceptualized within the tradition of Western politics, any proper analysis of extraterritoriality requires a broader perspective that encompasses other, non-Western forms of politics and dynamics of negotiation between diverse systems of laws. Finally, viewing extraterritoriality through the prism of the "state of exception"—which Agamben traces back to forms of dictatorship— might also fail to comprise the varied positive aspects of exception, such as messianism, an example raised by Agamben.[87]

The positive potential of extraterritoriality has also been articulated by the French philosopher Emmanuel Levinas, who in his essay, "Les Droits de l'Homme et les Droits d'Autrui" (The Rights of Man and the Rights of the Other), conceives of extraterritoriality as a vital space from which forms of dictatorship and totalitarianism can be countered.[88] In his view, any effort to defend human rights must rely on the understanding that these rights are essentially located outside the state. "The defense of the rights of man," writes Levinas, "corresponds to a vocation outside the state [in] a kind of extraterritoriality, like that of the prophecy in the face of the political power of the Old Testament." Extraterritoriality thus makes possible a "way to fight totalitarianism, which is defined in part by its denial of any 'outside the state.'"[89]

Revisiting Levinas's ethics, sociologist Zygmunt Bauman claims that the Levinasian "Other" is no more than a mirror image of the individual's personal responsibility. He argues that in today's world in which economy has gained independence from the state, rather than an extraterritorial ethics, it is "the real powers which decide the shape of things [that] have acquired a genuine ex-territoriality," making it more difficult to maintain a distinction "between the 'inside' and the 'outside' of the state ... in any but the most narrow, 'territory-and-population policing' sense."[90] Bauman, therefore, offers a different approach to extraterritoriality. In his view, extraterritoriality does not necessarily take the form of spatial delimitation or legal status. Rather, power itself can become "extraterritorial" as a result of what Bauman describes as the instigator process of modernity: the separation of time from space, and the treatment of the two as independent categories.[91] Building on Foucault's concept of the "Panopticon" as a metaphor of modern power, Bauman offers a model in which control is gained by "immobilizing [one's] subordinates in space through denying them the right to move and through the routinization of the time-rhythm they [have] to obey."[92] In today's world, notes Bauman, this has become a "principal strategy in [the] exercise of power."[93] In previous eras, power was bound by space. In our own day, as a result of technological advances that diminish the limiting effects of distance, power has "become truly extraterritorial, no longer bound, or even slowed down, by the resistance of space."[94]

A second effect of post-panoptical modernity is that we may no longer simply assume that supervised and supervisors are simply present: that they are "there" in fixed locations maintaining stable power relations. Rather, with the emergence of a type of "disembodiment," human labor no longer ties down capital to any physical place, enabling it to be extraterritorial, volatile, and also fickle.[95] According to Bauman, these new relationships encourage those in power to use techniques of "escape and slippage."[96] The ideal condition for them is now one of invisibility. Their optimal strategy is to reject territorial confinement and the regimes that it involves.

Reviewing the history of nation-state citizenship, Bauman distinguishes between the "solidity" of the modern and the "liquidity" of pre-modern forms. In the modern, "solid" era, he claims, nomadism was rejected in favor of territorial and sedentary configurations that are easier to dominate. In contemporary times, this has resulted in the reconfiguration of nomadism in the form of extraterritorial elites, which rule the sedentary majority:

> The contemporary global elites are shaped after the pattern of the old-style "absentee landlords." It can rule without burdening itself with the chores of administration, management, welfare concerns, or, for that matter, with the mission of "bringing light," "reforming the ways," morally uplifting, "civilizing" and cultural crusades.[97]

Bauman's view echoes to a certain extent the work of architectural theorist Keller Easterling, specifically in terms of the ways the economic power of elites relies on extraterritorial exemptions in relation to the expanding implementation of worldwide free-trade liberalism policy. Easterling locates these exemptions in so-called free zones—"spatial instrument[s] for externalizing obstacles for profit."[98] These are used by the market and the state, but also by non-state and non-market actors. According to Easterling, although such zones have ancient roots traceable to other early forms of extraterritoriality, only recently have they "emerged as a powerful global form," proliferating as an "extra-state legal habitat" that provides "the setting for secrets, hyper-control and segregation."[99] Easterling understands the current abuse of these extraterritorial zones as a recent mutation, however, noting their potential to become "alternative forms of urbanism."[100]

A positive outlook on the potential advantages of extraterritorialities is found in Agamben's own oeuvre. Despite the close connection between the conditions of extraterritoriality described above and Agamben's notion of the state of exception, Agamben himself never draws an explicit link between the two in his early writings dedicated to the latter concept.[101] When he does use the term, it is in the context of the Israeli-Palestinian conflict, where he offers the concept of extraterritoriality as a solution to the Palestinian refugee problem and to the Israeli-Palestinian conflict over Jerusalem. The problem, he claims, is a product of the current nation-state system, which is based on the triad state-nation-territory. To solve the problem, we must first re-examine and re-articulate the very concepts by which political subjects are represented. In Agamben's view, extraterritoriality (or "better yet a-territoriality") could serve as a generalized "model of new international relations."[102] Accordingly, Jerusalem could be governed by a mutual condition of extraterritoriality, creating a multi-faceted collective political space:

> Instead of two national states separated by uncertain and threatening boundaries, it might be possible to imagine two political communities insisting on the same region and in a condition of exodus from each other—communities that would articulate each other via a series of reciprocal extraterritorialities in which the guiding concept would no longer be the *ius* (right) of the citizen but rather the *refugium* (refuge) of the singular.[103]

Sari Hanafi seems to endorse Agamben's idea. Accordingly, his proposed solution to the Israeli-Palestinian conflict involves both Palestinian statehood and acknowledgment of the Palestinian refugees' right of return.[104] He then turns to the notions of extraterritoriality as a refuge: a way to avoid territorial division. Rejecting a territorial approach, he contends that a feasible two-state solution requires a reconceptualization of "a new model of nation-state … based on flexible borders, flexible citizenship, and some kind of separation between nation and state." As a solution, Hanafi proposes a new model of "two extraterritorial nation-states … with Jerusalem as their capital, contemporaneously forming, without territorial divisions, two different states."[105]

Extraterritorial Impasses: Background to the Gaza Freedom Flotilla

Extraterritorial Prescriptions to Palestine's Unrecognized Borders

The Israeli attempts to suppress the activists' Freedom Flotilla protest outside Gaza's territorial sea broadened the reach of the blockade deep into international waters. The resulting extraterritorial nature of the struggle embroiled Israel in various legal issues, which saw the activists claiming that Israel operated illegitimately by confronting the protesters beyond national jurisdiction. For their part, the Israeli authorities insisted that their efforts were necessary in order to defend its blockade of Gaza, and thus the State's own sovereignty, even if this involved straying into the high seas.[1] By doing so, however, Israel in effect extended its power outside its own territory, and even beyond sovereign Palestinian territory, carrying the conflict out into the "no-man's" reaches of open sea.

Although the flotilla incident marks a particular watershed in activists' resistance to the Israeli occupation, it is historic that the Israeli endeavor to tighten its hold over Palestine has been increasingly gravitating toward extraterritorial activities. The Israeli-Palestinian conflict is at source spreading chaotically over unrecognized borders and unacknowledged sovereignties. Instigated by struggle over territory and primarily interpreted in terms of land (holy, promised, sacred, plunder, dispossession, grab, etc.), however— and no less drastically—its boundaries and frontiers have concomitantly been shaped and consolidated by diverse forms of extraterritoriality. In fact, one might say that the fateful century-old geographical dispute actually took form within extraterritorial circumstances, and still today encompasses a wide range of extraterritorial phenomena. Throughout the process, the concept of extraterritoriality continues to offer shrewd and pliant legal terrain, ostensibly promoting the reciprocal development and adaptation of communities—invoking tolerance along with guarantees of immunity and protection—while instead adroitly tightening the screws of repression, occupation, and expulsion, along with any number of insidious arrangements that merely give further ballast to the ongoing a-symmetric coexistence.

On the ground, the fight over the exclusive right to land gave rise to a number of extraterritorial arenas involving diverse local and global actors. In addition, the boundaries of these extraterritoriality manifestations were not pre-given but fabricated, adapted, and modified deftly according to the changing political interests. The disputed territory is thus inseparable from its constitutive extraterritorial layers, superimposed on its arbitrary, tangible, and contested borders. To understand the conflict's territorial impasses, therefore, requires also learning its extraterritorial trajectories and underlying networks. While national borders are by definition visible, physical, and juridical entities, extraterritoriality is abstract and far more multifaceted, and asserts borders as if by stealth.

Some of the extraterritorial aspects and salient extensions can be detected in the various critical stages of its gradual evolution. Until the early twentieth century, Palestine had been under Ottoman rule for 400 years. Prior to the 1948 establishment of the State of Israel, in 1923, with the demise of the Turkish Empire following the First World War, control over the area officially devolved to Great Britain as part of the overarching framework of the Mandate system.[2] This governing method was devised by the international organization League of Nations, formed by the Allies subsequent to the Great War.[3] The Mandate regime was applied within various countries which, thanks to the war's outcome, had "ceased to be under the sovereignty of the States which formerly governed them."[4] Declaring a will to avoid colonization of the defeated territories, the said League's Article 22 defining the Mandate unfortunately left a wide margin of interpretation with its three distinct classifications, and imposed external control owing to the perceived inability of certain nations to achieve statehood through independent means.[5]

As regards Palestine, the chosen classification involved administrating "[c]ertain communities formerly belonging to the Turkish Empire" which "have reached a stage of development where their existence as independent nations can be provisionally recognized subject to the rendering of administrative advice and assistance by a Mandatory until such time as they are able to stand alone."[6] It should be noted that the lack of clarity of these definitions is imputed with contributing to a "legal vacuum,"[7] and throughout the Mandate, the complex issues of sovereignty and the scope of international authority remained vague and undetermined.[8]

Thus, while the interwar period is identified with "changes in attitude" toward imperialism, and aimed to bring an end to the system of extraterritorial colonies and revoke the former method of extraterritorial capitulations,[9] these extraterritorial arrangements persisted. Already in 1934, in an official review of practices of international law in Palestine prepared for the government of the United States. This review argued that despite the fact that "the mandates ... provided for the suspension of the existing capitulations upon the establishment of a judicial system guaranteeing the rights of both foreigners and natives[,] [t]he technical arrangements for exercising of these provisions [in Palestine] differ slightly."[10] Moreover, the Mandate system itself was presented as a way of shepherding nations toward compliance with international law, reminiscent of the modern deployment of extraterritorial measures through "judicial imperialism," whereby sovereignty was allowed on condition of conformity with Western standards.[11]

More generally, the involvement of the British and other intergovernmental organizations in determining the spatial division of the extensive historical area in question, while applying their power even beyond their (self-appointed) territorial jurisdiction, is indicative of the "extraterritorial nature of a sovereign's power"[12] that generated the Israeli-Palestinian conflict, and the establishment of a Jewish national land in the area, all of which was determined by external forces operating beyond their remit. On November 29, 1947, the UN General Assembly approved a plan of partition, according to which "[t]he Palestine state would be converted into two states linked together in an economic union and would become independent."[13] The UN resolution to divide the land into two separate states, one Arab and one prospective Jewish, was rejected outright by the Arabs (including Syria, Jordan, Egypt, and Iraq), who immediately launched a war against the budding Jewish state. That war meant that in 1948, the newly established State of Israel's borders no longer conformed to the original program while "[t]he rest of Mandate Palestine remained in legal limbo."[14] In fact, the Armistice Agreement of 1949 (known also as the "Green Line") established the borders of Israel as "comprising 78 percent of Mandate Palestine, including the entire Galilee and the stretch of Mediterranean coast that had been designated for the Arab state, except for the small coastal belt that became the Gaza Strip."[15] Moreover, in the wake of the war, "750,000 Palestinians became dispersed."[16] In hindsight, this significant outcome has been considered as "the birth of the Palestinian refugee problem," which has led an estimated third of this group of displaced Palestinians and their future descendants to still reside in assorted refugee camps in neighboring Arab countries, camps one could describe as extraterritorial in nature.[17]

Concomitantly, in many cases, the postwar agreements resulted in an elusive border demarcation. In particular, the agreement with Syria and Egypt outlining the demilitarized zones (DMZs) on the Israeli side left ample margins on questions of sovereignty, which frequently ignited armed border clashes, most notably between Israel and Syria in 1951, and then Israel and Egypt in 1955.[18] In the period between 1948 and 1956, violence frequently erupted around the newly formed frontiers, owing to large-scale cross-border infiltration.[19] By and large, these border crossings took place for various nonviolent reasons, and involved the sizeable quota of Palestinian refugees who wished to resettle, retrieve, or maintain family and work relations in their former lands. However, infiltrations were also carried out for the purpose of plunder and premeditated attacks on the Jewish state settlements.[20] For its part, Israel responded by adopting retaliatory policies, including military incursions beyond its borders, at first targeting civilians at the suspected sites of origin in the neighboring states, but as of 1953 shifting instead to overtly targeting military and police facilities identified as the source of the attack.[21] From early 1954, neighboring states embarked on organizing violent infiltration by activating trained squadrons aimed at terrorizing those living across the border as a means of destabilizing the occupying communities. These cross-border attacks—and the largely perceived ineffective counter attacks— were among the factors that enabled Israel to embark on the Sinai Campaign, also known as the Suez Crisis (1956).[22] At the end of this war, in which Israel managed to capture the Gaza Strip and Sinai, they promised military withdrawal on the condition that the newly established United Nations Emergency Forces (UNEF) would act as a "buffer" between Israel and Egypt, though exclusively stationed on the Egyptian territory.[23]

Within the state borders, in order to govern the expanding Israeli dominion over the land, "by September 1948, areas of the new State with a high concentration of Palestinian-Arab residents were declared closed security areas, administered by the Israeli army and subject to the Emergency Regulations that Israel adopted from the British Mandate's legal code."[24] Similarly relying on this set of rules, in the same year, Israel imposed a Military Government on the Palestinian inhabitants in specific territories in the north, south, and center.[25] Consecutive to the formation of the new State, Israel deftly allocated the remaining Arab population "a discrete set of individual rights and duties."[26] While this regime was dismantled in 1966, both personal and geographical extraterritorial forms for regulating the emergent multiple exceptions triggered by the evolving intricacies of the political framework were soon to reappear in light of Israel's sweeping victory in the June 1967 War, fought between Israel and its neighboring Arab countries, Egypt, Syria, and Jordan from June 5 to June 10, 1967. In the war's aftermath, Israel expanded its national territory to "three and a half times its original size." As a result, 1.2 million Palestinians came under Israeli rule in the newly occupied territories, consequently reshaping the Israeli-Palestinian conflict and the balance of power in the entire Middle East, and initiating a period of occupation that has continued until the present.[27]

Upon the war's termination, Israel introduced military oversight to be applied to the recently conquered territories of the West Bank, the Gaza Strip, and Sinai.[28] Among the exceptional factors were the seized lands of the Golan Heights and East Jerusalem. Initially defined as "occupied territories," soon afterward, these areas also came under the thumb of Israeli extraterritoriality, which was disseminated in the north by military decrees, whereas in Jerusalem through its incorporation to the city's western municipality, until the formal annexations in 1981 and 1980, respectively.[29] In the rest of the occupied territories, juggling between legal systems became a vital tool for enhancing State control, as well as a means for bypassing extraterritorial commitments that should have been applied, given the State's effective control over an "external" territory, in case the law of occupation was to be enforced.[30] For the West Bank, for instance, Israel cited the former annexation of the territory by the Kingdom of Jordan as a legal justification for claiming it to be "disputed land"[31] rather than an area under enforced occupation. Another prevalent line of legal argumentation in regard to both the West Bank and Gaza invoked by state officials, alas somewhat contradictory with the previous, was that of the "missing reversioner," advocating the invalidity of the former sovereignty of Jordan and Egypt's administration in these regions, due to their 1948 invasion of Mandatory Palestine.[32] On the basis of these mixed legal claims, Israel reinstated an amalgam of "Ottoman, British Mandatory, Egyptian, and Jordanian laws that [were] in place prior to the war, while adding an array of military orders published by military commanders," arguing that the latter "supersedes any [other] law"[33] and basically overrides all previous legislation.

While numerous Jewish settlements emerged within the decade which followed the war, with the rise of the rightwing Likud party in 1977, the government "began to establish settlements throughout the West Bank, particularly in areas close to the main Palestinian population centers along the central mountain ridge and in western Samaria."[34] In light of an ever-expanding initiative of Jewish settlement in the newly occupied territories—and in order to spare the Jewish settlers from the military jurisdiction or any other system of laws and instead ensure their inclusion into Israeli civil law "step by step"[35]—the State resorted to extraterritorial "personal" laws, thereby turning the settlers into "extraterritorial citizens, who, like diplomats, carry the Israeli law on their backs."[36] International law scholar, Neve Gordon, has argued that "by transforming Jewish citizens into turtles of sorts, i.e., creatures that are entitled to 'personal jurisdiction' (i.e., laws that follow people), Israel managed to create a situation whereby two ethnic groups sharing the same space have actually been subjected to radically different legal systems."[37]

In spatial terms, we can apply architect Eyal Weizman's description of these territories as "homogenous ethno-national enclaves" shaped by a unique "territorial ecosystem" whereby "various other zones—those of political piracy, of 'humanitarian' crisis, of barbaric violence, of full citizenship, 'weak citizenship', or no citizenship at all—exist adjacent to, within or over each other."[38] Viewing the Israeli attempt to "desperately ... separate the inseparable" to "multiply a single territorial reality and create two insular national geographies that occupy the same space,"[39] which in judicial terms, however establishes a regime "based on the existence of two separate legal systems in the same territory, with the rights of individuals being determined by their nationality."[40] Furthermore, Weizman emphasizes that the endeavor of the State to control the West Bank by securing their vertical supremacy has brought to a spatial top/bottom divide by which "the seized highland [of the West Bank dominated by Israelis] thus acquired an effective extraterritorial status."[41] According to Eyal Benvenisti, it is precisely through extraterritorial prescription of the Israeli laws that the State was able to claim that the legal absorption of the territories "does not amount to annexation"—a pretext that allowed it to legitimate its long process of assimilation of the occupied territories as congruous with international law.[42] Simply put, this procedure enabled the Israelis to informally "conquer" the Palestinian land through the (unequally applied) expansion of its jurisdiction.[43] It should be noted that in the aftermath of the 1973 Yom Kippur War (Known also as Ramadan War), Israel extended its borders even further, while eventually withdrawing its forces in line with postwar accords and peace treaties.[44]

Already in the subsequent year, the UN brokered two agreements of Separation of Forces between Israel, Syria, and Egypt, establishing two "area[s] of separation," devised to delimit territorial buffers between Israel, and each of these neighboring states to be manned by the UN's "Disengagement Observer Force," whereby the boundaries of neighboring countries acquired extraterritorial acreage.[45] In 1979, the Israel-Egypt Peace Treaty entailed not only Israel's withdrawal from territories it previously occupied in exchange for peace, but also the establishment of a buffer zone "for maintaining separation of forces," later to become a demilitarized zone (Area C). Moreover, another buffer zone known also as the Philadelphia route, stretching for 14 km at the border between Gaza and Egypt, was set to be exclusively controlled by the Israeli military.[46] A few years later, the 1982 Lebanon War saw Israeli gains in the southern part of the country, and was followed by partial Israeli withdrawal in 1985, though not without retaining a "security zone" controlled by the IDF and the SLA (South Lebanese Army), a strategy that held until the early 2000s.[47] In the aftermath, the UN drew a border of demarcation between Israel and Lebanon, known as the Blue Line, mandating power over the area via troops of the UNFIL (United Nations Interim Force in Lebanon), thereby increasing the control of the corps from their initial deployment in the area in 1978, with even greater investment after the Second Lebanon War of 2006.[48]

The impact of extraterritoriality as a legal device resurfaced in the form of a stipulation for ending occupation—and the conflict as whole—in a series of accords signed in the early 1990s between Israel and the Palestine Liberation Organization (subsequently rebadged as the Palestinian Authority), which marked an apex in relations between the two sides. For example, securing Israeli extraterritorial control is reflected in the "Declaration of Principles on Interim Self-Government Arrangements" (part of the Oslo Accords of 1993, originating from the "Middle East Peace Process" initiated at the 1991 Madrid Peace Conference), which stated that "[i]n order to guarantee public order and internal security for the Palestinians of the West Bank and the Gaza Strip, the Council will establish a strong police force, while Israel will continue to carry the responsibility for defending against external threats, as well as the responsibility for overall security of Israelis for the purpose of safeguarding their internal security and public order."[49] Accordingly, the subsequent Cairo Agreement on Gaza and Jericho (1994) specified the transfer of authority in these areas from the Israeli military government to the prospected Palestinian Authority's "Civil Administration" wing,[50] emphasizing however that its jurisdiction would "not include foreign relations, internal security and public order of Settlements and the Military Installation Area and Israelis, and external security."[51] It additionally stated that the "personal jurisdiction extends to all persons within the territorial jurisdiction referred to above, except for Israelis, unless otherwise provided in this Agreement."[52]

These provisions would be echoed in the Interim Agreement of the West Bank and the Gaza Strip (Oslo II, 1995), which superseded the former accord while specifying—for legal purposes—a division of these regions into three distinct types of control. Notably, even in Area A,[53] which designated an extensive autonomy to the Palestinian Authority, it included a clause reserving Israeli jurisdiction over resident Israelis and settlers on the said territories.[54] Accordingly, despite stating that in Area A "the Palestinian Council will have full responsibility for internal security and public order, as well as full responsibility for civil affairs,"[55] the agreement also imposed that "the IDF and Israelis will continue to move freely on the roads of the West Bank and Gaza. … Israelis may not in any circumstances be arrested or placed in custody by the Palestinian police, and may only be required to present identity and vehicle documentation. On roads that are jointly patrolled, any request for identification shall only be made by the Israeli side of a joint patrol."[56] Correspondingly, the Hebron Protocol, which divided the city to areas H-1 (under the auspices of the Palestinian Authority) and H-2 (within Israeli control), similarly ensured that the State's domestic extraterritorial laws applied to Israelis.[57] In fact, it was argued that the Oslo Accords "did not actually transfer meaningful authority over the occupied Palestinian Territory (OPT) from Israel to the PA. … In effect, the PA's competence and jurisdiction extended only to governing the Palestinian population in the territory, not the territory itself."[58]

Since then, although several attempts to promote peace accords that would end the conflict were doomed to failure, in each of these, extraterritorial arrangements, both in the form of personal laws (e.g., in the case of the settlers) and as a special spatial order (e.g., the proposal to create a territorial link between the West Bank and Gaza), were suggested as a binding condition for putting a halt to the territorial dispute.[59] Moreover, extraterritoriality was also invoked as a countermeasure at the hands of the Palestinian Authority in the face of Israeli reluctance to endorse a peace agreement. This manifested in the 2014 decision to seek extraterritorial jurisdiction by joining the International Criminal Court for the purpose of pressing charges of war crimes against Israel.[60] Interestingly, Israel instead failed to implement extraterritorial jurisdiction in the occupied territories, despite ratifying five Human Rights treaties in 1991, restricting the reach of its consequent extraterritorial human rights obligations to be applied in the State's national territory, while claiming these are not pertinent beyond.[61]

Furthermore, at the turn of the millennium, with the failure of the peace process, Israel occupied some areas of the territories allocated to the Palestinian Authority, while additional extraterritorial enclaves were created following a 2002 State decision to construct the "Israeli Barrier," a meandering palisade approximately 708 kilometers long.[62] Originally prospected to follow the aforesaid Green Line, in practice, the goal of securing Israelis within state borders from terror attacks was extended to include Jewish settlements in the occupied territories. To this end, its snaking course was redrawn to "run inside the West Bank, including East Jerusalem."[63] Consequently, a "Seam Zone" comprising the area between the new Barrier and the Green Line, corralling approximately 6,500 Palestinian inhabitants in its erratic path, "has been designated a 'closed military area,'" which entails severe restrictions on both residency and daily mobility.[64] "The lawless line", carved in order to represent the Barrier's prospected path, produced a sinuous "sliver of extraterritorial space."[65] The area is now conceptualized as:

> a mutual extraterritoriality, a condition of double enclosure. Settlements in the "special security zones," like the Palestinian communities in the "closed military zones," are territorial "islands" physically and legally estranged from their immediate surroundings. Under this arrangement, the traditional perception of political space as a contiguous territorial surface, delimited by continuous borderlines, is no longer relevant.[66]

Moreover, extraterritoriality is crucial for understanding the complex topography carved by the separation barrier through the occupied territories (the Israeli State's eastern borders). In the north, the geography of extraterritoriality was broadened, not only officially through the aforementioned separation zone, but also by the mounting numbers of the Shia Hezbollah militia guerrilla underground tunnels, which have been described as another "sphere of extraterritorial sovereignty."[67] This relates to the aforementioned broader assertion made by Weizman, who claimed that "the boundaries raised up by the conflict, making the ground below and the air above separate and distinct from, rather than continuous with and organic to, the surface of the earth" demonstrate the phenomenon's vertical spread into novel extraterritorial domains.[68] Actually, the borders of Israel push constantly beyond established territory into the extraterritorial: the separation zones in the north, the enclaves of the West Bank in the east, and the effective extraterritorial control over Gaza in the south. The settlement expansion into Palestinian territory is, therefore, also a story of frustrated jurisdiction and the exploitation of endless legal loopholes, and proves to be ultimately bound to extraterritorial orders and terrains.[69] To grasp all the complexities of this requires an extraterritorial mode of reasoning. In parallel, the *Mavi Marmara* incident in offshore international waters is a logical extension of the kind of conflict we are witnessing in the systematic reallocation of land as an "extraterritorial" domain.

Extraterritorial Prescriptions to Gaza's Closures

Governed for four centuries by the Ottomans, Gaza was conquered by the British in 1917. Consequently, the area was included within the ambit of the Mandate for Palestine, which was formally declared in 1920. Toward the termination of the 1948 Arab–Israeli War, the Egyptians—one of the adversaries in the armed campaign—gained control over the area, first administrating its inhabitants via a declared "All-Palestinian Government," while in practice subjecting it to the command of an Egyptian military governorship, later even overtly.[70]

The postwar borders separating the Gaza Strip from the newly formed Jewish State established in the armistice agreements were ill-defined and remained largely contested. Albeit nonviolent, during the first years, large-scale cross-border infiltration was a recurring phenomenon.[71] For instance, the poorly marked borders meant that farmers were tending their crops on lands that now belonged to Israel, turning these workers technically into illegal infiltrators, until Israel and Egypt reached an accord in March of 1950.[72] Meanwhile, however, the growing incidents of threatening incursions, plunder, and outbursts of violence, were often countered by military raids and the entry of Israeli Military forces into the strip.[73] The status of the DMZs specified in the accords was perceived differently by the two sides: while Egypt regarded these areas as a sort of "no-man's land," Israel awarded itself sovereign control. The conflicting views transformed these areas into a site of further infiltration and a source of strife.[74]

The growing friction around the borders was among the factors that drove Israel to taking part in a combined Israeli, French, and British attack on Egypt in 1956, known as the Suez Crisis.[75] In the course of this conflict, Israel succeeded in conquering the Gaza Strip and Sinai, vowing to withdraw on condition of a transfer of control over the area to the UNEF, which was created "ad hoc" to facilitate the participating forces' evacuation.[76] Though Israel demanded that the Gaza Strip remain out of Egyptian control, the UNEF allowed them back into the region, and the Egyptian authorities worked alongside the UN troops to help maintain Gaza.[77] Relative peace was upheld throughout the UNEF's ten-year deployment along the Egypt-Israel border, with very few cases of border crossing, most of which were done by farmers or shepherds.[78] The UNEF remained along the Israel-Egypt border and in Gaza from November 1956 until May 1967, when Egypt's demands and the subsequent UNEF withdrawal from the region was one of the first stages that precipitated the June 1967 War (known also as the Six-Day War) in the month that followed.[79]

Egypt retained command of the area for almost two decades until the June 1967 War, which resulted in the Israeli occupation of the territory and the imposition of its own military rule. From the 1970s on, assorted military settlements were gradually installed, later to become the first Jewish civilian settlements in the postwar Gaza Strip, paving the way for others.[80] In 1979, Israel and Egypt signed a peace treaty that redrew the south and eastern boundaries of the Gaza Strip, reconstituted in accordance with an old 1906 border agreement between the Ottomans and the British Empire.[81]

In 1994, following the Oslo accords, the Palestinian Authority was granted limited self-governing authority over Gaza, excepting Israeli settlements and military zones, however, representing a quarter of the Strip's land. In addition, Israel maintained exclusive control over accesses to and from the territory, thus in practice undermining Palestinian autonomy.[82]

Over the next thirty-eight years of occupation, until 2005, Israel exercised a continuous military presence in Gaza. During this time, its Palestinian residents remained stateless and without citizenship, deprived of basic civil and human rights, and excluded from democratic participation. (As previously outlined, they shared this fate with their fellow Palestinians in the West Bank ruled by Jordan, similarly captured during the June 1967 War).[83] In 2005, in the framework of the "disengagement plan," which was endorsed by Egypt, the Palestinian Authority, and Jordan at a summit meeting at *Sharem a-Sheikh*,[84] Israeli forces unilaterally withdrew from the Gaza Strip, evacuating both its military installations and twenty-five civilian settlements numbering some 8,000 inhabitants.[85] At this juncture, Gaza became nominally autonomous, under the jurisdiction of the Palestinian Authority. In the democratic legislative elections held in Gaza the following year, the Islamic party Hamas came to power, first forming a coalition, then replacing the secular and politically more moderate Fatah party.[86]

In real terms, however, Gaza has remained very much under Israeli control throughout the post-2005 period. Most importantly, Israel (with Egyptian collaboration) continues to hold command over all land, naval, and aerial pathways to and from Gaza.[87] In 2007, Israel imposed a form of closure on the Gaza Strip, severely limiting the movement of goods into the region. In January 2009, the Israeli authorities reinforced the closure by declaring a naval blockade over Gaza.[88] Israel has invoked security concerns to justify the closure in general, and the naval blockade in particular; however, many believe that it is largely motivated by political goals, collectively (and illegally) punishing the people of Gaza for having elected Hamas.[89]

Hence, the notion of extraterritoriality has been central to the aims and motivations of the flotilla organizers. According to their claims, Israel's effective control over Gaza, and its regulation of the passage of persons and goods through Gaza's borders, constitutes an illegal expansion of Israel's state powers beyond their proper jurisdiction.[90] The logic of Israel's control over Gaza has become especially convoluted since the "disengagement campaign." Gaza's territory has come to be defined by a series of Israeli actions and proclamations devised to isolate it from its immediate geographical environment, as well as from the other Palestinian territories in the West Bank.[91] During this period, the Israeli authorities have declared Gaza a "hostile zone" (2007), a "combat zone" (2008), and, during Operation Cast Lead (Known as the Gaza War), a "military enclosure" and "exclusion zone" (2009). Gaza's territoriality has thus come to be defined as constituted by the various exclusions and blockades to which it has been subjected.

The Freedom Flotilla organizers, primarily the IHH, invoked several different interpretations of the territorial closure imposed on the Gaza Strip, referring to it variously as an "embargo," a "siege," and a "blockade."[92] The same variations recur in dozens of passengers' testimonies, where the three terms are used interchangeably to describe the mechanisms of territorial domination that prompted the flotilla initiative.[93] They also arise, this time in legal terms, in the report submitted by the Turkish National Commission of Inquiry. According to the report, the different blockades are legally indistinguishable. Furthermore, the report claims that an effective blockade on Gaza preceded Israel's formal declaration of a blockade by at least two years.[94]

The flotilla organizers deployed a uniform rhetoric, articulating the closure mechanisms in undifferentiated legal-linguistic terms. Moreover, according to the Turkish National Commission of Inquiry, the naval barrier was "an integral part of the land blockade [and] must be examined in tandem."[95] Accordingly, they accused Israel of making artificial legal-spatial distinctions between its various restrictive measures (e.g., by distinguishing between forbidden "combat zones" and "hostile zones").[96] The organizers' rhetoric seems to imply that the different terms applied to Israel's policy are identical in meaning. Yet, in fact, each tactic may entail its own laws, ideology, conception of space, and border regime. This may suggest that in order to address the territorial separation imposed on the Gaza Strip, two separate conceptions of the spatiality of the closure must be taken into account. The difference between these two conceptions is captured by the distinction between a *blockade* and a *siege*.

The contrast between these two terms is in fact crucial to the question of the *legal* status of the naval closure imposed by Israel on the Gaza Strip—a question addressed by the various national and international committees of inquiry.[97] The Israeli Turkel Commission begins its report with precisely this question— that is, with the question of whether the blockade complied with international law, whether the Israeli military takeover operation was therefore legitimate,[98] and whether Israel was justified in launching the interception of the flotilla in extraterritorial waters, carrying the territorial conflict deep into the international high seas.[99] The committee begins its account of this issue with stressing the conceptual distinction between a naval blockade and a siege, a variance based on their allegedly different *spatial* features:

> Whereas a siege means the encircling of the enemy's military forces, a strategic fortress, or any other location defended by the enemy, and cutting it off from support and supply lines, a naval blockade describes a wider variety of operations.[100]

According to the committee, a naval blockade aims at "preventing the enemy from having access to the maritime area on which the blockade has been imposed … [and] from being able to receive supplies and assistance via that area."[101] According to these definitions, a siege could be perceived as a spatial tactic whose objective is the establishment of fully surrounding borders that would lock the enemy in a clearly defined, unified political space. A naval blockade, though site-specific, is determined not by a particular spatial structure or topography, but, rather by different practices of political control, by management of people and their circulation, and by other methods of maritime warfare.[102] Thus, while a siege exerts pressure on the interior of a territory, a naval blockade extends its regime beyond the territory in question. The implication of this view is that both types of spatial configuration inflict territorial separation, yet it was the naval blockade—applied against the backdrop of the Israeli–Palestinian conflict to tighten the borders of the Gaza Strip—which enabled Israel to claim that its operation in extraterritorial waters was legitimate.

The naval blockade, executed in the maritime space of the Gaza Strip, culminated in a process of fluctuating restrictions on border crossing, which imposed a land siege on Gaza.[103] As part of the disengagement plan, Israel withdrew from the Gaza Strip, but kept guard over the territory's borders, including Gaza's air-space and coast.[104] The Rafah crossing point, which is the only non-Israeli army-controlled access point for Palestinians to and from Gaza, was to be manned by the European Union Border Assistance Mission (EUBAM). Israel deployed closed-circuit cameras at the checkpoint, which allowed it to monitor people's movement in and out via live video footage,[105] and to retain the power to open and close the crossing according to its assessment of the security situation.[106]

The production of images has been an important part of the border regime imposed by Israel over Gaza. The Israeli authorities employ dozens of closed-circuit video surveillance cameras to monitor Gaza's borders and territory, helping Israel control the areas where it is not officially sovereign, and where its citizens and troops are no longer directly present. In this sense, Israel's extraterritorial dominion over the Gaza Strip is made possible by the circulation of images.[107]

It should be noted that the physical extension of Gaza's borders also involves delving beneath the surface. Already four years after the 1979 Israeli-Egyptian Peace Treaty, which bisected the southern border city of Rafah, Palestinian families split by the arbitrary partition seem to have been the first to construct underground tunnels linking Gaza and Egypt in order "to foster communication amongst extended family members." These tunnels were further deployed for smuggling, to address a variety of needs and economic interests.[108] During the first 1994 and second 2000s Palestinian uprisings widely known as *intifadah*, Israel argued that the tunnels were repurposed for warfare, and that as from 2001, tunnels were built with the objective of combating the State.[109] Since the 2005 disengagement plan, the creation and utilization of military tunnels has increased, and the system was further elaborated, in some places reaching depths of 25–40 meters to avoid detection.[110]

In correspondence, after the Palestinian elections of 2006 that brought Hamas to power in Gaza,[111] there has been a dramatic increase in the number of Palestinian rockets and mortar attacks on southern Israel. As the Israeli military was no longer stationed on the Gaza-Egyptian border, and the demand for weapons expanded as a result of internal Palestinian fighting and the ongoing Palestinian struggle against the Israeli occupation, the smuggling of weapons soared through the Gaza-Egypt tunnel network. Using a tunnel dug under the border with Israel, a Hamas guerrilla cell also captured an Israeli soldier.[112] Citing these events, Israel imposed further land-crossing restrictions on the Gaza Strip. However, in practical terms, the tunnels reshaped the spatiality of the conflict, literally making it deeper and more complicated by spreading underground. While, unlike the regulation of a shared air and sea space, state sovereignty over subterranean land is widely acknowledged, the depth of state control has yet to be decided, contributing to ongoing legal-spatial ambiguity.[113] Nevertheless, aimed at combating the imposed territorial isolation, these cross-border tunnels made the already contested territorial borders of Gaza even more unstable.

With the activity taking place inside these underground installations mostly immune (at least temporarily) to visual identification, the tunnel network could be viewed also as a direct response to Israel's aforementioned efforts to maintain control over the Gaza Strip remotely, via the use of surveillance cameras. The Palestinian tunnels literally created an underground zone exempt from the reach of Israeli scrutiny and its image-making apparatuses.[114]

On September 19, 2007, Israel declared the entirety of Gaza, including a 20-nm maritime zone,[115] a "hostile territory," and announced additional restrictions on the passage of goods, the supply of electricity, fuel, and the movement of persons. In some cases, the land-crossing was entirely closed, effectively applying a national lockdown from the outside.[116] Egypt worked with Israel to close the Rafah crossing, with passage allowed in exceptional cases only.[117] The fishing range in the Gaza maritime zone, which extended practically over 12 nm, was reduced during those years, and has been subjected to restrictions fluctuating by 3–6 nm along the maritime boundary.[118]

Even prior to the arrival of two flotillas flying Greek flags, a legal advisor of the Israeli Navy had already suggested imposing a naval blockade. This option was cited in a position paper from August 3, 2008, and similar recommendations were submitted by the Chief Military Advocate General, but it seems that, at the time, the attorney general wished to postpone the decision on this matter until further discussion.[119]

Nevertheless, on August 13, 2008, Israel declared the stretch of water near the coast of the Gaza Strip a "combat zone" or an "exclusion zone."[120] Invoking international humanitarian law as its mandate, the Israeli Turkel Commission asserted that this designation permits a party in conflict to constrain the activity of a neutral vessel, and even seize control of its communication systems.[121] Accordingly, "all foreign vessels in the area [were requested] not to enter the maritime zone adjacent to Gaza."[122] Still, between August and December 2008, flotillas continued to arrive, and six vessels were reportedly permitted entrance to Gaza.[123] According to the same report, the Israeli military had relatively limited options to inspect the incoming humanitarian flotillas, partly because these ships were neutral, and partly because the military could not legally use the "visit-and-search" power it employed when there were reasonable grounds to suspect an approaching vessel.[124]

On January 3, 2009, violence soared during the Gaza War in which a series of devastating attacks carried out by the Israeli military on Gaza reportedly killed 1,400 Palestinians: "The entire population of 1.5 million people has been trapped in Gaza.[125] ... [T]he 22 days of intense bombardment trapped tens of thousands of families in their homes."[126] In the course of the war, the Minister of Defense Ehud Barak ordered an additional naval blockade of the Gaza Strip coastline up to a distance of 20 nm from the coast.[127] Gaza's territoriality has thus come to be defined by the various exclusions and blockades to which it has been subjected, which had remained in force in the period preceding the 2010 flotilla initiative, and served as its background.[128]

Extraterritorial Images in Action: The Gaza Freedom Flotilla

The Takeover of Images in Extraterritorial Waters

On May 30, 2010 at around 10 p.m., several hours before the physical takeover of the flotilla, the Israeli military forces began to interrupt satellite communications to and from the flotilla vessels. The interruptions intensified later that night until a complete or near-complete blackout on communications was imposed.[1]

It is particularly significant that the Israeli operation commenced with an attempt to inhibit the transmission of images from the vessels, given that the production and distribution of images were among the flotilla's central aims. The flotilla was conceived as a high-profile media event designed to "alert the world to the crimes being committed against the Palestinians."[2] According to Bülent Yıldırım, a Turkish lawyer and the president of Turkish NGO, IHH, who was aboard the *Mavi Marmara*, "our aim was to reach Gaza or anchor on the high seas and make propaganda for about a month but they attacked us on the high sea."[3]

Gülden Sönmez, the IHH lawyer and a member of the organization's executive committee who was also aboard the *Mavi Marmara* attests:

> We aimed to sail from international waters to Egyptian waters, then on to Gaza [where we wanted to] deliver the aid, if possible. If Israel prevented the delivery, we would draw attention to the illegal blockade, broadcast live for a while through the media, and then return.[4]

To make broadcasting and media coverage possible, a large number of journalists and television teams were invited to take part.[5] A strong infrastructure for mid-sea live broadcasting was installed. The engineers who operated the onboard broadcast "took account of every possible situation about the system" and worked to ensure that "the course of the flotilla could be watched uninterrupted on the IHH website."[6] To prepare for the battle over images, the IHH rented two Turksat frequencies for the live broadcast, one of which, known only to the IHH, the Foreign Press Association (FPA), and Turksat itself, was meant to serve as backup in case of attempts to block the broadcast.[7] In addition, the activists brought with them an abundance of personal communications equipment. According to some estimates, the *Mavi Marmara* held 546 passengers and 29 crew members at the time of the struggle, and no fewer than 600 laptops, 800 video cameras, and 1,200 mobile phones.[8]

For some of the activists, the presence of this ostensible array of communications devices was precisely the best means to signal the expedition's peaceful intentions. According to activist Alexandra Lort-Phillips, "the vessels were covered with cameras to witness the voyage. I don't know what else the Freedom Flotilla could do to make sure it was clear it was a peaceful mission."[9] For the Israeli forces, however, the deactivation of this very equipment was pivotal to their raid: one of the military's primary aims was to obtain complete control of the images and limit their distribution—to keep the images quarantined, as it were, within carefully pre-set borders.[10] To achieve this, a large-scale information operation was devised. Its aim was to halt any type of image production by seizing all communications devices and materials onboard the vessels. A special military division was assigned to confiscate all digital images and pre-empt their reproduction and circulation.[11]

The first virtual encounter between the adversaries in extraterritorial waters— the first stage of the Israeli army's inception of the flotilla—therefore consisted of bombarding the area with electromagnetic waves to jam the transmission of any records of the unfolding events, and thus pre-empt their circulation. "For about half an hour [now] the Israelis have been harassing us," a reporter announced in one of the last transmissions documented abroad the *Mavi Marmara*, referring not to any physical force directed toward the activists themselves, but to the Israeli efforts to jam their signals.[12] Another Turkish reporter, Ayşe Sarıoğlu, described the ensuring chaos: "Our satellite connection was frequently failing and the internet kept disconnecting. The more they jammed, the more we elevated our receivers."[13]

The confrontation between Israeli forces and the activists was therefore primarily a clash between two logics of information flow—one devoted to producing a strictly monitored territory of limited communications in extraterritorial waters, the other dedicated to expanding the information flow as part of the protest agenda. As the confrontation unfolded, these conflicting

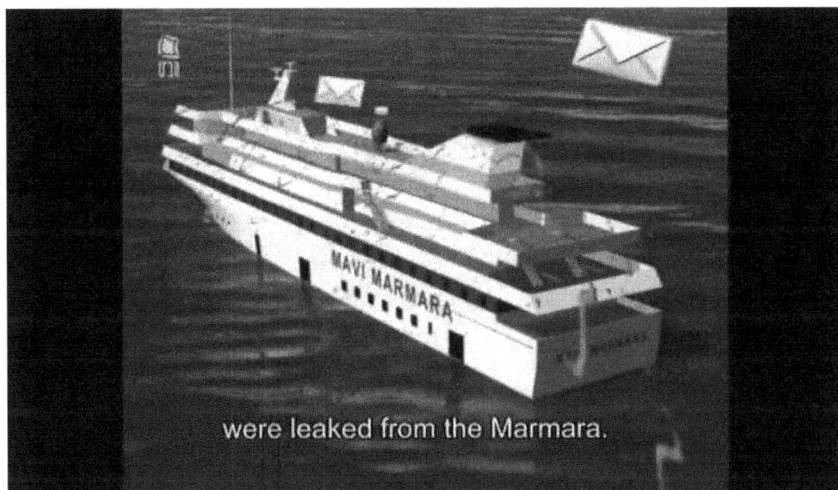

were leaked from the Marmara.

Figure 2 The events leading up to and throughout the flotilla incident are recounted in the video, as presented by the team of experts led by Maj. Gen. (res.) Giora Eiland in the IDF's internal inquiry. The image above illustrates the IDF's electronic screening. Still from: IDF, "Video Timeline of the Flotilla Incident," (English Version), YouTube Video, 21:18 mins., May 22, 2011, https://www.youtube.com/watch?v=z31G esVrBjc&feature=youtu.be.

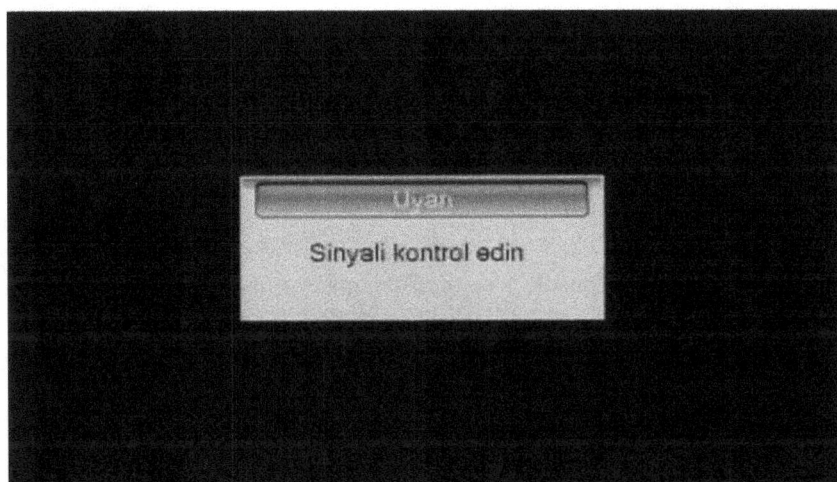

Figure 3 The image above is a still taken from IHH documentary recounting the incident presented by a witness, illustrating the IDF's electronic screening. Still from: IHH, "Freedom: Last Destination—*Mavi Marmara*," Vimeo Video, 91 mins., October 5, 2012, http://vimeo.com/50824956.

logics generated complex perceptions of the role played by images. Indeed, the invisible stream of images soon became an organizing principle of the lethal fighting that took place onboard. One of the activists, and an IHH attorney, Cihat Gökdemir, reported:

> The first two combat boats came very close ... [a]fter a few minutes a helicopter approached from the stern side to the wheelhouse deck. It created a huge wind and a lot of noise ... I thought the helicopter was coming to break down the radio transmitter of the ship, which was on top of the wheelhouse, so I ran toward the wheelhouse deck ... I saw a few other people climbing the stairs with me. ... The helicopter was about 9–10 meters high and it didn't have a flag, coat of arms or any such sign. It stayed up there for about a minute and then opened fire. We thought this firing too was "aiming at the satellite systems." This is why people had gathered not right on top of the wheelhouse where there was an opening, but further back, near the satellite antennas. Personally, I thought "if they're sending them on board, they will probably land right on top of the wheelhouse. After this first shooting some of our friends fell down, but we still thought that they were using plastic bullets; and since we had never seen plastic bullets, we believed injuries from plastic bullets weren't significant, that the main target of the attack was the satellite systems."[14]

As this testimony indicates, the ensuing battle was largely determined by the activists' need to protect and sustain the flow of visual evidence. This overlapped with the physical struggle onboard such that the two became barely distinguishable, and it was no longer clear to what degree military power was mediating the image stream or to what degree the images facilitated and shaped the physical struggle. Indeed, reports about the deadly encounter portray a tangled relation between the shooting of live ammunition and the visual record of the fight under way. Prior to the event, some of the activists had debated whether, in the event of an attack on the flotilla, they would choose to document the conflict or defend the boat. Activist Ken O'Keefe, who was aboard the *Mavi Marmara*, described the dilemma:

> When I was asked, in the event of an Israeli attack on the *Mavi Marmara*, would I use the camera, or would I defend the ship? I enthusiastically committed to the defense of the ship. I am a huge supporter of non-violence. In fact I believe non-violence should always be the first option. Nonetheless I joined the defense of the *Mavi Marmara*, understanding that we may very well be compelled to use violence in self-defense.[15]

The implied distinction between filming and active resistance would soon be contested, however. Reports claimed that men were killed holding cameras, some even "using them to film the Israeli invaders when they were shot."[16] According to several eyewitness reports, the director of the ship's press room, Cevdet Kılıçlar, was last seen stepping outside to take pictures.[17] One of the testimonies quotes his last words:

> I helped others carry one of the injured down. As I was climbing up, right in front of the pressroom door I saw our martyr Cevdet Kılıçlar. Cevdet told me "brother I sent the images." I think he had managed to send some of the images/videos of the first attack via satellite or Internet—this is what he must have meant.[18]

From the Israeli testimonies, one soldier reported being badly beaten with large cameras tripods.[19] Another reported being photographed and videotaped extensively while he was being beaten with batons, making him feel like he was "in the middle of a press conference."[20] This pattern was repeated in other soldiers' testimonies.[21] The activists, for their part, describe continuous and indiscriminate attempts to disrupt the live broadcast:

> We climbed upstairs to the 3rd floor. The staircase was all bloody. I went out from the stern side door to the deck where we had the live broadcast. Live broadcast was going on, but I didn't know if the world did actually receive it. I stayed there for a minute; from the stern deck, port side, I looked up the wheelhouse deck and saw one of the terrorists/pirates pointing with his gun at the live broadcast equipment, and saw the red light on the cameraman. I thought he was trying to shoot the cameraman, so I ran there on the narrow port side deck. ... A cameraman dragged me and said, "stand still in front of me, I'll record this" and I did what he told me; I shielded him and he recorded. I stood straight to shield the cameraman and also to see the helicopter sending troops down to our deck. ... But in a minute or so the cameraman behind me fell down. I squatted down near him and saw that he was shot from his right arm.[22]

According to one activist, the injured onboard the *Mavi Marmara* were evacuated only when the Israelis discovered that "satellite images of what happened on the ship [were spreading] around the world"; only then, the activist continues, did the soldiers "begin to play the role of 'the good guy' [and try] to save the lives of the wounded."[23] In contrast, the Israelis authorities claim that such attempts were taking place all along, and only continued in a "more managed way" once the takeover was complete.[24]

Around the same time, starting at 5:10 a.m., an additional Israeli force (provided by Masada, the special operations unit of the Israel Prison Service) boarded the ship. A two-step arrest procedure got under way, with all passengers searched for data storage devices and some being handcuffed. Almost all of

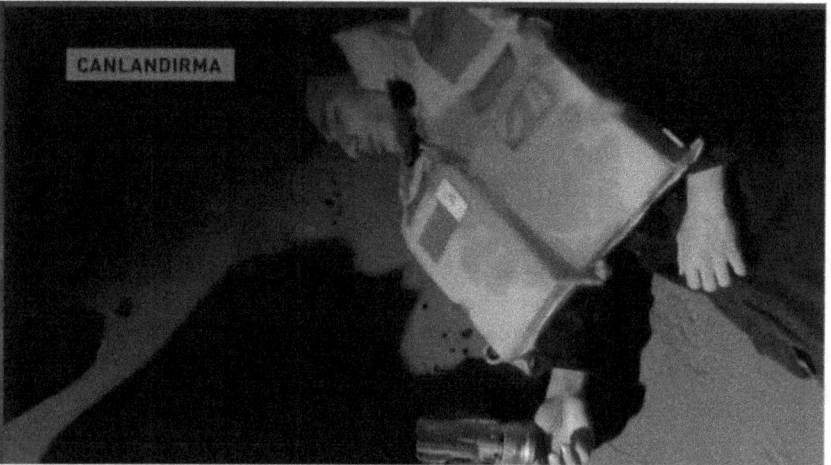

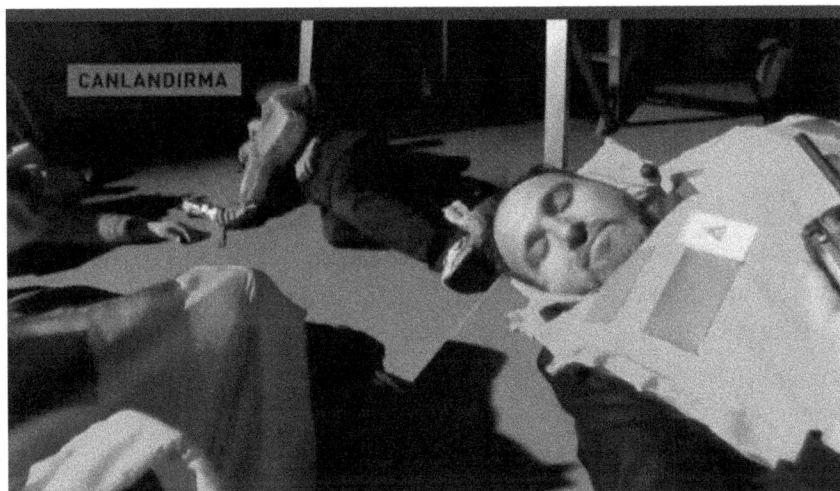

Figures 4a–d Stills taken from the IHH documentary staged re-enactment of the incident. IHH, "Freedom: Last Destination—*Mavi Marmara*," Vimeo Video, 91 mins., October 5, 2012, http://vimeo.com/50824956.

these devices—an estimated number of 2,600—were sequestered.[25] Thus, while the wounded were being treated and evacuated, Israeli forces were also busy confiscating memory cards, cameras, mobile phones, hard discs, videos, and diskettes from the hundreds of flotilla passengers, and removing all recordings from the ships' security cameras. According to the Turkel Commission Report, the same helicopters that evacuated the wounded were also used to transport some of the confiscated media for use by the Israeli military's Spokesperson's and Advocacy Department. All other materials were transferred to the IDF's Document and Technological Capture Collection Unit upon the flotilla's arrival at Ashdod Port.[26] In fact, various sources suggest that the Israeli military's censorship policy only escalated during and immediately following the confrontation itself. Prior to the raid, the Israeli military invited a group of journalists to accompany its forces. However, in the course of the raid, it prevented them from broadcasting and publishing their reports. Moreover, a year later, Colonel Shai Stern, then the Israeli military's Deputy Spokesperson, revealed in the course of a military conference: "In the flotilla incident we were involved in the very initial planning of the takeover operation. … For the first time in the IDF history, the military allocated helicopters to the [Spokesperson's] unit to enable it to produce operational coverage and then transfer materials to the media as quickly as possible."[27]

Incidentally, this censorship effort was self-defeating, given Israel's primary goal of preventing images of the event from circulating internationally: during the first twelve hours after the raid was launched, numerous images capturing events as they unfolded were streamed by the activists and distributed extensively in the international media, while remaining blocked for Israeli viewers.[28] Moreover, it seems that, accidently, the efforts to block the flotilla communication eventually degraded the ability of the invited press to communicate visuals from the sea.[29]

Thus, while Israel's censorship efforts failed to prevent the events from being documented, they successfully impeded public access to the evolving documentation. What happened on the upper deck, where the fighting took place, was filmed from numerous angles by dozens of cameras (with videos, stills, CCTV frames, and aerial shots)[30] as well as by action cams mounted on the soldiers' helmets.[31] The surreal and somewhat unprecedented proliferation of visual recording devices turned the raid into an event in which "hyper-representation" became a core feature and—especially for the flotilla organizers—a key objective of the entire enterprise. And yet, despite the surfeit of visual evidence actually produced, barely five minutes of video material documenting the confrontation remain accessible to the public. Hours of video and an untold quantity of stills remain sequestered. The estimated several hundred hours of recordings withheld by the Israeli authorities are now categorized as "classified information" for reasons of "national security,"[32] and continue to remain under exclusive Israeli control.[33] In terms of the cameras on the ship, some of them, smashed by the soldiers,[34] were quickly rendered inoperable by the Israeli forces. Notably, while the ship's passengers themselves were detained only temporarily, their property (visual material) was unlawfully seized and remains in custody.[35] As a result, the international judicial inquiry into the events had to rely on the forensic reports produced by the Israeli and Turkish investigative bodies. In the absence of the relevant visual documentation of events, the UN report had to weigh up the conflicting narratives presented by each of the two adversary parties. In short, although it was known to exist, the multiple visual evidence was replaced in the hearings with second-hand verbal testimony describing it.[36]

When the images reached territorial soil by means of the hijacking the ships' electronic communications, and then by confiscating the activists' collective digital memory, the Israeli military effectively appropriated all visual evidence of the event and made it national property. Its goal was to ensure that all this evidence would remain "extraterritorial," that is, to keep it both outside of the public domain and also beyond the reach of international legal proceedings.

Simply put, while it is common knowledge that the evidence exists, it remains inaccessible to the international investigative bodies, and countries other than Israel.[37]

What little accessible footage remains shows only fragments of the actual struggle on board the *Mavi Marmara*. The publicly available evidence, most of which was released by the Israeli military, has been the visual basis for the various attempts to "expose the truth"—by governments, NGOs, the media, and individuals. Moreover, this material has served as actual evidence in various official inquiries and investigations. As noted, however, the publicly available footage amounts to no more than a few minutes of videotaped material. Rather than revealing what actually happened, it is an almost ephemeral trace of the event, testifying from a distance, as it were, to the existence of the censored footage.[38]

Since the publicly available images are so fragmentary, they are prone to multiple interpretations, and have been used variously to support different narratives, often of contrary political outlooks and objectives. Paradoxically, it is precisely the *absence* of visual material that has allowed the scant footage that remains to generate an atmosphere of permanent investigation, fueling rival interpretations based on identical visual data.[39] There is a complex set of relationships between the publicly available images and the functions they have been assigned within the various narratives adjoined to them. In some cases, these uses simply underscore the relationship's fundamental dependence on perspective. In others, however, the distance between image and narrative becomes so great as to make the relationship either weak or downright contradictory.

The video footage publicly available at present consists of three types of material:

1. The last images broadcast live from the ship by the activists at the time of the confrontation. These images were transmitted via the complementary Turksat satellite frequency installed by the flotilla organizers, which reportedly continued broadcasting until 7 a.m. on May 31.[40]
2. Clips edited by the IDF Spokesperson's and Advocacy Department, and released about 12 hours after the event. These clips are based on footage filmed by the Israeli military, along with material confiscated from the activists, and were evidently edited to serve Israel's propaganda purposes.[41] One of these clips, released by the military at a later date, is cited as "based on findings by the Eiland Team of Experts," and "breaks down the events of

the flotilla using a timeline that alternates between 3D models and footage captured throughout the incident."[42]

3. A very small number of images smuggled by the activists and released after the event.

The section below presents an assessment of each set of these images in turn. The overarching aim is not to try and reconstruct the events in the order they occurred (most of the visual data we have were released by the Israeli army, so it would be playing into the military's game to base one's view of the event on this partial and tendentious selection). Rather, it will explore, first, the uses to which both sides have put the few publicly available images, and, second, the relationship between these uses and the confiscated images that remain inaccessible to the public.

(a) The Live Broadcast

The first images from the confrontation to circulate in the media were the very last ones broadcast from the ship while satellite communications were being interrupted. These are short sequences in color, visually disrupted and distorted.[43] They feature live accounts of the attack by such individuals as news reporter Jamal al-Shayal of *Al-Jazeera*[44] and IHH director Bülent Yıldırım.[45] The live broadcast by the activists includes several images of the physical altercation, among them two clips, each a few seconds long. One shows a soldier aiming his M-16 rifle horizontally and firing at an off-camera target, apparently from very close range. Another shows soldiers kicking an off-camera individual on the floor. The interruptions to the live broadcast are clearly visible in these clips, forcing the viewers to observe the documented clash through the filter of the further battle between the activists' broadcasting systems and Israeli military's signal-jamming technology. The narrative of the original event thus forks off in two overlapping directions, and the visuals of the aggressions are filtered by competing technologies. The violence conveyed by images becomes inseparable from the violence wrought upon the images themselves.

Two additional segments show a soldier allegedly being stabbed by one of the activists.[46] Though initially shown by the activists as evidence for the Israeli assault,[47] the stabbing scene was later broadcast by Israel's largest commercial television channel, Channel 2, to back the Israeli military's version of the events.[48] The latter scene was also edited by the Israeli military in the "timeline" clip in order to highlight what they allege was the excessive violence in the activists' response to the military's incursion.[49]

Clearly, all the images were frequently employed in conflicting ways by the opposing sides and were sometimes antithetical, even within the same agenda. In more than one case, the activists' use of the images contradicted the verbal testimonies of their colleagues. For example, the clip that shows soldiers as aggressors kicking and shooting was used to expose the military's brutality: with graphics superimposed on the moving images, the activists claimed that the clip depicted the close-range execution of one of the slain flotilla passengers, Furkan Doğan.[50] Instead, the statement submitted to the criminal court in Istanbul, accusing the Israeli military of initiating the violence, claimed that "Furkan Doğan and İbrahim Bilgen were killed before any of the soldiers boarded the ship *Mavi Marmara*."[51] This latter claim was meant to prove that the military attacked the activists before encountering any violence on the part of the passengers; clearly, however, this claim contradicts the attempt to show that Furkan Doğan was gunned down on the ship, that is, after the soldiers descended from the helicopters.[52]

As the above case illustrates, the very same images were often used by both sides in support of their respective versions of the event. That the images could be utilized in such a way, however—that they could be used to support divergent takes on the events—only indicates that they were often so rudimentary as to preclude any conclusive interpretation. The images that stood at the center of such bitter fighting, the images that inspired such careful efforts by those who wished to capture or to defend them, often turned out to provide the flimsiest of evidence. Their importance as factual documents, their ability to support claims of fact, has turned out to be highly dubitable.

(b) Clips Released by the Israeli Military

The material made available by the Israeli military is intriguing in a number of ways. In one piece of footage—a minute and 5-second-long clip, which is in color but without sound, taken in long shot from aboard the ship—a Morena-type military vessel is seen approaching the *Mavi Marmara*. Passengers aboard the *Marmara* are shown wielding clubs and waving a chain, throwing objects, and using a water-hose to spray IDF soldiers located below them on a Zodiac boat. At the same time, a flash of light can be seen. On the Israeli military website, this clip is described as evidence that the activists assaulted the soldiers. Using instructive graphics overlaid on top of the footage, the Israeli military claims that the flashing (presumed to be explosions) object thrown at the soldiers was a stun grenade.[53] However, this contradicts the testimony of "the most senior

[IDF] officer in charge of taking the *Mavi Marmara*" who admits that he ordered the use of flash grenades (a type of stun grenade devised to both temporarily deafen and blind an opponent) should the military's Morena boats be met with resistance.[54] Parts of the same clip appear in a documentary, produced by the IHH, intent on reconstructing the events based on eyewitness testimony.[55] Here, the footage is presented as proof that the activists tried to prevent the soldiers from boarding the ship, yet the documentary claims that it was the soldiers who threw grenades from the Zodiac boats onto the *Mavi Marmara*.[56]

Another piece of footage released by the Israeli military—a clip taken in medium shot, 2:10 minutes in length, again in color and without sound—was edited out of footage purportedly taken from a security camera installed onboard the *Mavi Marmara*.[57] The clip is heavily edited, with constant temporal jumps and without a single sequence lasting longer than 15 seconds. In one 10-second segment, activists are seen using slingshots and throwing an object overboard. The other segments mostly show activists holding clubs, gathering on the deck, and reacting to various off-camera occurrences.[58] Parts of this clip, too, are included in the IHH documentary to illustrate the activists' testimonies, in particular their accounts of how they tried to prevent the soldiers from boarding the *Marmara*.[59]

Two other clips released by the military are in grainy black and white. One was taken in a long shot, the other in an extreme long shot. The first, 1:01 minutes long and with sound, was reportedly taken from a naval boat; the other, 00:54 minutes long and silent, shows aerial footage.[60] Both clips present, from different points of views, soldiers rappelling down from helicopters and being attacked by activists. Some of the activists appear to be using clubs, or what instructive graphics added by the Israeli military describe as metal poles. A soldier is seen thrown from the upper deck to a lower one by the activists. The two sequences may overlap at some points, and short segments from each appear in the IHH documentary to illustrate the activists' testimonies about the takeover, the evacuation of the wounded, and their own responses to these developments.

The "timeline" clip put together by the Israeli military incorporates much of the footage described above. The clip is heavily edited, combining the above black-and-white footage and accompanied by a voiceover of the Israeli version of the events. The clip also includes very short segments from the other footage described earlier—the clip shot from the *Mavi Marmara* in which a military Morena boat is seen approaching; the footage taken from the ship's security cameras; and the two segments in color, seemingly taken from the live streaming, which show a soldier beaten and stabbed. This representation also draws from a clip that features some of the footage described earlier but other material is otherwise unavailable to the public. These include black-

and-white segments, apparently taken from an Israeli navy boat, in which the military Morena boat is seen approaching the *Mavi Marmara* and being sprayed by a water-cannon. Also incorporated are very short pieces of aerial footage, including a black-and-white segment, again taken from a navy boat, in which what appear to be rifle crosshairs are visible mid-screen. In this segment, a soldier is seen abseiling down to the vessel and is then attacked by a group of people holding clubs, while another soldier is thrown from an upper onto a lower deck. Interestingly, the same segment also appears in the IHH documentary, where it is used to illustrate the activists' claim that the soldiers had already begun shooting from the Israeli helicopters before the takeover of the vessel had gone under way. At a later point, the documentary shows sections from these clips as an activist describes how he, together with others, managed to "throw some of the soldiers overboard to prevent them from shooting" and how "some of [the soldiers] may have jumped by themselves to avoid falling into our hands."[61]

(c) Smuggled Images

The main piece of video evidence smuggled from the *Mavi Marmara* was filmed by activist Iara Lee on a camera memory card that eluded the Israeli military's bodily searches.[62] Her footage testifies visually to the complexity of the act of visual documentation itself onboard the ship. The footage reveals very little of the actual physical confrontation.[63] Military Zodiac boats are shown approaching the *Mavi Marmara*; gunshots are heard,[64] and a soldier is seen pointing his gun upward and shooting; several objects are thrown at the soldiers, including a large case, and a flickering light flashes quickly while another loud noise is heard. Many of the passengers are seen holding metal bars and poles, and there are shots depicting red stains.[65] Later, soldiers are seen descending on ropes from a helicopter while three activists aim slingshots and fire at the helicopter for about 40 seconds. Toward the end of the recording, just before the takeover is complete, a group of activists holding metal poles is seen crowding the stairwell leading to the ship's entrance and protecting the door from inside. Gunshots are occasionally heard, probably coming from outside (off-camera). One activist is shown standing near the round window of the already-smashed entrance door, and as what sounds like a gunshot is heard, the man is seen either ducking or falling down.[66] As noted, however, the actual confrontation is hardly seen. Most of the footage presents the evacuation of the injured to the ship's inner galleries and various attempts to provide medical care.[67]

Iara Lee's footage reveals the presence of photographers aboard the ship, both amateur and professional. From the beginning of the assault, barely a sequence goes by without a photographer caught in the frame. As a result, we, the viewers, cannot but reflect on the ways in which the event we observe was documented; our experience of the event is always mediated by our contemplation of the photographers' work. Whereas in the beginning of Lee's footage, the photographers seem to apply routine documentary conventions in taking photos of the wounded from the sidelines or looking down from above, once the capture is in full effect, they can no longer be separated from their subjects. In many cases, those taking pictures of the wounded from close range are forced to stop in order to make way for evacuators and medical help. Photographers are seen documenting their own colleagues while they themselves are looking for shelter. The unity of photographer and subject culminates in a piece of footage in which a photographer is seen turning his camera toward himself in extreme close-up in order to document himself lying-down wounded.

The army's eventual confiscation of the footage changed the photographers' role, however, from being producers of actual (that is, viewable) documentation, to being directly symbolic of the act of requisition: with most of the documentary footage confiscated and stored out of the public domain, the photographers' presence in the available footage is a significant portent of the sheer mass of images that are now kept from view.[68]

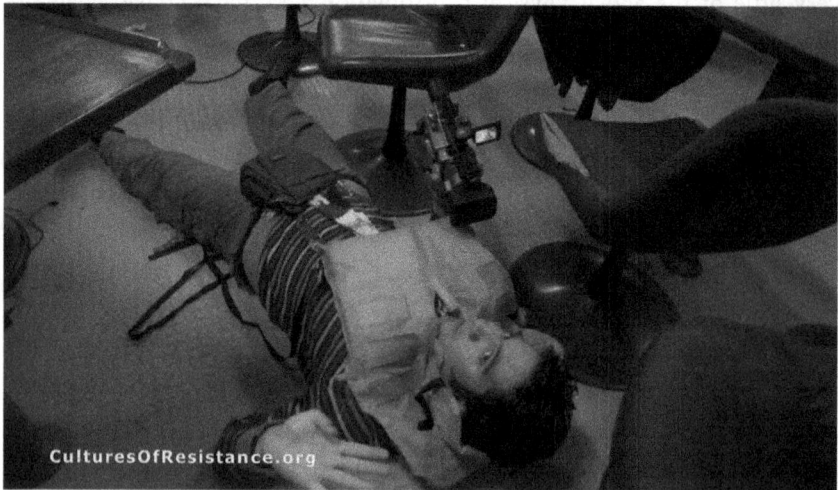

Figure 5 Still from: Culture of Resistance Films, "Israeli Attack on the *Mavi Marmara* (1 Hour Raw Footage)," YouTube Video, 62 mins., June 11, 2010, http://www.youtube.com/watch?v=vwsMJmvS0AY (CulturesOfResistance.org).

Extraterritoriality and the Battle over the Images

As it stands, Israel's state archives currently contain confiscated visual evidence that may determine whether violations of human rights occurred during the assault. Yet for reasons of "national security," this evidence has been stored away at the Israel State Archives, and remains beyond the reach of international law and of states other than Israel. This means that the evidence is, paradoxically, held in a legal distance that is extant but at the same time absent: we know it is there, but it is inaccessible and therefore useless. This generates a situation of crucial imbalance in the process of resolving the event's legal and political implications.[69]

More generally, my project adopts the Gaza flotilla raid as an impactful case study to illustrate a specific "geography of vision," whereby the military sees and interprets specific images (whose invisibility is considered vital to security) and imposes a veto on their disclosure to the public, claiming their ban is in the interest of "national security." Thus, the state accrues digital archives of acts of violence whose contents are co-authored by the military and by activists alike, records that remain off-limits, even (and specificly) when claims of human rights violations are raised.[70]

What is particularly remarkable about the archives is the question of "co-authorship" of the contents: it is an amalgam of documentation produced by the military acting "in the name of the law," and by the activists, staging a spectacle to challenge the system of the sovereign legislation, yet obliged to do so within the pre-set terms of that same law. The moment the activists' images are expropriated as a parallel testimony, the resulting co-authored archive becomes a liminal record lying between documented "history" (comprising evidence that may be used to incriminate the civilian co-authors) and a visual inventory that is placed out of bounds and is inaccessible to the very persons involved, or to the outside legal bodies initiating the inquiry.

Another significant feature of the co-authored archive of the flotilla incident concerns post-production and intellectual property. Although the archive is, strictly speaking, co-authored, the state has appointed itself the sole legal proprietor of all the material documenting the event. All the other co-authors are not only denied access to the archive, but may even be incriminated by the fruits of their own work. Moreover, now that the images have become "spoils of war," their status has changed from that of crucial historical documentation—particularly as the collective effort of recording events determined the nature of the confrontation and the way in which it unfolded—to that of mere illustrations of various political claims. Their ability to convey information, to impart genuine knowledge of the events, was thrown into doubt. The primary question regarding these materials was no longer "What do I see?" but "How can this image help me establish the story I wish to tell?"

Given these general features of the flotilla incident, I wish to suggest that the incident and its aftermath may be best understood through the notion of *extraterritoriality*, which seems to have shaped not only the event's *legal* dimensions (including the legal aspects of its concrete spatial geography) but also its *visual documentation*.

By confiscating images documenting the event, the Israeli military created an archive of visual documents that is "extraterritorial," in the sense of being outside of the public eye and beyond the reach of international and national legal mechanisms. In many cases, both the activists and the Israeli government defended their actions by citing images Israel has not been willing to release. In such cases, the documentation has remained "present at a distance," publicly invoked in the service of certain political purposes, yet relegated to an "extraterritoriality" in which the normal workings of the legal and political order are suspended under the tutelage of the Israeli law.

It is worth noting that my use of "extraterritoriality" here diverges from the term's ordinary sense, of a sphere beyond the reach of some legal jurisdiction. Rather, the extraterritoriality of both the archive of images and Gaza itself follows a more complex logic, one in which (1) the state exercises direct control over some object (the archive of images; Gaza's territory and population), regulating it, preventing others from having access to it, etc.; and (2) the state nevertheless does so while exempting its own actions, either partially or completely, from the scrutiny of legal mechanisms and from the public eye, perforating our visual knowledge about its own violations. In the case of the expropriated archive of images, the result is a regime of representation in which the images are removed from the public field of vision; to the extent that they remain present in the public discourse, it is only via the indirect (and unverifiable) verbal representations provided by the state at its own unregulated discretion. The extraterritorial images' most basic capacity, their power to represent or signify, is revoked. Under most conditions, these images remain out of scope, even though their content—the visual evidence they contain—continues to play a role in public life. However, when the images are mediated by alternative substitutes, "at a distance," as it were, they inevitably become subject to loose interpretation, reimagining, and manipulation; their absence opens room to misinformation and disinformation efforts.

Examples of Similar Images Used by Both the Activists and the IDF to Convey Contradictory Meanings:

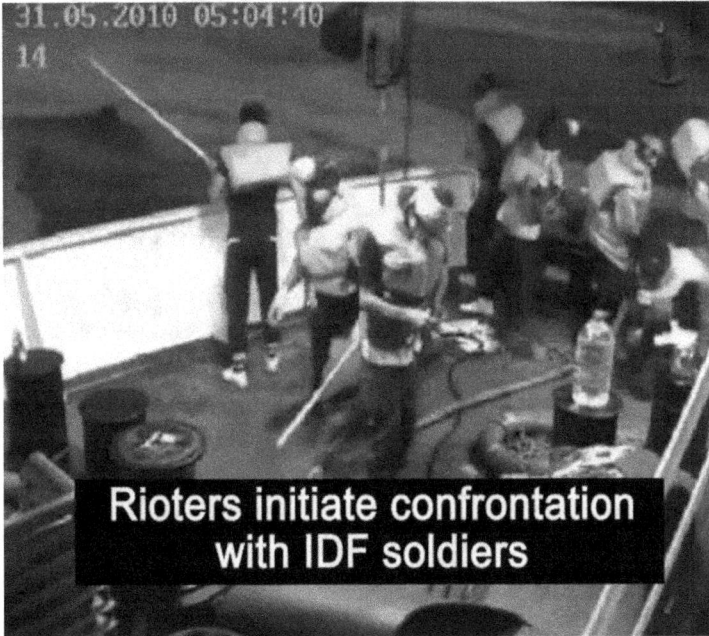

Figure 6 Still from: IDF, "Flotilla Rioters Prepare Rods, Slingshots, Broken Bottles and Metal Objects to Attack IDF Soldiers," YouTube Video, 2:24 mins., June 2, 2010, https://www.youtube.com/watch?v=HZlSSaPT_OU: "Rioters initiate confrontation with IDF soldiers."

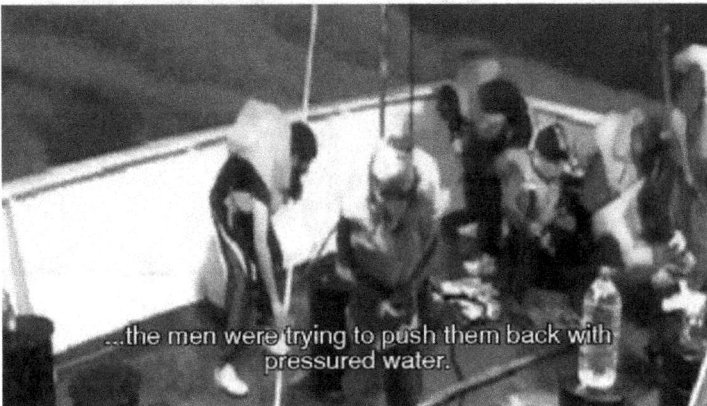

Figure 7 Still from: IHH, "Freedom: Last Destination—*Mavi Marmara*," Vimeo Video, 91 mins., October 5, 2012, http://vimeo.com/50824956. Activist testifies: "When the soldiers tried to board the ship by dropping rope ladders … the men were trying to push them back with pressured water."

Figure 8 Still from: IDF, "*Mavi Marmara* Passengers Attack IDF before Soldiers Boarded Ship," YouTube Video, 1:10 mins., June 2, 2010, http://www.youtube.com/watch?v=B6sAEYpHF24: "Activist waving metal bars later used for hitting soldiers."

Figure 9 Still from: IHH, "Freedom: Last Destination—*Mavi Marmara*," Vimeo Video, 91 mins., October 5, 2012, http://vimeo.com/50824956. Activist testifies: " ... the men were trying to push them back with pressured water" (voiceover).

Figure 10 Still from: IDF, "*Mavi Marmara* Passengers Attack IDF before Soldiers Boarded Ship," YouTube Video, 1:10 mins., June 2, 2010, http://www.youtube.com/watch?v=B6sAEYpHF24: "Metal chain … "

Figure 11 Still from: IHH, "Freedom: Last Destination—*Mavi Marmara*," Vimeo Video, 91 mins., October 5, 2012, http://vimeo.com/50824956. Activist testifies: "So that the soldiers could not board the ship … " (voiceover).

Figure 12 Still from: IDF, "Timeline of the *Mavi Marmara* Incident," YouTube Video, 21:18 mins., May 22, 2011, http://www.youtube.com/watch?v=z31GesVrBjc: "While falling, one of the soldiers is stabbed in the stomach and hand" (IDF Narrator's voiceover).

Figure 13 Still from: IHH, "Freedom: Last Destination—*Mavi Marmara*," Vimeo Video, 91 mins., October 5, 2012, http://vimeo.com/50824956. Activist testifies: "Of course at first we were able to throw two to three soldiers to the lower deck by such prevention" (voiceover).

Figure 14 Still from: IDF, "Timeline of the *Mavi Marmara* Incident," YouTube Video, 21:18 mins., May 22, 2011, http://www.youtube.com/watch?v=z31GesVrBjc: "As soon as the IDF light boats approached the boat, IHH activists crowded together at the side of the ship" (IDF Narrator's voiceover).

Figure 15 Still from: IHH, "Freedom: Last Destination—*Mava Marmara*," Vimeo Video, 91 mins., October 5, 2012, http://vimeo.com/50824956. Activist testifies: "For a moment I thought that they all came only for me" (voiceover).

The *Mavi Marmara* Trial: From Absent Images to Absent Defendants

Background

The extraterritorial logic of the flotilla event seems to have extended to the legal proceedings and tactics taken up by the flotilla organizers both before and after the Israeli takeover of the boats. Since the takeover occurred mid-sea in extraterritorial waters, and since, paradoxically, international naval law revolves around the national affiliation of vessels,[1] the national identity of the *Mavi Marmara* has been at the center of the legal actions taken by the organizers against Israel. The *Mavi Marmara*'s free-floating identity has been articulated in different ways in the various legal charges brought against Israel, depending on the particular courts or legal bodies before which the case has been taken. In this way, the *Marmara* has anchored both the flotilla organizers' claim for universal justice and the legal, diplomatic, and even cultural processes occurring at the distinctly national level. The IHH bought the *Mavi Marmara* from the City of Istanbul.[2] Two days before setting sail, presumably for reasons of regulatory convenience, the boat gave up its official Turkish affiliation, registering instead under the flag of the Comoro Islands, a tiny archipelago in the Indian Ocean. Ironically, it was the organizers' choice of a "flag of convenience"—a step often taken to circumvent legal requirements and avoid minimal human rights standards[3]—that allowed them to press charges against Israel for the most serious crimes recognized by international law. The *Marmara*'s original Turkish affiliation was the basis for charges brought before the criminal court in Istanbul. Yet, it was the boat's new national affiliation that enabled the organizers to appeal to the International Criminal Court (ICC) at The Hague. Had the *Marmara* remained a Turkish boat at the time of the takeover, the IHH could not have gone to the ICC, since Turkey (like Israel) is not a signee of the Rome Convention and is therefore not an ICC member. However, due to the boat's arbitrary registration under the Comoran flag, the IHH was able to bring its charges of "crimes against humanity" before the international court. While the appeal to the ICC was submitted on May 14, 2013, on behalf of the government of Comoros, represented by the Turkish IHH's law firm, the request to open an investigation did not pass the ICC's preliminary filtering process and was eventually entirely dismissed in early stages by the Chief Prosecutor, though not before November 29, 2017.[4] According to the ICC, it was not the gravity of the crimes but rather the inaccessible evidence which contributed to the court's decision in its pre-trial investigation:

> In the decision the prosecutor has, however, found that although there is a reasonable basis to believe that crimes within the ICC's jurisdiction were committed by the Israeli Defense Forces ("IDF") on board the *Mavi Marmara* and the other two vessels, "the information available does not provide a reasonable basis to proceed with an investigation of the situation."[5]

In Turkey, however, full-fledged trial proceedings were conducted, on which the next section will focus.

The *Mavi Marmara* Trial

In 2012, two years after the incident, criminal charges against four Israeli senior commanders, allegedly the leaders of the military interception of the Gaza flotilla, were presented before the Seventh Court of Serious Crimes at the Çağlayan Courthouse in Istanbul, Turkey.[6] An indictment signed by an Istanbul prosecutor was brought against former Israeli Military Chief of Staff Gabi Ashkenazi, former Head of Military Intelligence Amos Yadlin, former Commander of the Israeli Navy Eliezer Marom, and former Air Force Commander Avishai Levy, for the alleged crime of planning and leading the attack. The indictment chose to base its legitimacy on an "extraterritorial" claim, namely, that Turkish territorial jurisdiction applies to Turkish maritime vessels, such as the *Mavi Marmara*.[7] Held in the absence of the defendants, who were declared fugitives, the hearings commenced on November 6, 2012.[8]

The IHH played a significant role in getting the case to trial, hiring barristers to represent the victims, funding the invitation of dozens of international witnesses to arrive in Turkey in order to testify, and conducting extensive efforts to present the case to the media. Their inclusion in the trial was made possible by an invocation of an extraterritorial law, namely the "principle of universality" which allows the prosecution in Turkey of crimes committed abroad against foreign citizens.[9] The prosecution, for its part, demanded nine consecutive life sentences for each of the defendants.[10]

The indictment charged the defendants with numerous violations, including premeditated murder, attempted premeditated murder, aggravated assault, assault, aggravated looting and torture.[11] In the six hearings held on May 26, 2014, the court also issued arrest warrants for the four defendants, reflecting the claim that the *Marmara* incident took place on Turkish soil.[12] Since both Turkey and Israel had signed the European Convention on Extradition agreeing to mutually respect extraterritorial law enforcement, it was claimed that Israel would be obliged to extradite the defendants in case of conviction. In tandem, the Turkish branch of Interpol reportedly requested that the General Secretariat of Interpol issue arrest warrants and a "red notice" for the suspects, yet these were never respected by the State of Israel.[13]

Some have criticized the Istanbul court for trying the four commanders *in absentia*, in potential violation of international human rights law.[14] Israeli officials denounced the trial, arguing it was merely performative in nature—a "show trial," "political theater," a "unilateral political act with no judicial credibility."[15] The IHH retorted by stressing that it was deliberate absence—the forced deprivation of visual evidence—that not only occasioned the trial itself but also shaped the nature of the testimonies. In its condensed report on the trials, lawyer Cüneyt Toraman is quoted as stating, "[t]he victims' cameras were seized, but those who shot the footage are in front of us as witnesses or victims now."[16] The act of giving testimony was thus presented as an alternative to the absent visual evidence. A later IHH report on the legal actions taken against Israel explicitly cites the absent images as validating the recourse to trials *in absentia*:

> There is no impediment to continuing the trial and the hearings. Because the Turkish and foreign complainants and victims testifying in the hearings saw and experienced the events that took place during the attack, they are the witnesses of the human rights violations and of the crimes dealt with in this case. Though the victims' cameras and the recording devices on the ship were seized by Israeli soldiers, it is extremely important for the realisation of a fair trial that the statements of those who have made these records are received immediately while they are still alive, and that all the evidence of the event is collected with all the details thereof and brought before the legal authorities.[17]

Against this backdrop, the international media reported that, contrary to normal juridical procedures in Turkey, the trial would be officially documented and recorded, but not broadcast.[18]

From the very beginning, then, the trial was conceived as the production of an official inaccessible archive. Since documentation of the flotilla event had been removed from visibility by the Israeli government, the trial had to replace visual evidence with verbal description: witnesses were now orally testifying as to what they had filmed on the night of the incident.[19] The court's documentation of the juridical proceedings helped their testimony regain a visual dimension— although, as I shall later explain, this new visual dimension would become out of reach as well. The missing archive of the flotilla event, co-authored by the Israeli military and by the activists, is being used to generate yet another inaccessible visual archive, this time co-authored by the activists and by the Turkish legal system.

My main claim in the following section is that to better understand the Istanbul trial, we must comprehend the extraterritorial logic of representation underlying certain of its aspects, including the following: (a) The court proceedings relied on, and were in turn documented by, visual images produced by sometimes overlapping, sometimes competing, legal systems. (b) The images' evidentiary content may have both indicated and affected the competition between the legal systems involved: for example, if the court documentation had been made public, this would have shown that the European standards allegedly adopted by the court had not been assimilated in practice.[20] (c) The images were made inaccessible to public scrutiny. (d) Representatives of the legal systems hold exclusive rights to the images. (e) The inaccessibility of the images may affect the ways in which the event they document is perceived and imagined.

Since I, like others, lack access to the court's visual documentation, my main tasks in what follows are, first, to trace the ways in which the creation of the trial's documentation has itself been an outcome of the encounter between negotiating law systems; second, to examine the evidentiary value of the court-produced images and their potential effect on the legal validity of the proceedings. As I hope to show, the visual images produced and used by the Istanbul court ended up exposing certain shortcomings of the court itself and its legal proceedings. Although the images were produced by representatives of the law, they exposed violations that were carried out in the name of the law and contested the legitimacy of its procedures (from an unchallenged prosecution process at start, to the outright exposure of the lack of independency of the court in accordance to political interests). Here, again, I offer that the notion of the "extraterritorial image" can help to explain some features of the phenomenon in question.

The following sections pursue these tasks by combining legal storytelling with an examination of how justice was documented by the court cameras. I will juxtapose the actual proceedings with written Turkish criminal law and fair trial procedures, while describing verbally what presumably exists on the audio-visual records in the court archive.[21] In a sense, my own work here becomes an example of the ways in which the existence of "extraterritorial images"—in this case the court documentation—could incriminate their creators if the images become open to public scrutiny.

Extraterritorial Images and "Access to Justice"

(a) *The Concept of Access to Justice*

In the course of the *Mavi Marmara* trial, which lasted from November 6, 2012, to December 6, 2016, the Turkish court in Istanbul itself became the unwitting creator of "extraterritorial images" by producing audio-visual records of the eventually dismissed court proceedings—only to then restrict access to them. To understand both the reasons for this in-court documentation and the implications of its later suppression, we first need to look briefly at the strained relationship between the Turkish legal system and the European Union.

For decades since the 1950s, Turkey has been making a concentrated effort to join the European Economic Community upon which the European Union was built.[22] Reforms in the country's legal and judiciary system have been a major part of this effort ever since the country's application.[23] A fundamental condition for EU membership is that candidates must be monitored by the EU commission.[24] To examine Turkey's progress, the country's justice system has therefore been subjected to ongoing investigations and annual reports.[25] A crucial aspect of EU monitoring of states seeking membership is the concept of "**access to justice.**" On the most basic level, "access to justice" requires that citizens be provided equal access to courts of law. In a broader sense, however, "access to justice" may also refer to the ability to monitor the legal system from outside, and ensure that it properly administers justice. For example, principles of "access of justice" may cover vital measures required for tracing the ways in which the justice system operates: for example, public access to court records and proceedings, as well as to legal information connected with the investigation (both pre- and post-trial).[26] According to Seda Kalem Berk, the concept itself made its first appearance in the Turkish legal literature in tandem with the acceptance of Turkey's candidacy for full EU membership.[27] While originally, the 1982 Turkish Constitution did not explicitly include a constitutional right of access to juridical or other government information, in 2004, to harmonize "along the line of the legislations of the European Union," a Turkish version of an information right was introduced as a law.[28]

In a strategic plan developed by the Turkish Ministry of Justice (MoJ) in order to comply with EU requirements, the Turkish government expressed its will to "provide and introduce all opportunities that are necessary for the people to easily have the access to justice they need [in order to] seek their rights effectively."[29] The 2013 Istanbul Declaration further states, "[i]t is now universally accepted that the principle of transparency is a fundamental component of the juridical process in states that uphold human rights and the rule of law."[30] The Declaration further notes that "subject to judicial supervision, the public, the media and court, those who concerned should have reliable access to all information pertaining to judicial proceedings, both pending and concluded," and that "poor or biased media coverage can undermine public confidence in the judiciary and raise concerns with regard to judicial independence."[31]

Similarly, according to the Right of Information Law (adopted in 2003 but in effect since 2004), Turkish citizens enjoy a right to access any governmental and juridical information available on the internet. When the original documents cannot be provided, the law allows citizens to access visual copies and sound recordings. The law does not apply to criminal cases, however, ostensibly in order not to "obstruct judicial duty" or to "endanger crime prevention or investigation"—to name just a few pretexts. These considerations are readily cited by the authorities in order to deny access to records concerning criminal proceedings.[32]

In its evaluation reports, the European Court of Human Rights has repeatedly pointed out Turkey's systematic violations in this area, most frequently involving infringements of the right for a fair trial.[33] Despite the implementation of a raft of reforms in mid-2012—including the directive that judiciaries provide more documentation of their rulings—court proceedings in Turkey continue to lack transparency. Defendants' limited access to prosecution files has been described as contrary to "international fair trial standards,"[34] and some have noted, even prior to a July 2016 failed coup attempt against the regime, the tendency of prosecutors and judges to avoid criticizing government policies, "sympathizing with radical ideology," and adhere to "state-centered attitudes."[35] Journalists reporting on or being critical toward sensitive investigations or court proceedings risk prosecution, and the situation has only deteriorated over the last few years.[36]

In July 2012—the same month the above legal reform was adopted—the ruling Justice and Development Party (AKP) proposed a "sweeping constitutional amendment that would restrict coverage of the judicial system, national security, and other public issues, along with vaguely defined topics such as 'public morals' and 'others' rights."[37]

The EU's judicial concerns with Turkey became stronger yet when on February 26, 2014, then-Turkey's prime minister, Recep Tayyip Erdoğan, approved a bill limiting the independence of the judiciary and empowering the MoJ, at the expense of the Supreme Board of Judges and Prosecutors (HSK).[38] These fears culminated with the Turkish government's introduction of new measures "curtailing fundamental rights" in response to the aforementioned 2016 coup attempt.[39] In the immediate aftermath, Turkey declared a state of emergency, which served as a pretext for the mass jailing of some estimated 150,000 people, among them some 3,000 judges and prosecutors, along with hundreds of journalists. In most cases, all of these incarcerations were conducted without official indictments or any access to evidence in their justification. Following the arrests, around 110,000 public sector employees were summarily dismissed, including 4,238 judges and prosecutors; reportedly, the "[d]ecisions were taken without an individual assessment being provided in all cases."[40]

The EU commission reports from 2016 onwards outline the growing stranglehold, showing particular concern regarding the predicament of the judiciary, which is the source of glaring violations. The reports describe the wide-ranging "changes to the structures and composition of high courts" as "serious concern" and incompatible with European standards. Since the coup attempt, the reports find:

> Judges and prosecutors continued to be removed from their profession and in some cases were arrested. This situation worsened following which one fifth of the judges and prosecutors were dismissed and saw their assets frozen ... Turkey has further extended for certain offences the pre-trial detention to 30 days without access to a judge against ECHR case law and an important part of the judiciary is subject to these measures.[41]

Further, the reports note:

> The HSYK [Supreme Board of Judges and Prosecutors, now named HSK] launched several cases against prosecutors and judges dealing with high-profile cases. Such decisions, especially on judges and prosecutors involved in high-profile cases, create a suspicion of interference by the HSYK in their judicial tasks. Self-censorship appears to be spreading among judges and prosecutors who are wary that any decision undermining the interests of the executive may affect negatively their careers.[42]

Repeated instances revealed the government's despotic control, including the reversal of verdicts that did not fit the purge policy, coupled with disciplinary actions against the judges and prosecutors who defied the procedures that were published in the media.[43]

One aspect criticized by the European Commission throughout the years was the fact that Turkish courts did not have any mechanisms for recording verbatim the testimony of witnesses or presented evidence.[44] Until that point, hearings were recorded mainly in the form of "minutes": court records composed of the judge's notes. Since 2002, the latter have been documented electronically, and thus automatically preserved via the UYAP, Turkey's National Judiciary Informatics Program—a system initiated as part of the effort to adhere to the EU demand to overhaul Turkish justice.[45] The program promotes the use of information and computer technology in the judiciary, enabling all courts to share judicial proceedings via electronic networks.[46]

The Turkish MoJ's active efforts to adopt EU norms of access to justice are reflected in a report concluding the Program for Better Access to Justice in Turkey, a two-year (2003/4) project initiated by the European Union. Among other objectives, the program addressed the need to provide both audio and visual records of court proceedings. According to the report, the installation of full recording systems in Turkey's felony courts (to be funded by the European Union) was awaiting EU approval. Listing the program's expected advantages, the report notes that:

> [Since] evidence will be recorded thoroughly, the possibility of reaching the truth in criminal justice will increase. Not only the submissions and arguments but also the gestures of the parties will be recorded, which will lead to an increase in the quality of justice. Judges and prosecutors will spend more time investigating the facts of the case and will not be facing the difficulty of entering all the evidence and submissions by the parties into the court record through a court stenographer.
>
> . . .
>
> The administration of criminal justice will be swift, all the visuals and sounds recorded via this recording systems will be archived and could be checked whenever a dispute arises as to their accuracy. In addition to these benefits, [the program will] reinforce one of the fundamental principles of criminal law, namely the directness of evidence.[47]

The reform is also manifest in Articles 52, 58, 81, 87, 140, 180, and 196 of the new Turkish Criminal Procedure Code, No. 5271, in effect since June 1, 2005.

The new code requires penal courts and prosecutors to use both sound and visual recording systems for certain procedures. Recording witnesses's statements live is now allowed, and in some cases even compulsory,[48] and court minutes must record even evidence unobtainable by the courts.[49]

The criminal proceeding of the *Mavi Marmara* trial, which lasted for nearly half a decade, took place in Istanbul's Seventh Aggravated Criminal Court.[50] Initially, the IHH announced that 490 witnesses would voice their experiences before the court in a trial open to the public.[51] Accordingly, the hearings were set to be comprised of the testimonies of eyewitnesses who experienced the incident firsthand onboard the *Mavi Marmara* and the accompanying fleet. Since the court reserved the exclusive right to film and record the courtroom proceedings, and limited all outside access to the resulting audio-visual documentation, my analysis attempts to reconstruct selected aspects of the trial based on trial reports and on my own attendance at the hearings, alongside other reports from the trial.[52] In parallel, I will provide my own reflections on the relationship between how justice appears and how it is administered in court.

According to some, the fact that the trial was held in a Turkish court shows a failure of international law. Elsewhere, it has been argued that the Turkish government made "a significant effort to safeguard the values of international law ... [demonstrating] that national courts can play a role in making international law effective" on home soil, and in changing "the double standard of international law."[53]

By providing some examples, I propose a somewhat more complex view, namely that the trial exposed various faults and dysfunctions inherent to certain judicial aspects of the Turkish justice system charged with failing to comply with the most basic prerequisites of a fair trial according to both European standards and international law. Prompted by the criticism of the EU Commission, the Turkish MoJ claims to have formally rectified some of these shortcomings; in practice, however, many of these flaws remained apparent throughout the trial. I propose that this gap between the written letter of the law and the way justice has been administered in practice is precisely what the audio-visual recordings of the proceedings reveal.

(b) The Courthouse and the Courtroom: Spatial Aspects of the Production of Justice

The İstanbul Seventh Aggravated Criminal Court Courthouse was inaugurated in 2011 as part of a comprehensive juridical reform undertaken in order to meet EU membership standards. According to the Turkish MoJ, the court building was erected as part of an extensive modernization scheme launched in 2003 for the construction of dozens of modern courthouses throughout the republic. The scheme was carried out ostensibly to augment the "physical capacity of courthouses in the framework of determined [EU] principles," taking into account "contemporary architectural aspects," with the aim of furnishing juridical services with "advanced technological facilities."[54]

From the start, the national press described the Istanbul "Justice Palace" as being "one of the most costly construction projects in Turkey" and "the largest of its kind in Europe."[55] Irrespective of the declared aim of improving the technological capacities of the nation's courthouses, these boasts betray the superiority/inferiority complex at the heart of the relationship between Turkey and Europe.[56] The emphasis on size and expense, both symbolic and concrete, indicate that the juridical reforms would carry not only legal significance but also have ostensible symbols in the form of ambitious built environments that would embody the underlying architecture of the contemporary state justice system. Despite the hulking dimensions of the new courthouse complex, the hearings actually took place in courtrooms that were often too small for the crowds they attracted. As a result, much of the audience remained outside the courtroom, contravening the court's pretense to secure the trial's open and public nature.[57] Against this background, it is worth recalling the Istanbul Declaration, published the same year that the second hearing took place, which announced a commitment to juridical transparency. The principle of public proceedings implies that ... "the court should ... ensure that the public and the media can attend court proceedings"; that "adequate facilities should also be provided for the attendance of the public ... taking into account the ... interest in the case and the nature of the hearing"; and that "public access to court hearings is a fundamental requirement in a democratic society."[58]

The court's spatial arrangement involved a further flaw that had serious implications for those attending the hearings: stationary microphones were located at various points in the courtroom, including the witness stand and the judge's bench, while several mobile microphones were used, for example by the translators for non-Turkish-speaking witnesses, and by the plaintiffs' lawyers.[59] The latter used the usual counsel seats on the left side of the courtroom, but due to their number—usually more than a dozen at any given time—many were also occupying the front gallery. Consequently, the public was relegated to the remaining space at the back of the courtroom. Alarmingly, without exception, the microphones in the courtroom were used exclusively for the court's internal audio-visual system; none were used to amplify the speakers, which made the hearings barely audible for the attending public. Despite the claim of conducting an open trial, the court thus gave primacy to its own documentation of the legal procedure, neglecting its duties toward the public. The importance given to the task of documentation was also indicated by the fact that the trial was filmed by four security cameras aimed at the judge's bench, the witness podium, the defense lawyers, and the empty seats of the absent defendants, all of which are shown in real-time on a multi-frame monitor mounted above the judge, enabling the audience to see his face as well as those of the witnesses. Intriguingly, for the audience, the presence of the images on the screen in conjunction with the inaudibility of the proceedings merely emphasized the performative and gestural aspects of the trial underway, like watching a silent film.

(c) *Territory on Trial*

While the above scenario is indicative of the administration's general inadequacies, the *Mavi Marmara* trial in particular embodies an even more fundamental issue—the question of *who* is on trial. According to the Turkish criminal code, only individuals (and not collective entities such as states) are considered liable for criminal prosecution and a court trial. Turkish law also prescribes that no one shall be held responsible for the acts of another individual.[60] The hearings of the *Mavi Marmara* incident reveal a different reality, rhetorically at least, for the testimonies captured by the court cameras focus not on the four accused individuals, but on the State of Israel as construed by the victims. Through a process of personification, the State itself is pictured as a murdering lawbreaker and fit to be incarcerated. By criminalizing the Israeli occupation and blockade, the sentence of the trial promises, as it were, to release the Palestinian territories from the hold of this villain.

Consequently, despite the fact that charges were brought against four Israeli individuals, their physical absence from the courtroom also carries juridical significance. As the witnesses repeatedly made evident in their testimonies, this was a trial against Israel, and the Israeli state would eventually be punished.[61] On the second hearing, for example, witness Mary Ann Wright testified that "the *Mavi Marmara* trial is of historic importance because this is the first time Israel is standing on trial as a murderer."[62] Another witness, Joe Meadors, testified:

This is the first time that Israel is being called to account for its actions. The United States has refused to do this for decades. But the Turkish state has acted honestly by being willing to file this case against Israel.[63]

Refika Yıldırm, the widow of *Marmara* victim Necdet Yıldırım, stated on the witness stand, "Israel has taken such a valuable thing from us that I want them to be executed."[64] İsmail Songür, who lost his father, Cengiz Songür, added:

Now, the entire world and Europe in particular have seen [what Israel had done]. ... This trial is the first in history because people used to think that it is never possible to try Israel. They used to think that Israel is even more powerful than the United States. But we know that Allah is more powerful than Israel and the United States ... Israel should be aware of this now ... We don't have any demands, such as an apology or compensation from Israel. We want the termination of the blockade on Gaza.[65]

In tandem with the testimonies, statements tweeted from the court by the IHH's public relations office, intended to mediate the trial to non-Turkish speakers, described the witness testimonies as follows: "All different nationalities came to Istanbul to seek justice for the crimes committed against them by Israel."[66] As noted by IHH lawyer Cihat Gökdemir, who became also a witness in the trial, "[t]he real goal of the *Mavi Marmara* victims is not to receive compensation but to ensure that Israel is convicted in court."[67] Accordingly, the significance of the trial's outcome was construed in political and national terms:

The importance of the *Mavi Marmara* case [is that] Israel's [illusional] immunity will disappear [and its] impunity from [accountability for] grave international crimes will not be tolerated ... Israel will be held responsible for its crimes for the first time and this will set an example.[68]

This view was endorsed by another witness, David Schermerhorn, who summed up, "[t]he real purpose of these hearings is to hold Israel accountable."[69]

The trial's political and national significance was again underscored in an exchange during the third hearing, in which witness Ciğdem Topcuoglu claimed, "[a]ll means are justified in the fight against the Zionist occupiers. They have to abandon the Palestinian lands." In response, one of the plaintiffs' lawyers stated emphatically, "[t]his trial is not just a criminal case; it is first and foremost an effort to liberate the Palestinian lands. May the US be cursed, may Israel be cursed!" The crowds at court responded with a wild round of applause. Sara Colborne, head of the Palestinian Solidarity Campaign, wrote in her report from the hearing, "[v]ictims of the *Mavi Marmara* attack have also repeatedly made clear that another essential demand that must be fulfilled is the lifting of Israel's siege on Gaza."[70] Similar statements were made online in an IHH twitter feed dedicated to reporting from the court: "[The] lawyers are defending the rights not only of the *Mavi Marmara* victims but also the Palestinians."[71]

(d) *The Absence of Cross-Examination*

In a report by the Turkish MoJ on the unique features of the Turkish justice system, in keeping with the EU Commission's definitions, judges are defined as those entrusted with the task of reaching juridical decisions based on the claims of the litigating parties.[72] In a later report dedicated to the "Administration of Justice and Protection of Human Rights in Turkey," issued a year after the trial commenced, judges and prosecutors are imputed with having given "precedence to the protection of the state over protection of human rights." This practice carried serious implications for the defense's cross-examination, at times in outright violation of the prerogatives of the defense counsel.[73] Frequent complaints arose regarding the lack of judicial independence and the absence of so-called direct questioning as a form of cross-examination, an omission sometimes voiced by the judges themselves.[74] Turkish criminal court procedures accord judges a leading role in the trial, and they have primary interrogation powers. Hence, while attorneys are permitted to put direct questions to the witnesses, it is the judge who has the primary obligation to establish the truth. To reach their verdict, judges are therefore allowed to summon witnesses of their own choosing and present evidence to the court as they deem fit.[75]

In the *Mavi Marmara* case, the judge's poor fact-finding process was disturbingly evident throughout the hearings: no examination or efforts were made to impartially evaluate the claims made in previous judicial investigations—by the United Nations, by Israel, or in the media. Most crucially, no investigation was made into whether any of the violence had been pre-planned by the organizers.

Instead, the hearings took the following format: the presiding judge asked the witnesses to recall their experiences of the incident, asking very few questions about particular aspects of the case. Interrogation of witnesses was rare, and the judge abstained from summoning witnesses on his behalf (his prerogative according to Turkish law). Moreover, the judge omitted to interrogate when witnesses made contradictory claims that evidently called for further clarification. To note just a few examples, one of the witnesses testified that passengers were "throwing weapons into the water," without clarifying whose weapons these were. Another witness complained that his interrogation onboard by the Israeli soldiers became more aggressive once they discovered he was carrying his weapons license, yet he was never asked why he had it with him on a journey for which weapons were strictly prohibited. Another witness, Muhamed Latifkaya, told the court that he urged the other activists not to resist, but he was not asked whether their reaction was the result of unprovoked aggression or not. Such questions were never asked, either by the judge or by the defense lawyers. Furthermore, it was never clear to what extent the testimonies directly addressed the actual felonies with which the suspects were being charged: aggravated assault, assault, torture, etc.[76] Throughout the hearings, little effort was made by the prosecution, the judge, or the witnesses, to connect the defendants to the felonies cited in the indictment.

It is worth noting that early in the course of the hearings, the judge ordered the court clerk to cease dictating the witnesses' statements (a standard requirement of the Turkish court system), presumably because (he considered) the testimonies were no longer relevant to the case.[77] As a result, the only full record of the hearings is provided by the court's audio-visual system, despite the fact that Turkish law considers written minutes to be the basis upon which the fairness of a trial is determined.[78]

Furthermore, although three defense lawyers had been assigned by the Istanbul Bar Association at the behest of the court, the three (Alev Peken, Murat Bozkurt, and Uğur Kasapoğlu) were hardly ever present at the same time.[79] During the hearings, none of the lawyers took notes or made comments. Most strikingly, none of them ever undertook cross-examinations, with the result that the entire case became a series of almost uninterrupted performances orchestrated by the prosecution. The failure to cross-examine is at odds with Article 201 of the reformed Turkish Criminal Code (TCCP 2005), which:

> introduced for the first time into the Turkish legal order the possibility for the defense counsel to address direct questions to witnesses or experts during the trial, ... changed the practice of examining witnesses to conform to the principle of a fair hearing (as stated in Article 6 of the European Convention on Human Rights), and regulated the right of confrontational questioning.[80]

However, years after Article 201 came into force, the EU Commissioner discovered that the practice of cross-examination has rarely been implemented, reportedly due to inexperience on the part of judges, prosecutors, and defense lawyers.[81]

A necessary condition for the existence of a fair trial is the principle of "equality of arms"—the idea that in a criminal trial, the prosecution and the defense must enjoy equal rights.[82] In reality, however, only attorneys representing the plaintiffs addressed the witnesses, and their questions tended to strengthen rather than question their testimonies. The defendants' physical absence was thus exacerbated by the complete absence of cross-examination—a core aspect that determines their misrepresentation in court.

The audio-visual documentation of the court hearings thus reveals a disturbing picture: the defense's silence through the long hours of court hearings, and the paucity of its argumentation, seem to have turned its lawyers into mere extras. At the same time, the testimonies on behalf of the plaintiffs emerged as prolonged monologues, involving little if any genuine dialogue or exchange.

(e) *Mistranslation and Misinterpretation*

Another aspect in which the court revealed its incompetence is regarding the issue of translation and interpretation. Concerns about the accessibility and quality of interpretation services in court were addressed by the Turkish MoJ as part of Turkey's juridical reform strategy, which tackled numerous issues, including the cultural-political rights of minorities in Turkey—for example the Kurdish minority, which for many years was denied the right to use the Kurdish language in court proceedings.[83] The reform thus aimed to safeguard the right of communication via regulated interpretation services. In particular, the MoJ acknowledged that qualified interpreting was essential to the system, and that "court interpretation is a highly demanding profession requiring special training and skills." The Ministry duly pledged a thorough overhaul of its provision of interpretation services.[84]

Qualified legal interpreters must not only to be fluent in all the languages involved, but must be able to translate from one language into another while preserving the integrity of the message, with due attention to dialect, accent, cultural meaning, body language, and gestures, as well as being skilled in legal terminology. An EU Directive from 2010 states that providing legal interpretation and translation services is a "basic obligation for member states." As part of the judicial reform, the Turkish authorities thus pledged to find and train objective and reliable interpreters with an excellent command of the languages in question, with the goal of meeting EU standards by the end of 2010.[85]

From its earliest stages, the *Mavi Marmara* trial was supposed to include dozens of witnesses from thirty-seven countries, with foreign witnesses scheduled to testify before Turkish ones right from the first hearing, indicating their importance to the court. For this reason, proper translation and interpretation services were paramount to the proceedings, but in practice, they fell far short of the required standards of quality and accessibility.[86] In some cases, the initial choice of translators and interpreters failed to meet the cited standards of "professional training" and "objectivity." For example, the person translating the testimonies of witnesses from the UK was the IHH lawyer Ms. Rabia Yurt. In another instance, one of the court security guards was summoned to translate a testimony by an Arabic-speaking witness. And in some instances, no translator could be found at all, for example in the case of Indonesian witness Surya Fachrizal, who was obliged to communicate his testimony in English. Repeatedly, the translations were poor and incompetent, such as when the lengthy sentences of five witnesses from Greece (testifying on May 20/21, 2013) were reduced to a couple of words in Turkish. Worse still, blatant mistranslations were a common occurrence: one witness's reference to "Semitic" people was translated with the Turkish word *simit* (a kind of bagel), turning entire parts of the testimony into utter nonsense.

While this example may seem trivial, another episode of mistranslation involved a complete inversion of the plaintiffs' reply from "no" to "yes" when the lawyers asked a Greek witness whether the passengers had weapons onboard. Surprised by the answer, the judge posed the question two more times, and the interpreter repeated his mistake. Since the traditional written court minutes are summarized and dictated by the judge for the record of the court procedures, they immortalize the mistranslated answer.

The above examples illustrate clearly enough how the Istanbul trial failed to meet accepted standards of fairness. This means that we are left with only the audio-visual records of the sessions to expose these systemic failures. The skewed reality is, however, that by making these records "extraterritorial"— that is, excluding them from public access and scrutiny—the Turkish court has effectively ensured that no direct record of these failures is publicly available.

(f) *Lack of Independency of the Court and Court Documentation of the Political Theatre*

According to Article 9 of the 1982 Constitution of the Turkish Republic, which was enforced during the *Mavi Marmara* trial, "[j]udicial power shall be exercised by independent and impartial courts on behalf of the Turkish Nation."[87] Article 11 adds that "[l]aws shall not be contrary to the Constitution." However, in real terms, the result of the *Mavi Marmara* case firmly proved that in point of fact, the court in Turkey is a theater of justice staged by the government in accordance to its political agenda.[88] Already in 2013, it was reported that due to an initiative led by Former US President Barack Obama on the backdrop of the deteriorating civil crisis in Syria, Israel's prime minister, Benjamin Netanyahu, apologized over the phone before President Erdoğan and the Turkish people "for the errors that may have led to the loss of lives" during the *Marmara* incident.[89] It was further communicated that in return "Turkey had agreed to drop all charges against the Israeli commanders."[90] The announcement on the inter-state agreement thereby straightforwardly confirmed that a symbolic apology at the national level—combined with material compensation for the dead, delivered by the Israeli side—will be matched with the creation of a new amnesty law, retroactively exempting the Israeli commanders from all legal claims over crimes that allegedly took place in the extraterritorial waters, as well as preempting other possible civil lawsuits against individual Israeli soldiers who participated in the raid.[91] However, despite the awareness of the formal announcement, the trial at İstanbul's Seventh Aggravated Criminal Court would continue for another three years in light of the suspension of the final agreement between the two states, as the conditions for the settlement were not yet ripe. Finally, on June 27, 2016, Israel and Turkey signed an ex-gratia reconciliation deal, heralding the normalization of relations between the two countries,[92] and on September 30, Israel duly transferred 20 million dollars in compensation. At that point, the legal proceedings were closed.[93] Actually, the underlying motivation for the solemn accord was a canny combination of security and business interests, specifically a prospective lucrative gas deal between the two states.[94] The agreement's legality was swiftly questioned by experts in international law, among them Rodney Dixon, who claimed:

> [T]he universal jurisdiction is imperiled with this agreement which exonerates persons responsible for the commission of serious international crimes and frees them from accountability.[95]

He emphasised that a decision by Turkish court to discontinue legal proceedings in terms of the agreement would violate the rule of international law, be in conflict with a peremptory norm, and would also violate the right of the victims to access to justice. Paradoxically, at this point, the governmental agreement to grant political immunity to those indicted *in absentia* became the subject of debate within the framework of formal examination of evidence before the trial judges. To the extent of even determining its inner timeframe, for example, it was reported:

> Within the court hearing, the plaintiff legal team, victims and family members of the martyrs had defended that the agreement between Turkey and Israel

does not affect the case and the *Mavi Marmara* criminal case should continue on. The chief judge had taken the objections of the legal team and victims into consideration and had decided to continue the hearing to the 2nd of December.[96]

Interestingly, the theatrical tone of the proceedings—which the Israeli side had encouraged since its inception, despite the furious opposition of the organizers and supporters, toward the trial's end—was also publicly denounced by the plaintiff's counsel, which stressed the troubling effects of the court's evident partiality. In one of the last hearings that took place on December 2, 2016, the IHH international media relations officer Mustafa Özbek began his press release thus:

> [T]he presiding judge gave his opinion to the accusations that "the case should be abated on the grounds of the Turkey-Israel agreement." The hearing lasted for 12 hours non-stop as the courtroom was packed with people, some of whom were standing. The presiding judge's behaviors and expressions could be interpreted as comments reflecting bias, because he expressed that he "will award case abatement regardless." The wife of an activist killed on board fainted and an ambulance was called. Due to the ensuing chaos the hearing adjourned at 10 pm, to be continued on 09.12.2016.[97]

Furthermore, this time, it was the victims' families that denounced the court for a lack of judicial independence, and for buckling to political objectives outside the court's remit. Addressing the judge of the trial as representative of a government whose political interests had tainted the proceedings, their communication ran thus:

> The families of the victims, who claimed that the court is being influenced by outside political forces, said that "we have so far heard in the political platforms that 'the right-holders are those who hold blood.'" While to this day we have not received a single dollar in compensation, this is not a claim for damages but a criminal lawsuit.[98]

Most urgently, at this point, the counsel of the plaintiffs officially imputed the court with improper administration of justice. Eventually, the *Mavi Marmara* case spawned fresh criminal imputations against the State of Turkey: the initial enthusiasm toward the Turkish state for its role as a paladin of international justice was now replaced with calls to prosecute Turkey for the trial's dismal lack of fairness, and to pursue indictment in the international courts:

> "[Victims from] Turkey … can claim damages against Turkey for "violating the right to a fair trial, to a fair hearing by an independent and impartial tribunal,

to seek justice" in the European Court of Human Rights if and when the case is abated on the grounds of the agreement made with Israel.[99]

There are very few reports on the final hearings, presumably since at this point, the government strove to avoid coverage, preferring a media blackout as the trial came to a halt.[100] One of the last reports available on the closing two days of the hurriedly truncated trial describes an atmosphere of tumult and dissent. The original legal threats were now accompanied by feverish condemnations, and in some cases, events deteriorated into physical clashes. One reporter described the experience as follows:

> At the final hearing on Friday, a large crowd of the plaintiffs' lawyers and victims' families were packed in the courtroom. Tensions rose when others were not allowed inside, sparking protests and shouts of "*Allahu akbar*" (God is greatest). The judge summoned the riot police to remove one co-plaintiff who refused to leave the courtroom. The families of the victims and lawyers chanted in protest and walked out before the verdict was read.[101]

According to the journalist's account, given that the galleries and press benches had been cleared beforehand, it may be assumed that the verdict was delivered— the judge reading out his decision, as dictated by government doctrine—only to the documenting cameras. Subsequently, the arrest warrants issued by the court in 2013 for the defendants were purportedly lifted.

After the Turkish Government had pulled the plug of the political performance played by the Turkish Justice System, the documentation of the trial could be understood as another image making of political spectacle by the authorities, withdrawn from public view, particularly when it could serve as evidence to the blunt violations of the law by its representatives.

Figure 16 Photograph of statue of blind-folded Goddess of Justice at entrance to the İstanbul 7th Aggravated Criminal Court, Istanbul, Turkey.[102]

Images as Court Evidence

Our understanding of the phenomenon of "extraterritorial images" may be enriched by an awareness of the legal history of images, both as legal evidence and as a way of documenting legal proceedings. In what follows, I will consider the attempts of legal systems to control images by looking on how images have been perceived, conceptualized, articulated, and applied by such systems.

Regarding the history of images as evidence, I will focus on the diverse legal uses of images in common law systems—from attempts to downplay their evidentiary value at the expense of a merely illustrative role, to their full acceptance as self-authenticating evidence (that is, as evidence whose truth is not subject to further proof beyond themselves). Regarding the history of images as documentation, I will concentrate on cases of historic international significance.[1]

The presentation of photographic images in courts can be traced back to the nineteenth century and has developed ever since with the evolution of technologies of image production and reproduction. The invention of photography had a tremendous influence on systems of justice. As soon as the technology appeared, some recognized it as "a new form of representation that challenged received notions of original and hearsay evidence." Despite doubts concerning the reliability of photography expressed by jurists, many claimed that the new "pictorial realism" would make possible a "new judicial photographic realism," a new "means for presenting facts" by way of "machine-made testimony."[2] Already in the 1840s, British police initiated the use of photography for criminal identification, while a year later the French police included daguerreotypes of criminals in its files.[3] The use of photography was soon extended to additional aspects of criminal investigations: reconstruction of crimes, documentation of evidence at the crime scene, identification of fingerprints and handwriting by means of photo analysis, and more. In the second half of the nineteenth century, these applications turned photography into a forensic practice and a powerful judicial tool.[4] Within two decades of its invention, photography was routinely employed in courtrooms across the United States, England, and France within ever-expanding legal contexts.[5]

Until the final decades of the nineteenth century, photography was technologically constrained by the need to develop the photograph immediately upon exposure (if the collodion dried prior to development, the image would be damaged). This made outdoor photographing more challenging, resulting in an overwhelming preference for studio photographs. The invention in 1880 of the "stable dry plate," which made it possible to postpone the development process to a later time, gave rise to "incriminating photographs," as the new technique made it possible to "take photographs without the subject's knowledge." The new technique also led to a "new way of establishing [legal] truth: the emergence of a 'culture of construction' within the courtroom. Evidence was now something not only to be found, but to be made."[6]

The emergence of photography as a source of visual evidence spawned a legal discourse whose goal was to determine the status of such images in courts. Jurists' responses to the invention ranged from early enthusiasm ("photographs as objective machine-made truth") to skepticism that emphasized the human agency and manipulation involved in the process.[7] From an early stage, it was understood that photographs could not be viewed as mere replications of reality, and that the accuracy of photographic representation was therefore often debatable.[8]

Since judicial facts have been said to comprise "both facts and the means to bring such facts to the attention of the tribunal," the emergence of photography was soon followed by an examination of its epistemic status as legal evidence.[9] Prior to the nineteenth century, English courts mainly relied on "material" objects (handwritten documents, instruments of criminal offense, etc.) as "primary evidence" in "trials by inspection."[10] In *The Rationale of Judicial Evidence*, philosopher and jurist Jeremy Bentham proposed to classify such evidence as "real evidence," providing the following definition:

> All evidence of which any object belonging to the class of things is the source; persons also included, in respect of such properties as belong to them in common with things.[11]

Bentham further proposed to apply this category to any physical evidence "made present to the senses of the judge himself" but unclassifiable under the existing categories of "personal," "testimonial," or "documentary" evidence.[12]

In the early eighteenth century, however, with the emergence of a distinct "law of evidence" to regulate the use of evidence in court, oral and written testimony took precedence as primary forms of evidence.[13] In particular, oral testimony emerged as the privileged form of evidence.[14] By the mid-nineteenth century, legal evidence mainly consisted of oral testimonies and written documents (depositions, contracts, etc.), whereas images were hardly used to establish judicial claims.[15] When photographic images did appear in courts, they were usually thought of as "evidentiary aid" and played a merely illustrative role. Photographs were on a par with forms of symbolic visual representation such as maps, charts, and diagrams; its evidentiary role was thus circumvented.[16] Under common law systems, images, including photographic ones, were classified as "demonstrative evidence." Early case law contained absolutely no discussion of what evidential standards governed the admissibility of demonstrative evidence as a separate category of proof. Later definitions vary, and courts have been inconsistent in their assessments.

The common law of demonstrative evidence began to develop more fully in the United States. According to some scholars, US courts in the late nineteenth century were almost indifferent to the need of any evidential theory to justify the use of other visual images such as diagrams or models, which were viewed as purely demonstrative displays. Such demonstrative evidence was understood as an "illustration of tautological, mathematically confirmable proof, something in the nature of what we might call scientific proof."[17] Even late in the century, the category of demonstrative evidence did not have a stable meaning, though some judges considered it conclusive: "evidence that offered the highest possible degree of proof."[18] According to other scholars, demonstrative evidence was understood as theatrical props, a form of evidence only "derivatively related to material fact,"[19] used only for illustrative purposes and not as independent proof.[20]

The aforementioned paradox of photography—the fact that it is both a mediated artifice and an innovative means of representation—was met in the legal context with the claim that photographs "could not provide definitive evidence about their mode of manufacture" and that it was therefore necessary "to look not at the product but at the process."[21] Consequently, the courts demanded that "before a witness could use such a visual aid, he was required to authenticate the image and verify that it in fact offered a correct representation of whatever was at issue."[22] While such demands are often made regarding the admissibility of every form of evidence, it led some judges to hold photographs to especially stringent standards of authentication.[23]

The early view of the relationship between photographs and other types of visual evidence ("models, maps and diagrams") is illustrated in *A Treatise on the Anglo-American System of Evidence in Trials at Common Law* (1889) by legal scholar John Henry Wigmore, which classifies photographs as "non-verbal expression" and therefore as "demonstrative evidence," as distinct from verbal "testimonial evidence."[24] The category of "demonstrative evidence" also appears in the legal writings of American lawyer Melvin Belli, who with some qualification defines such evidence as "the type of evidence imparted directly to the senses without the intervention of a testimony."[25] In 1940, Dean McCormick similarly described demonstrative evidence as "all phenomena which can convey a first-hand sensuous impression to the trier of fact ... [a]s opposed to those that serve merely to report secondhand sense impressions."[26]

Pointing to the enormous influence of the category of "demonstrative evidence" yet also to its limitations, law professor Robert D. Brain claims that the category was too broad, lacking "any coherent legal theory justifying the inclusion of real, documentary, illustrative, and demeanour evidence under [that] one heading."[27]

Nineteenth- and early twentieth-century approaches to the evidentiary value of photographs were problematic in several ways, then: early jurists viewed photographs as mere illustrations of verbal testimonies and underestimated the persuasive power of images and their capacity to reaffirm impressions. Above all, they failed to recognize the objectifying power of the camera— the impossibility "to express in words everything that a photo depicts"; for this reason, they failed to recognize that "the photograph [was] still further evidence" that could go beyond verbal testimony.[28] As a result, approaches to the legal status of photographs oscillated between those who viewed them as objects with autonomous evidentiary value, capable of "speaking" directly to the senses and thus of serving as "sheer proof," and those who viewed them as human artifacts requiring human mediation in the form of persuasive verbal interpretation:

> In practice, however, the two conflicting approaches sometimes coexisted, for despite an effort to make photographs the operative equivalent of other kinds of visual evidence, the doctrine was only partially successful. That is, even though it ignored the widespread belief in photographic truth, the awareness of the photograph's special probative power could not be suppressed entirely.[29]

Once photographs were allowed into the courtroom:

> it was no longer clear ... where illustration ended and proof started or who was illustrating what: the photograph illustrating the testimony or the testimony illustrating the photograph.[30]

In fact, it has even been claimed that, whereas theorists often accorded photographs secondary status, in practice, this innovative form of representation was perceived as substantial evidence almost from the moment it was invented.[31]

The conflicting approaches to "demonstrative evidence" and the inconsistent definitions of the category itself presented difficulties for scholars who sought to explain its role in the evidentiary process. Eventually, in the advent of modern attempts to replace the common law of evidence with statutory evidence codes, the category was abandoned altogether.[32]

In the twentieth century, growing acceptance of photographs as substantial legal evidence was in large part a result of certain technological developments. Early in the century, changing attitudes were largely a response to the discovery of X-ray technology, which exceeded the capacity of natural human vision and therefore stood in a new relation to human testimony and verbal description. The introduction of other new technologies such as 16-mm film (early 1920s),[33] color photography (early 1940s), and videotape (late 1950s) did not confront the courts with similar challenges regarding the evidentiary status of photographs.[34] It was not until the introduction of surveillance cameras in the late 1960s that another major doctrinal shift occurred:

> Surveillance cameras, just like X-ray machines, provided valuable images for which no verifying eyewitness could be provided. However, unlike X-ray machines, surveillance cameras needed no one to speak for them in court. They produced traditional photographic evidence that conveyed intuitive information readily accessible to the jury. Thus, for the first time, the courts faced machine-made visual evidence that no longer was required to be coupled with human agency to express what it contained.[35]

To allow the admissibility of surveillance footage in courts, the American appellate court recognized "machine-made pictures as reliable representations of what they depict."[36] The principles invoked in support of this decision have come to be known as "Silent Witness" theory.[37] According to the older "pictorial testimony" doctrine, for a photograph to be admissible in court, a "sponsoring witness"—a person with personal knowledge of that which was depicted in the photograph—had to testify to the photograph's accuracy. According to "silent witness theory," by contrast, the photograph could "speak for itself" and, as such, was substantive evidence for what it portrayed, independently of the input of any sponsoring witness.[38] Photographic material thus became admissible as independent, self-authenticating evidence, "based on the presumed reliability of the photographic process."[39] Silent Witness theory acknowledged that the admissibility of photographic images could be subject to various criteria ("relevance," "authenticity," "fair representation"); these, however, were to be determined by the particular facts of any given case.[40]

From the twentieth century, hardly a trial takes place without the use of images, while the latter have gained recognition as among the most effective forms of evidence. The accuracy of photographs can even be established circumstantially (without the addition of either expert or witness testimony), as in cases of automatic cameras. In time, similar rules have come to apply to filmed and videotaped images as well: "the tape recording is not admissible as an illustration ... but as evidence itself ... the tape becomes mechanical hearsay, admissible as long as the correct foundation be laid as to the truth and accuracy of the recording process."[41] Though perhaps classifiable as "secondary" evidence, "with proper foundation [it] could be viewed as 'substantive or real evidence.'"[42]

The same principles applying to traditional photographic images have also come to govern the admissibility of digital photographs as evidence:

> Digital photographs still need to be authenticated by a witness, and it is up to the opposing counsel to question the authenticity of the evidence. Should there be any indication that the photograph is not what the witness states it represents, the evidence can be accorded less probative value or weight by the jury.[43]

Even in the age of digital photography, then, evidentiary uses of technology are still structured around verbal rhetoric, prioritizing language over pure vision as a way of "opening our eyes."

Whether press cameras should be allowed to document court proceedings has been debated from the early twentieth century. Courts have often expressed the fear that cameras would alter the trial process and put witnesses at risk, that the media might misuse camera footage, and that visual documentation might commercialize the legal procedures and compromise the defendants' right to a fair trial.[44] Based on such concerns and others, justice systems have imposed various restrictions on photography, filming, and videotaping in courtrooms.[45]

Another important debate (though one less often discussed outside the professional legal discourse) has concerned the visual documentation of court cases by the legal system itself. The question of courtroom documentation predates the age of photography.[46] For some, however, the advent of the camera represented a new potential for ensuring the existence of fair legal procedures.[47] According to legal scholars Collins and Skover, legal events, both legislative and judicial, are transformed by the medium through which they are communicated and documented, since different media—from oral language, handwriting, and print, to photography, filming, and videotaping—are capable of recording different types of information.[48] Legal proceedings were harder to preserve in preliterate societies. The invention of writing made it possible to preserve legal processes; such preservation was still limited, however, given the slow and cumbersome nature of early writing technologies and the sheer rarity of literacy. The age of print marked a revolution in this field, as in others, and in time written evidence joined and even surpassed oral testimony as a leading form of evidence. By the eighteenth century, print "ushered in a new legal culture," replacing living memory with the dead letter.[49] The advent of print increased "reliance on the fixed rules of published law," replacing "the fluid memory of the oral way and the comparatively flexible rules of custom."[50] They even claimed that archetypal notions of Anglo-American jurisprudence are intimately linked to print.[51]

The invention of the camera marked yet another watershed moment in legal history. Despite the widespread prohibition on photography in the courtroom, especially in criminal trials, the introduction of cameras has been closely linked to several developments in both domestic criminal and international law.[52] Let me illustrate this claim by reference to a few cases, both historic and more recent, each representing a certain politics of representation.

Historically, the Nuremberg Trials (November 1945–October 1946) represented one of the earliest efforts by a court to audio-visually record its own criminal procedures. The court presented several reasons for its pioneering decision to document the proceedings. In particular, the documentation was described as an attempt to raise international consciousness of the atrocities committed by the Nazis and to shape the collective memory of the international community.[53] I wish to suggest, however, that another novel purpose of the trial's audio-visual documentation was also to prove to the German public that the Nazi leadership was being given a fair trial. This way of using the camera became one of the Nuremberg tribunal's most important legacies.[54] The audio-visual documentation of the Nuremberg Trials marked the genesis of a certain kind of legal-judicial image production—the creation of images in order to later use them as evidence for the court's proper conduct, on the basis of which further judicial assertions could be made.[55]

It has been argued that the documentation of the Nuremberg Trials affected the trials themselves, prompting their organizers to redesign the architecture of the Nuremberg Palace of Justice in which the hearings were held. Whereas traditional juridical practices protected the accused from the public eye in order to avoid an excess of emotions, here the accused stood in full frontal view of a mass international audience. It has even been argued that it was "the new configuration of the courtroom [that] allowed the emergence and contestation of the novel charges of crimes against humanity and later genocide."[56]

The 1961, Adolf Eichmann trial set another precedent for the use of cameras by a legal system to document its own proceedings. Kidnapped in Argentina by the Israeli Mossad, former S.S. officer Eichmann was brought to Israel in 1960, where he was put to trial the following year for his part in the Nazi genocide of European Jewry. Prior to the trial, the Israeli government hired a production company to film the entire trial.[57] Though the courtroom itself was not reshaped to accommodate the documentation, the trial was set up as a public performance. The venue chosen for the trial was the 800-seat People's Hall (*Beit Ha'am*) Theater in Jerusalem.[58] The tension between the trial's two objectives—legally valid procedures on the one hand, performative dramatization on the other—was evident in the special filming arrangements:

> Filming was authorised under strict conditions: cameras were to be located in three concealed corners of the hall, special noise-reduction measures were to be taken, and the presence of cameramen in the courthouse was to be kept minimal. … [A]ll copies were to be released simultaneously to all interested parties on an equal basis, the price of copies was to be fixed and controlled, and the entire record was to be handed to the government at the end of the procedure. Defined a "public service", profits were to be donated to charity. These terms stipulate, in effect, that coverage of the Eichmann trial was not to be traded or benefited from, at least not in the commercial sense.[59]

As in Nuremberg, the precedential decision to film the legal procedures was given two main justifications: the desire to generate wide publicity, and the need to make the legal process accessible to public evaluation in order to ensure that justice was being served without bias or prejudice. According to some, the main concern was the latter rather than the former: "[the] concern was thus the propriety of the legal process rather than the place it would take in history."[60] The trial was broadcast extensively abroad, but it was clear that the filmed coverage would have little immediate impact on the local audience, as Israel had no television broadcast services at that time. Moreover, when the idea of filming the proceedings was first introduced, it was claimed that the purpose was to provide archival footage for future use rather than immediate regular reportage.[61] According to the presiding judge at the Eichmann trial, Supreme Court Justice Moshe Landau, the documentation had to be "accurate and fair"—in my terms, it had to produce images of a fair trial—in order to serve as future proof for the validity of the legal procedures.[62]

Because of a blunder made by Israeli government officials, it eventually turned out that the production company hired to document the trial was not contractually obligated to film the proceedings in their entirety. Fearing that partial documentation would represent the proceedings as incoherent, the Voice of Israel, Israel's official radio broadcasting service (then a subdivision in the Prime Minister's Office) stepped in to record the entire proceedings.[63] The recordings were to be kept for "safekeeping in the State Archives or in some other national institute." Officials claimed that "it would be an irretrievable loss if for whatever reason such audio recordings were not preserved by the State of Israel and the Jewish people," emphasizing the importance of such records as an educational device for future generations.[64] Supreme Court Justice Landau signed a decree stating that the proceedings would be "machine-recorded," and that the resulting record would have the same validity as written court protocols.[65] The audio-visual documentation thus officially received equal weight as the actual court protocols.

Both the Nuremberg and the Eichmann trials made pioneering use of filmed footage as substantial evidence—so much so, that in Nuremberg, the prosecutor preferred film over summoning witnesses to the stand as a way to support his claims. His stated reason for this preference was that witnesses might fail to control their emotions; we may assume, however, that the preference was at least equally motivated by the expectation that filmed evidence would make the defendants feel guilty and express their sense of guilt, which would then be used as further evidence against them. The same strategy was later used in Jerusalem, where Eichmann was made to view filmed footage of Holocaust atrocities.[66]

The turn to documentary filming practices in both Nuremberg and Jerusalem made possible yet another mode of image production—the production of images that blended the criminal and the political. On the one hand, the way in which the proceedings were documented molded the defendants in the image of common criminals. On the other hand, the documentation was carried out by state authorities and not by the media, marking the genesis of new practice in which filmed documentation could replace written court protocols, serving not only as legal evidence but also as a political instrument used to validate the court and its actions.

Both the Nuremberg and Eichmann trials had the declared goals of protecting human rights. Both trials also show, however, how the court can preserve to itself the exclusive right to use cameras and thus create a power imbalance contrary to basic human rights and to legal transparency. Moreover, once the production of the documentation is produced by the court itself via automatic security cameras, without the mediation of professional filming personnel, the court can more easily assert control over the resulting documentation. Moreover, as soon as the footage is taken by security cameras, it becomes easier to treat it as objective, as a self-authenticating artifact of "pure vision."

In recent decades, many courts followed the precedent set in Nuremberg and Jerusalem, using audio-visual technologies to document their proceedings. The practice has taken special prominence in cases of international law violations and crimes against humanity. A notable instance has been the proceedings of the International Criminal Tribunal for the Former Yugoslavia (ICTY). In 1994, the ICTY judges decided to record and publicize the proceedings in order to "make sure that justice would be seen to be done, to dispel any misunderstanding that might arise as to the role and nature of the proceedings, and to educate the public."[67] In recording the proceedings, the court followed an explicit set of conventions characteristic of the "genre." Though each of the three purpose-built courtrooms contained six cameras with zooming and tilting capabilities, the four video directors in charge of the filming were subjected to specific guidelines. For example, there had to be no panning or zooming visible on screen, and the directors had to cut away from any visibly distressed court participant. Witnesses had the right to avoid identity exposure by having their voice and facial features distorted. In addition, the production process itself had to be open and visible (perhaps to ensure the impression of a fair trial): all court participants were to see what the courtroom director was filming. The footage was recorded live but broadcast with a thirty-minute delay to protect court participants.[68] Other international criminal courts have adopted similar practices of audio-visual recording, each contributing to the "genre" by adding its own restrictions. In 2009, the Joint Tribunal of the Khmer Rouge (also known as the Extraordinary Chambers in the Courts of Cambodia [ECCC]), a special Cambodian court set up to prosecute leaders of the Khmer Rouge regime for the killing of 1.7 million and backed by the UN, resolved to document its own judicial proceedings. Inspired by the ICTY, the ECCC adopted the following standards:

> the presence of cameras did not force upon the proceedings an ordinary media standard of transparency. It facilitated the widening of the spatial and temporal framework of the judicial narrative, which was up to the judges and prosecutors to render audible for the greatest number of people. They did this by determining which counts of the trial seemed representative of the history under indictment, what punishments were called for, and what reparations were required.[69]

In other instances, court-created images helped make the proceedings more accessible to those to whom the trial was of most concern. For example, the audio-visual archive set up by the International Criminal Tribunal of Rwanda (ICTR, created in 1995) has been of tremendous value given Rwanda's low literacy and almost nonexistent internet accessibility rates.[70]

Audio-visual recording of court proceedings has also been used by the Special Court for Sierra Leone and in East Timor.[71] It is precisely the accusation that such international tribunals constitute the victors as just that encouraged in these cases a "rigid adherence to the requirement of proof beyond reasonable doubt" and "the development of transparent and consistent rules in the treatment of evidence."[72] The advanced audio-visual policy pursued by these courts is likely to have represented their efforts to produce images that would become evidence for the fairness of the trials.

While it has been argued that "the goal of the modern trial is the rectitude of an ultimate decision achieved through rational process of presentation," the paradox is that in order to achieve such a goal, "modern law has to ultimately fall back on notions of exclusivity, exclusion and closure."[73] In the context of internationalized criminal justice, this paradox helps us understand the role played by the current economy of images in the effort to present such trials as fair. In many cases, it seems that national interests overpower the goal of accessibility and transparency, with the production of certain images entailing the exclusion of others. A clear instance of the latter phenomenon is provided by the International Criminal Court (ICC), the first permanent court of its type, established in 1988 on the basis of the Rome Treaty. While the ICC's legal proceedings are recorded and made public, a careful look at the ICC's own regulations reveals the explicit statement that "the ICC's audio-visual records may be released to broadcasting unless ordered otherwise." Here again, all broadcasts are to be "delayed by 30 minutes in order to protect sensitive information." The ICC Chamber may prohibit audio-visual documentation and broadcast based on various considerations, among them concerns of national security raised by the member states.[74] While using the audio-visual images as evidence for the validity and fairness of the legal procedures, the courts also reserve to themselves exclusive editing and distribution rights which risk undermining those same goals. Of course, operating according to this clause does not compel one to abuse it, though it is in our interest to keep its use in check.

Epilogue: Extraterritorial Images

The endeavor of the State to control the extraterritorial image is further challenged by the ways in which technological advances contest perceptions of the state territory as bounded spaces. In 2014, the story of an unprecedented civil lawsuit against the Israeli army was exposed on the weekend news edition of Israel's main commercial TV channel, Channel 2.[1] The lawsuit was filed by Sergeant Major M, the first Israeli commando who rappelled down from the helicopter onto the *Mavi Marmara*—the largest vessel of the freedom flotilla. Beaten badly with clubs and poles, then flung from the upper deck to a lower level of the vessel, Sergeant Major M was seriously wounded. His identity could not be established in the official Israeli documentation of this scene, filmed from an Israeli navy boat in extreme long shot, and released by the Israeli's military Spokesperson's Unit after the incident. Yet, his face was clearly visible in still images taken by the *Marmara* activists, which were among the very few to be leaked from the boat and which have been circulating worldwide ever since.

In his news interview, Sergeant Major M reported that he was still haunted by the incident: "I have been living with it ever since … We are at risk of being injured, of being killed, that is something we take into account. But I, as a fighter, am doing my job and I expect that the system will support me." Stating his accusations and conveying the agony inflicted on him by the loss of control over his exposed image, Sergeant Major M's charge against the Israeli military—the first of its kind—was the negligence that allowed his image to leak and circulate widely, causing him "irreversible harm" and preventing him from leaving the country out of fear of prosecution or assassination. His report of being haunted by the event—of "living with it ever since"—seems to refer, then, not to memories of the event itself, but to the publicly exposed images which revealed his identity and perpetually placed him at the scene.

Sergeant Major M took great pains to stress that the failure to protect his image was his sole complaint: "I very much love the army, and I don't regret for an instant my participation in this incident. If it were to happen once more, I would definitely go down that rope again."[2] Like many other elite soldiers, he was willing to die in action, yet he was not willing to sacrifice his life while still living—to lose ownership of his own image, created while he was serving his country. The interview with Sergeant Major M, conducted with his face darkened, emphasizes the illustrative character of the convention of darkening the interviewee's face as an attempt by the State to censor certain images in order to limit their identifying and evidentiary power. Paradoxically, his image can still be easily found online due to its former publication in global networks.

The model of extraterritorial representation and extraterritorial images offered here may be employed to analyze the meaning of this particular episode. What emerges here very clearly is the willingness to sacrifice life, including one's own, both in order to document and in order to not be documented.

Moreover, for Sergeant Major M, the military's inability to prevent an image showing the incident and its executors from becoming visible, its failure to control the image's territorial reach and keep it legally excluded—in other words, its failure to make the image "extraterritorial"—represented not only a breach of contract but a most serious crime. The special conditions of the extraterritorial maritime space in which the takeover operation was set to take place were supposed to enable the military to gain full control over the event's documentation. By making the images extraterritorial, protected from visibility under the laws of the State, the military was able to enhance their ability to evade responsibility for the documented actions, which other legal systems would, in all likelihood, consider crimes. These goals and conditions were presumably discussed with the soldiers prior to the flotilla takeover; Sergeant Major M was therefore under the impression that the system had failed him. The image, now openly accessible beyond Israel's borders, has confined him to the borders of the Israeli State. The State's territorial law has become both his shield and his prison. Such circumstances reveal how those equipped with weaponry and thus with the power to physically control the situation also expect to be in control of the visual evidence, to use national state law in order to keep it out of reach. In such cases, extraterritorial images are tools used to prevent the State's representatives (soldiers, officials, etc.) from becoming criminals in other territories or in the eyes of international law.[3]

By appearing with his face darkened during his TV interview, it was as if Sergeant Major M was regaining his anonymity, if only within his country's borders. By doing so, the TV station added yet another censored image that alluded to the confiscated documentation of the original incident. Just as the violence on board the *Marmara* was mediated via censored images, this testimony was communicated via yet another form of suppressed representation.

After the interview was initially broadcast, further information about the lawsuit was impossible to obtain and its progress, if any, was never covered again in the media. The logic of extraterritorialization I have just described is hardly unique to the *Mavi Marmara* case. It is discernible in various other historical episodes, some less recent, some are more so. One urgent example seems especially apposite to the present discussion: the case of the classification of the visual documentation of the US killing of Osama bin Laden, who headed the Islamist Al-Qaeda organization and was reportedly assassinated, along with his son and three other individuals, in Abbottabad, Pakistan, on May 1, 2011.[4] Since the visual representation of this case has been addressed in visual and legal critical scholarship, it may provide another opportunity to situate the logic of representation which produces what is termed here as the "extraterritorial image" in the broader context of critical theory that addresses the effects of power relations and authority on what is allowed to be seen, and what is withheld from view. The US Navy SEAL operation was to capture Osama bin Laden, the former leader of the Al-Qaeda organization behind the coordinated terrorist attacks on America on September 11, 2001. His death was first officially announced on May 1, 2011.[5] Addressing the nation on a televised broadcast, then-US President Barack Obama highlighted on top of his speech that "[t]he images of 9/11 are seared into our national memory."[6] Articulating the attacks' consequences in dramatic visual terms, he added, "[a]nd yet we know that the worst images are those that were unseen to the world,"[7] referencing the unexposed and probably undocumented pain of individuals over the loss of loved ones. In practice, while refraining from showing any visual evidence throughout the broadcast, a choice that predates the persistent government policy to rule out any access to the recordings of the killing(s), his statement is underlined by other unexposed, however certainly documented images. Specifically, ones which not only bear a sentimental value, but rather form a legal perspective, and have a much greater evidentiary weight.

In this context, it should be noted that US officials reported that during the raid "three other men—one of bin Laden's sons and two couriers—were killed" as well as "one woman" who was killed when she was "used as a shield," and that "two other women were injured."[8] This pithy description of the scene revealed nothing with regard to how the event unfolded, nor anything about whether the conduct of the US operatives was in compliance with international law. It was further announced that soon afterward, bin Laden's body was dropped from an aircraft flying over the Arabian Sea: hence the man was "buried at sea" out of respect for the codes of "Islamic funeral."[9] Thus, the extraterritorial killing of bin Laden, executed under the title Operation Neptune Spear, was reported to conclude with a burial in the extraterritorial waters, which served as the space that would conceal all physical evidence, neutralizing in advance requests for an autopsy report on the actual cause of death, or the DNA of the deceased for the purpose of identification.

The fact that the assassination was monitored while involving some of the United States' "most sophisticated technology," including satellite surveillance and a stealth drone "capable of flying undetected at high altitude taking photographs and sending real-time video," facilitating the White House viewing of "real-time footage of the target" was promoted on international media platforms.[10]

Holding back any footage of the lethal exchange inside the compound, the government instead published a photo of the event allegedly being viewed in real-time in the White House "Situation Room" on an (off-screen) monitor by former President Obama, in the company of his National Security team. In his investigation of the White House's official imagery, Liam Kennedy indicates how the released photo epitomizes the growth of this type of image, carefully calibrated to "promote the illusion of access and transparency."[11] Highlighting the growing distance between "official images" and the accompanying official verbal statements issued when national security concerns are involved, the international legal scholar Jothie Rajah describes how:

> In this image, the US is pictured as an omnipresent watcher; managing territory beyond its borders. The image subsumes the world to a US sphere of action and control with no suggestion that this expansive jurisdiction needs to be explained or justified. Extraterritorial power is seamlessly presented as taken-for-granted; the proper order of things.[12]

In his analysis of the photograph, Kennedy discusses the broad and multiplied exposure of the photo and its gained iconic status, and argues that it is "the illusion of transparency" that strives to distance violence to an "elsewhere."[13] He adds that the case reflects a request posed to the public by the Obama administration to "believe without seeing."[14] Applying here the extraterritorial prism, the now-iconic Situation Room image significantly demonstrates how evidence was substituted with a visual "aid" devised to publicly ordain the version of the forces on the field by providing a form of evidence, whereby the head of state is seen along with the country's most senior government executives as witnesses of the operation. In purely judicial terms, as object of evidentiary information in regard to how the operation was actually carried out, the officially released image hardly reveals anything. In fact, the Situation Room photo is the ultimate visual proof of how the act of viewing the evidence itself is replaced with an image of the Authorities witnessing the event, and hence serving as proxies both for the judiciary system and for the very people they claim to serve.

Furthermore, despite the widespread concerns over the legality of the killings, and outspoken doubts regarding the way the operation actually unfolded, Rajah finds that "with bin Laden's death, demands for disclosure have been minimal, suggesting a collapse of the state/society antagonism."[15]

It should be noted that as early as May 2, 2011, the day after the reported incident, the Judicial Watch filed a Freedom of Information request to the DoD demanding "all photographs and/or video recordings of Osama bin Laden taken during and/or after the US military operation."[16] The request was subsequently denied when in April 26, 2012, the US district court ruled that the images could "remain secret."[17] Further appeals against "withholding of images of Osama bin Laden's dead body" were similarly rejected.[18] In the process of the efforts for the release of the documents, it was declared that they "may not have been properly classified."[19] And, more strikingly, that "within hours of its filing a May 13, 2011, FOIA lawsuit seeking photos of the deceased Osama bin Laden, US Special Operations Commander, Admiral William McRaven permitted his subordinates via email to 'destroy' any photos they may have had 'immediately.'" Addressed to "Gentlemen," McRaven's email instructs that:

> one particular item that I want to emphasize is photos; particularly UBLs remains. At this point—all photos should have been turned over to the CIA; if you still have them, destroy them immediately or get them to the [redacted].[20]

The efforts of officials to keep control of the narrative, and to swap the classified evidence with a redacted version that glorified the violence, came to a head a few months after bin Laden's assassination: in 2012, it emerged that CIA agents had provided confidential information on the operation to Hollywood director Kathryn Bigelow and the screenwriter Mark Boal for the forthcoming thriller on the capture of bin Laden, *Zero Dark Thirty*.[21]

The elusive ties between "entertainment and propaganda" in the context of the US "Military Hollywood entertainment complex" are not new, and parallels have also been drawn to infotainment via the term "militainment," used to define the practice of representing military themes using popular cinematic conventions in a way that lauds the DoD.[22] From this perspective, we can see how evidence might be blanked out with the help of so-called big screen techniques, repurposed to publicly appear only after it has been professionally turned into fiction.

In response to the authorities' selective disclosure, a FOIA was issued by the Judicial Watch group for all "unredacted records of all communications to and from United States personnel and the filmmakers of the movie *Zero Dark Thirty*."[23] The CIA in turn responded that the filmmakers' access to the classified information was aimed to "help promote an appropriate portrayal of the agency and the bin Laden operation."[24] The scale of this policy that determines how and to whom information may be released is evident from the court ruling. For example, in the case of a certain Mr. Al Baluchi (a Pakistani citizen in the custody of the CIA at the Guantánamo Bay Detention Center), it was revealed that "the United States has provided more information to the filmmakers of *Zero Dark Thirty* about a detainee than it has to his defense counsel."[25]

Modern power has long been rather identified with an "all-seeing eye" and with the capacity to enforce and gatekeep the borders of visibility to legitimize its actions. This idea applies also to today's ever-expanding state control over visual evidence that could bear witness to violations committed by representatives of the law themselves. It is prevalent that advanced weapon and surveillance systems capable of recording are being widely deployed by armies, landing them in the "unique positions—not available in the past—to acquire and maintain high-quality monitoring information regarding all stages of the operation."[26]

The question of the extraterritorial image leads us to reflect on the visual-judicial discontinuities that come to light with the political and international spatial model applied by the state system. These empower states with the ability to sift through any visual documentation, covering its involvement in international disputes, declaring certain critical evidence confidential to international judicial inquiry—rendering its methods and acts of offensive violence invisible. At least in terms of volume, the dramatically growing inventory of visual evidence produced and possessed by states seems to indicate a similar trend with regard to the amount of visual proof aggregated yet withheld from view: access to that material is permitted only to representatives of the law, depending on their position within the system. This concealment of invaluable visual evidence of international significance is exercised under the guise of the national law system, increasing both uncertainties and discursive barriers in regard to state operations.

Although my analysis of extraterritoriality has pivoted on the particular case of the Gaza Freedom Flotilla, which cannot be fully understood without recourse to the language of extraterritoriality, the concept suggests a far wider application, such as how the state apparatus wittingly enables the evidence of crimes—in this case of considerable international gravity—to be airbrushed out of the picture, particularly in cases where competing legal systems (including that of international law) are in conflict.

The Gaza Freedom Flotilla incident is riven with multiple layers of extraterritoriality, and its aftermath seems to be framed not only by how extraterritoriality governs the particulars of the event's spatial geography and its legal aspects, but also its *visual topography*. Put differently, my claim is that the concept of extraterritoriality is part of a distinct *model* or *logic of representation*, and that this logic has been influential in shaping the cases in question. Examining extraterritorial practices through their diverse cross-disciplinary definitions reveals their varied applications and transformations across time and space, exposing how the phenomenon offers a vital tool for unraveling the way political events unfold and register in our time, and a key for deciphering current spatial-political orders.

Unfortunately for the powers that be, the suppression of the *Mavi Marmara* images has not only made their public impact more complex, but has increased their incriminatory potential, since the void created by their current invisibility allows room for speculations of every kind. The handful of images available merely provides fodder for competing claims and opposing narratives. Moreover, the "disappeared" images have been reconstructed in other media, including the discussed trial *in absentia*.

Furthermore, despite the images' inaccessibility, the very knowledge that they exist but are archived out of sight added to their potential for incriminating their co-creators. These factors contribute to their continued presence on the public radar, prompting an unhealthy climate of ambiguity that not only thwarts legal solutions, but meanwhile fosters a media environment of festering misinformation, whereby hard visual evidence is regularly supplanted by second-hand illustrations. By dint of their deliberate removal from critical public scrutiny, the resulting status of the images thus offers an important prism through which to peel back the complex layers of extraterritoriality, along with its side-effects, intended or otherwise.

Interestingly, images can become extraterritorial even when the conflict between competing legalities takes place within a single system. As the trial in Istanbul has shown, the court documentation itself served as evidence for the system's failure to adhere to officially acknowledged legal standards for judicial proceedings. Though the Turkish court has prevented access to its own documentation of the trial, this same documentation could potentially provide evidence of the court's various failures in the *Mavi Marmara* Trial—in particular, its failures in the light of the EU standards ostensibly adopted by the Turkish legal system—raising issues over the fairness of the court's procedures. Here, once more, the presence of an extraterritorial logic of representation offers a critical aid for construing the key role of images in the nexus between different, parallel, or competing legal systems.

What the research presented here illustrates is the multiple inter-connections between various forms of what is now widely termed "extraterritoriality." Rather than being a single static form, as a practice, extraterritoriality invariably involves a specific logic of representation that produces a variety of manifestations, exploring features glaringly revealed in the class between the presence and absence of visual rendition in the Gaza Freedom Flotilla saga.

Indeed, due to rapid technological developments, we live in times of great flux of changing information models, and while many major publishers are private corporations, we cannot risk confining our understanding of communication in the grip of governmental power. However, just as nation-states and state's laws continue to regulate the flow of people and commodities through extraterritorial ways and means, I suggest that the logic of extraterritoriality offers a unique prism to grasp how states and institutions forcibly regulate information across borders. The all-too-frequent restrictions that states impose on the visual documentation of acts committed by representatives of the law in the context of contemporary inter-state conflicts results in a lack of accountability on the international level. Moreover, states are constantly elaborating how their army's information operations combat power, striving "to gain and maintain information superiority at decisive points." Information supremacy is defined as "the operational advantage derived from the ability to collect, process, and disseminate an uninterrupted flow of information while exploiting or denying an adversary's ability to do the same."[27] In light of this overtly ambitious and technological capacity to marshal visual production on the battle scene, the re-conceptualizing of the legal-visual mechanisms used to support it becomes an urgent priority.

Simply put, if the "territoriality" of an image lies in its visibility, metaphorically speaking, then *excluding* it from view and limiting its "territorial reach" and visibility entails "extraterritorializing" that image, de-situating and alienating it from itself. If the evidentiary impact of an image resides in its signification, in the *Mavi Marmara* case, its ability to signify is subordinated to the goal of securing a pro-State propaganda tool that also impinges on the judicial spheres legal connotations. Herein lies the risk: that visual culture is co-opted at its most concrete level to serve the State or other forces and their extraterritorial agenda.

Notes

Introduction

1 According to the Turkel Commission Report, Part 1, *The Public Commission to Examine the Maritime Incident of 31 May 2010*, Israel, 2010, accessed July 7, 2011, https://www.gov.il/BlobFolder/generalpage/downloads_engl/en/ ENG_turkel_eng_a.pdf, the participating organizations were Canadian Boat to Gaza, European Campaign to End the Siege on Gaza, Irish Ship to Gaza, *Rumbo a Gaza* (Spain), Ship to Gaza (Sweden), the International Committee to Lift the Siege on Gaza, *Un Bateau Français Pour Gaza* (France), and US Boat to Gaza (p. 136). See also IHH, "*Mavi Marmara:* Gaza Freedom Flotilla," Department of Research and Publication, 2012, accessed April 10, 2020, https://www.ihh.org.tr/public/publish/0/79/mavi-marmara-freedom-flotilla. pdf, 13–14.

2 See Turkel Commission, Part 1, p. 36; IHH, "*Mavi Marmara:* Gaza Freedom Flotilla," 39.

3 The Israeli government tactic to prevent the initiative was to offer the activists the opportunity to transfer the humanitarian supply after security inspection at the Ashdod port over land. See Israeli Ministry of Foreign Affairs, "IDF Forces Met with Pre-Planned Violence When Attempting to Board the Flotilla," May 31, 2010, accessed July 30, 2020, https://mfa.gov.il/mfa/pressroom/2010/pages/israel_navy_ warns_flotilla_31-may-2010.aspx.

4 Turkel Commission, Part 1, p. 138.

5 IHH, "*Mavi Marmara:* Gaza Freedom Flotilla," 51.

6 Ibid., 50.

7 Ibid., 68.

8 See, e.g., Turkel Commission, Part 1, pp. 129–30.

9 Gilly Cohen, "The IDF Unit Whose Role is to Make a Headache for the Enemy," *Haaretz*, November 30, 2012, accessed July 6, 2020, https://www.haaretz.co.il/news/ politics/1.1876589.

10 Moustafa Bayoumi, ed., *Midnight on the Mavi Marmara: The Attack on the Gaza Freedom Flotilla and How It Changed the Course of the Israel/Palestine Conflict.* (New York: OR Books, 2010), 76.

11 Turkel Commission, Part 1, p. 129.

12 Ibid., 178.

13   See Israel, Knesset State Control Committee, Protocol No. 263, June 14, 2012, accessed
     April 11, 2020, https://www.mevaker.gov.il/he/Reports/Report_105/8587988a-92b8-
     4bd3-849d-8cab24f2d527/7685.pdf. The translation from Hebrew is mine.

14   The upper deck where the violent struggle took place was considered "the live
     broadcast" deck. IHH, "*Mavi Marmara:* Gaza Freedom Flotilla," 67. The use of
     excessive force is emanant based on the autopsy reports. See Turkish National
     Commission of Inquiry, *Report on the Israeli Attack on the Humanitarian Aid
     Convoy to Gaza*, pdf, February, 2011, accessed March 10, 2012, https://reliefweb.int/
     sites/reliefweb.int/files/resources/Full_Report_1621.pdf.

15   UN, *United Nations Convention on the Law of the Sea*, December 12, 1982, accessed
     February 20, 2020, https://www.un.org/depts/los/convention_agreements/texts/
     unclos/unclos_e.pdf, 57.

16   See also Maayan Amir and Ruti Sela, eds., *Extraterritorialities in Occupied Worlds*
     (Santa Barbara, CA: Punctum Books, 2016), 27.

17   The inquiry was headed by retired IDF Major General Giora Eiland. The report was
     submitted to IDF Chief of Staff Gabby Ashkenazi. See IDF announcement, "Maj.
     Gen.(Res.) Eiland Submits Conclusions of Military Examination Team Regarding
     Mavi Marmara," 2010, accessed August 9, 2020, https://idfspokesperson.wordpress.
     com/tag/giora-eiland/.

18   The Turkel Commission was chaired by retired Supreme Court Justice Jacob Turkel.

19   Israel State Comptroller's Report, *A Critical Review of the Application of the
     National Security Committee Law and the Handling of the Turkish Flotilla*, 2012,
     accessed April 11, 2020, https://www.mevaker.gov.il/he/Reports/Pages/
     105aspx?AspxAutoDetectCookieSupport=1, 61–153.

20   Adalah.org, "The Legal Center for Arab Minority Rights in Israel, Supreme Court
     Rejects Far-Right-Wing Politicians' Petition against Decision to Close Investigation of
     MK Haneen Zoabi and Sheikh Raed Salah for Participating in Gaza Flotilla," December
     24, 2012, accessed August 9, 2020, https://www.adalah.org/en/content/view/8232.

21   Guy Peleg, "Commando Unit Warrior Is Prosecuting: 'I Thought They Were Going
     to Execute Me,'" *Channel 2 News*, April 11, 2014, accessed April 16, 2014, http://
     www.mako.co.il/news-law/legal/Article-6cf8a45b4e15541004.htm.

22   UN Human Rights Council, *Report of the International Fact-Finding Mission to
     Investigate Violations of International Law, Including International Humanitarian
     and Human Rights Law, Resulting from the Israeli Attacks on the Flotilla of Ships
     Carrying Humanitarian Assistance*, September 2010, accessed October 12, 2012,
     http://www2.ohchr.org/english/bodies/hrcouncil/docs/15session/A.HRC.15.21_
     en.PDF; UN, *Report of the Secretary-General's Panel of Inquiry on the May 31, 2010,
     Flotilla Incident*, September 2011, accessed April 9, 2020, https://www.un.org/
     unispal/document/auto-insert-205969/.

23   The Palmer report was first leaked to *The New York Times* on September 1, 2011,
     forcing the UN Secretary-General to present the report officially the following day.

See Tamar Feldman, "A Tale of Two Closures: Comments on the Palmer Report Concerning the May 2010 Flotilla Incident," *European Journal of International Law* (blog), September 20, 2011, accessed July 5, 2013, http://www.ejiltalk.org/a-tale-of-two-closures-comments-on-the-palmer-report-concerning-the-may-2010-flotilla-incident.

24 IBH/FOCA, International Bureau of Humanitarian NGOs and Friends of Charities Association, *Timeline and Inconsistencies Report*, 2010, accessed January 15, 2013, https://www.globalresearch.ca/new-side-by-side-gaza-flotilla-timeline-report-discredits-israeli-version-of-events/21356, 30.

25 International Criminal Court, "ICC Prosecutor Receives Referral by the Authorities of the Union of the Comoros in Relation to the Events of May 2010 on the Vessel *Mavi Marmara*," 2013, accessed May 15, 2013, http://www.icc-cpi.int/iccdocs/otp/Referral-from-Comoros.pdf.

26 ICC, "Statement of the Prosecutor of the International Criminal Court, Fatou Bensouda, on Concluding the Preliminary Examination of the Situation Referred by the Union of Comoros: 'Rome Statute Legal Requirements Have Not Been Met,'" November 6, 2014, accessed November 8, 2014, http://www.icc-cpi.int/en_menus/icc/press%20and%20media/press%20releases/Pages/otp-statement-06-11-2014.aspx.

27 ICC, "ICC Prosecutor Receives Referral"; ICC, *Situation on the Registered Vessels of the Union of the Comoros, the Hellenic Republic, and the Kingdom of Cambodia*, (ICC-01/13), December 2, 2019, accessed July 29, 2020, https://www.icc-cpi.int/RelatedRecords/CR2019_07299.PDF.

28 See the congressional report by Carol Migdalovitz, *Israel's Blockade of Gaza, the Mavi Marmara Incident and Its Aftermath*, US Congressional Research Service, 2010, accessed March 1, 2012, http://www.fas.org/sgp/crs/mideast/R41275.pdf.

29 The report of the Turkish inquiry was published in February 2011, a month after the publication of the Israeli Turkel Commission Report, parts of which the Turkish report addresses. See Turkish National Commission of Inquiry, *Report on the Israeli Attack*. On Kayseri trial see, for example, "Turkish Court Rejects *Marmara* Victim's Family's Compensation Plea," *YNET News*, December 12, 2013, accessed September 16, 2014, http://www.ynetnews.com/articles/0,7340,L-4469745,00.html.

30 See Interpol Red Notice Removal Lawyers, *Report: Turkish Prosecutor Seeks Interpol Notice for Flotilla Attackers*, October 13, 2011, accessed January 15, 2013, http://interpolnoticeremoval.com/tag/istanbul-public-prosecutor-mehmet-akif-ekinci/; See also IHH, Indictment Files, 2012, accessed January 14, 2013, https://www.dropbox.com/sh/l0zl7g242zi1bu9/qFM6mGnflj; "Report: Israel Paid $20M to Turkey as Compensation for *Mavi Marmara*," *Jewish Press*, October 2, 2016, accessed July, 2018, http://www.jewishpress.com/news/breaking-news/report-israel-paid-20m-to-turkey-as-compensation-for-mavi-marmara/2016/10/02/;

Procedural Agreement of Compensation between the Republic of Turkey and the State of Israel, June 28, 2016, accessed August 9, 2020, https://www2.tbmm.gov.tr/d26/1/1-0754.pdf.

31 IHH, *The Mavi Marmara Case-Legal Actions Taken against the Israeli Attack on the Gaza Freedom Flotilla on May 31, 2010*, 2012, accessed April 29, 2014, http://www.ihh.org.tr/fotograf/yayinlar/dokumanlar/134-Mavi%20Marmara%20Hukuk%20Raporu%20-%2010%20Aral%C4%B1k%202012%20-mavi-marmara-legal-report.pdf; The Electronic Intifada, "Spain Prosecutor Requests ICC Referral of Case against Israel's Netanyahu for 2010 Flotilla Attack," January 17, 2013, accessed June 18, 2014, http://electronicintifada.net/blogs/ali-abunimah/spain-prosecutor-requests-icc-referral-case-against-israels-netanyahu-2010; Herb Keinon, "Sweden Looks into Israeli Actions toward Its Nationals Involved in Flotillas to Gaza," *The Jerusalem Post*, June 26, 2014, accessed September 16, 2014, http://www.jpost.com/Diplomacy-and-Politics/Sweden-looks-into-Israeli-actions-toward-its-nationals-involved-in-flotillas-to-Gaza-360737; IHH, "International Panel Held in LSE about *Mavi Marmara*," November 29, 2016, accessed October 10, 2017, https://www.ihh.org.tr/en/news/international-panel-held-in-lse-about-mavi-marmara.

32 See, e.g., Bayoumi, *Midnight on the Mavi Marmara*; Özgürlük Filosu, *Mavi Marmara Gazze* (Istanbul: IHH Kitap, 2011); Ferry Nur, *Mavi Marmara Menembus Gaza*, Jakarta: Kesaksian Seorang Relawan, IHH, 2010; M. Şefik Dinç, *Kanili Mavi Marmara*, (Istanbul: Kalkedon, 2010); *Feu sur le Marmara*, directed by David Segarra (Venezuela, 2010); *Mavi Marmara: The Inside Story*, (2011; Tehran: Press TV); IHH, "*Mavi Marmara* Art Exhibition Opens," August 4, 2010, accessed May 1, 2013, http://www.ihh.org.tr/en/main/news/0/mavi-marmara-art-exhibition-opens/220. About the premiere of the play *Ölüyoruz, Demek ki Yaşanılacak* [Dying to Give Life], written by Sedat Doyan and directed by Bedir Avşin, see IHH, "*Mavi Marmara* is on the Stage!," February 7, 2011, accessed July 30, 2020, https://www.ihh.org.tr/en/news/mavi-marmara-is-on-the-stage-275.

33 See, e.g., IHH, "Freedom: Last Destination—*Mavi Marmara*," Vimeo Video, 91 mins., October 5, 2012, accessed July 1, 2013, http://vimeo.com/50824956, or the IDF Habat – Unit of Technological Education and Training, "Timeline of the *Mavi Marmara* Incident," YouTube Video, 21:18 mins., May 22, 2011, accessed July 1, 2013, http://www.youtube.com/watch?v=z31GesVrBjc.

34 The claim that extraterritoriality should not be understood simply as a derivative of territoriality has been made with regard to antiquity. Richard C. B. Johnsson, "Non-Territorial Governance, Mankind's Forgotten Legacy: A Review of Shin Shun Liu's *Extraterritoriality: Its Rise and Its Decline*," in *Panarchy: Political Theories of Non-Territorial States*, eds. Aviezer Tucker and Gian Piero de Bellis (London: Routledge, 2015), 188–213.

35 Giorgio Agamben, *State of Exception* (Chicago: University of Chicago Press, 2005), 59.

36 Giorgio Agamben, *Means without End* (Minneapolis: University of Minnesota Press, 2000), 23.

37 Turkish National Commission of Inquiry, *Report on the Israeli Attack*, 78–81; *B'Tselem* "Reality Check: Almost Fifty Years of Occupation," June 5, 2016, accessed April 9, 2020, https://www.btselem.org/sites/default/files/sites/default/files2/201606_reality_check_eng_0.pdf.

38 A publication by the IHH Research Department notes at different points that the flotilla set sail in order to "end an ongoing embargo on Gaza." A press release dated April 3, 2010, included in the same publication, states that the flotilla is "a coalition bringing together a number of organisations and movements working to break Israel's illegal blockade." The same publication stated that the Free Gaza Movement initiative was launched by "an umbrella organisation established by pro-Palestinian groups and human rights advocates to increase public awareness of the blockade on the Gaza Strip ... [in order] to break the siege of Gaza." IHH, "*Mavi Marmara:* Gaza Freedom Flotilla," 8, 13, 33.

39 According to the Turkel Commission Report, the Israeli military planned to deploy a second-wave force whose task was "(a) to bring the flotilla vessels to Israeli ports; (b) to make a list of the persons on board and to deal with the magnetic media that would be found on board the vessels." The Israeli troops searched for both weapons and magnetic media. Some of the magnetic media gathered at this stage were transferred to Israel by helicopter to be used by the IDF Spokesperson's Unit. The rest of the material was transferred to the Document and Technological Capture Collection Unit upon the ship's arrival at Ashdod Port. See Turkel Commission, Part 1, pp. 129, 176, 178.

40 *The People's Law Dictionary*, s.v. "In Absentia," accessed February 6, 2013, http://legal-dictionary.thefreedictionary.com/in+absentia.

41 See, e.g., Jonathon Burch, "Turkey Tries Israeli Military over Gaza Ship Killings," *The Daily Star*, November 5, 2012, accessed April 23, 2020, http://www.dailystar.com.lb/News/Middle-East/2012/Nov-05/193962-turkey-to-try-israeli-top-brass-in-deadly-flotilla-raid.ashx#axzz2IRZw5noP. It should be mentioned that Turkish Criminal Procedure Code Article 196 prohibits visual and audio recording inside the justice building as does Turkish Criminal Code Article 183: Republic of Turkey, Turkish Criminal Procedure Code (Istanbul: Beta Publishing House, 2009), accessed April 23, 2020, https://www.legislationline.org/ download/id/4257/file/Turkey_CPC_2009_en.pdf, 98.

42 European Commission, "Standard Summary Project Fiche Project number: TR 05 01.01, Better Access to Justice in Turkey," January 1, 2005, accessed April 20, 2020, https://ec.europa.eu/neighborhood-enlargement/sites/near/files/pdf/fiche-projet/turkey/2005/pf-2005-01.01-better-access-to-justice-in-turkey.pdf.

43 See, e.g., Robert D. Brain, "The Derivative Relevance of Demonstrative Evidence: Charting Its Proper Evidentiary Status," *U.C. Davis Law Review* 25:4 (1992): 957–1027.

44 Peleg, "Commando Unit Warrior Is Prosecuting".

45 Macon Phillips, "Osama bin Laden Dead, the White House," May 2, 2011, accessed June 1, 2020, https://obamawhitehouse.archives.gov/blog/2011/05/02/osama-bin-laden-dead.

46 UN, *United Nations Convention on the Law of the Sea*, December 12, 1982, https://www.un.org/depts/los/convention_agreements/texts/unclos/unclos_e.pdf. See also: Mireille Hildebrandt, "Extraterritorial Jurisdiction to Enforce in Cyberspace? Bodin, Schmitt, Grotius in Cyberspace," *University of Toronto Law Journal* 63:2 (2013): 196–224.

Chapter 1

1 *Cassell's Latin Dictionary, Latin-English/English-Latin*, eds. James R. V. Marchant and Joseph F. Charles (New York: Funk & Wagnalls Company, 1953), s.vv. "extra," "territorium."

2 *Guide to Latin in International Law*, Aaron X. Fellmeth and Maurice Horwitz, s.v. "extra territorium jus dicenti impune non paretur," accessed March 26, 2020, https:// www.oxfordreference.com/view/10.1093/acref/9780195369380.001.0001/ acref-9780195369380-e-755. It should be mentioned that while extraterritorial practices were claimed to be ancient, the use of the term itself is found later, for example in the writing of German jurist Georg F. Von Martens. See Georg Von Martens, *The Law of Nations: Being the Science of National Law, Covenants, Power, etc. Founded Upon the Treaties and Customs of Modern Nations in Europe*, trans. William Cobbett, 4th ed. (London: William Cobbett, 1829), 119–120.

3 Shih-Shun Liu, *Extraterritoriality: Its Rise and Its Decline* (1925; repr., New York: AMS, 1969), 23; Shalom Kassan, "Extraterritorial Jurisdiction in the Ancient World," *The American Journal of International Law* 29:2 (1935): 237–47.

4 Kassan, "Extraterritorial Jurisdiction," 240.

5 See Liu, *Extraterritoriality*, 24; Kassan, "Extraterritorial Jurisdiction", 245; Michael B. Walbank, *Athenian Proxenies of the Fifth Century B.C.* (Toronto: Samuel Stevens, 1978).

6 Theodor Mommsen, *History of Rome*, trans. William Purdie Dickson (1895; repub., Project Gutenberg, 2005) https://www.gutenberg.org/cache/epub/10706/ pg10706-images.html, 199. Cf. Liu, *Extraterritoriality*, 24–5; Kassan, Extraterritorial Jurisdiction, 246.

7 See Liu, *Extraterritoriality*, 23–4; Kassan, "Extraterritorial Jurisdiction", 241; André Dollinger, "Herodotus on Proteus," An Introduction to the History and Culture of Pharaonic Egypt, 2000, accessed August 7, 2013, http://www. reshafim.org.il/ad/egypt/herodotus/proteus.htm: "After him, they said, there succeeded to the throne a man of Memphis, whose name in the tongue of the

Hellenes was Proteus; for whom there is now a sacred enclosure at Memphis, very fair and well ordered, lying on that side of the temple of Hephaistos which faces the North Wind. Round about this enclosure dwell Phoenicians of Tyre, and this whole region is called the Camp of the Tyrians. Within the enclosure of Proteus there is a temple called the temple of the 'foreign Aphrodite,' which temple I conjecture to be one of Helen the daughter of Tyndareus, not only because I have heard the tale how Helen dwelt with Proteus, but also especially because it is called by the name of the 'foreign Aphrodite,' for the other temples of Aphrodite which there are have none of them the addition of the word 'foreign' to the name." See also Herodotus, *Histories*, trans. A. D. Godley (Cambridge, MA: Harvard University Press, 1920), 401–3. Interestingly, it has been suggested that the Peregrines' ability to live according to their own laws ended when they received Roman citizenship. See also Johnsson, "Non-Territorial Governance," 188–213.

8   Kassan, "Extraterritorial Jurisdiction", 241, mentions the immigration of the Jews into Egypt from the land of Canaan and the migration of the nomadic Mentin tribe to Goshen, where they lived under independent rule.

9   Ibid.

10 Johnsson, "Non-Territorial Governance," 188–213.

11 Liu, *Extraterritoriality*, 31.

12 Ibid., 23.

13 Ibid., 27–9; Cf. Pär Kristoffer Cassel, *Grounds of Judgment: Extraterritoriality and Imperial Power in Nineteenth-Century China and Japan* (Oxford: Oxford University Press, 2012), 9. Liu claims that "[i]n the absence of any views of territorial sovereignty … racial consanguinity was treated as the sole basis of amenability to law." Liu, *Extraterritoriality*, 28. Johnsson disagrees however: "This cannot be entirely true, as the Alamanns (Alamannis), apparently, seceded from Lombard laws to establish Alamann laws. It rather seems like ethnicity was just one basis for how people decided what laws to live under, perhaps even the dominant, but evidently not the sole basis." Johnsson, "Non-Territorial Governance," 191.

14 Liu, *Extraterritoriality*, 32.

15 In a late nineteenth-century report, Edward A. Van Dyck, Consular Clerk of the United States at Cairo, writes, "These treaties [between Christians and Muslims] received, however, a name different to that given to treaties that were concluded by the Christian powers among themselves. Instead of being called treaties they were called capitulations, i.e., letters of privilege, or, according to the Oriental expression, imperial diplomas containing sworn promises." The early capitulations, Van Dyck stresses, were not reciprocal but only grants of privileges and immunities. See Edward Van Dyck, *Capitulations of the Ottoman Empire*

since the Year 1150: Part 1 (Washington DC: Government Printing Office, 1881), 12, 24. According to Liu, *Extraterritoriality*, 56, the objective of the capitulations was to regulate the conditions under which Europeans were to do business in the Levant; the interests of Muslims, whether at sea or abroad in a Christian country, were ignored in the scramble to encourage European commerce at home. According to Eliana Augusti, the capitulations were granted based on an explicit promise to keep peaceful relations with the Ottoman rulers, subject to the understanding that any violation may result in a unilateral revocation of the privileges. Eliana Augusti, "From Capitulations to Unequal Treaties: The Matter of an Extraterritorial Jurisdiction in the Ottoman Empire," *Journal of Civil Law Studies* 4:2 (2011): 294.

16　Van Dyck, *Capitulations of the Ottoman Empire*, 25. This definition is almost entirely opposed to recent articulations of extraterritoriality as related to "law at a standstill." Whereas older articulations used this definition to enhance the autonomy of foreigners, contemporary articulations use it to diminish and even to deny such autonomy. In Latin, these treaties were commonly referred to as capitulations as they contained a series of articles which were called capitula, i.e., "chapters." Andreas T. Müller and Friedrich F. Martens, "The Office of Consul and Consular Jurisdiction in the East," *The European Journal of International Law* 25:3 (2014): 878.

17　Liu, *Extraterritoriality*, 48–9.

18　Kamram Hashemi, *Religious Legal Traditions, International Human Rights Law and Muslim States* (Leiden, The Netherlands: Brill Publishers, 2008), 100. It should be noted that scholars disagree in regard to the specific time period in which the letter was written and its place of signature, as well as on other aspects relating to this document. Ibid.

19　Rachel Scott, *The Challenge of Political Islam: Non-Muslims and the Egyptian State* (Palo Alto, CA: Stanford University Press, 2010), 16.

20　Such quarters are also mentioned in Van Dyck's report. The Arabic word "Funduk," he writes, was used to designate the quarters inhabited by Pisans, Genoese, and other foreigners who traded in the cities of the Levant. The names of some quarters still retain reference to the nationality of their erstwhile denizens. For example, the city of Sidon still contains the Khan el-Afrange, i.e., "the Home of the French." See Van Dyck, *Capitulations of the Ottoman Empire*, 89.

21　Liu, *Extraterritoriality*, 58. In some cases, such specially designated quarters for foreigners were called "farms." Augusti, "Extraterritorial Jurisdiction in the Ottoman Empire," 291. On capitulations for citizens of the Italian republics in the period between 1150 and 1200. See also Van Dyck, *Capitulations of the Ottoman Empire*, 12–13. For a first-hand account of the capitulations regime in the Ottoman Empire, see, e.g., Van Dyck, who writes, "the agents of Ottoman public force cannot enter the residence of the foreigner without the assistance of the consul or the delegate of the consul of the power on which the foreigner depends." Ibid., 43.

22 M. L. Roy Chowdhury, "Principles of Law in the Mughal Empire," *Proceedings of the Indian History Congress* 10 (1947): 367–70.

23 Nandini Chatterjee, "Reflections on Religious Difference and Permissive Inclusion on Mughal Law," *Journal of Law and Religion* 29:3 (2014): 11; Bernard S. Cohn, "Some Notes on Law and Change in North India," *Economic Development and Cultural Change* 8:1 (1959): 79–93.

24 According to Liu, *Extraterritoriality*, 32, imperialism could not have been the origin of extraterritoriality, "inasmuch as the notion of territorial sovereignty was as yet unknown when extraterritoriality took its root." In addition, Liu claims, imperialism itself is based on a later idea of territorialism. Nevertheless, when exploring the notion of extraterritoriality in the nineteenth century, Liu identifies it with a kind of imperialism. See also Johnsson, "Non-Territorial Governance," 188–213.

25 Cassel, *Grounds of Judgment*, 5.

26 Augusti, "Extraterritorial Jurisdiction in the Ottoman Empire," 296.

27 Ibid., 288.

28 Ibid. Augusti refers here to claims made by Antoine Pillet.

29 Sarah Abrevaya Stein, *Extraterritorial Dreams: European Citizenship, Sephardi Jews, and the Ottoman Twentieth Century* (Chicago: University of Chicago Press, 2016), 2.

30 Turan Kayaoğlu, *Legal Imperialism: Sovereignty and Extraterritoriality in Japan, the Ottoman Empire, and China* (Cambridge, UK: Cambridge University Press, 2010). Liu writes, "In the Far East, extraterritorial rights have been enjoyed by foreign Powers in China, Japan, Korea, Siam, Borneo, Tonga and Samoa. The earliest grant of such rights made by China to Great Britain was contained in the supplemental treaty of July 1843. The first treaty entered into by Japan was that of March 31, 1854, with the United States, but it included no provision regarding extraterritorial jurisdiction. Of all the European treaties the Russian one, dated January 26/February 7, 1855, appears to have contained the earliest germs of extraterritorial jurisdiction in Japan. In Korea, Japan was the first foreign Power to secure extraterritorial rights. The formal establishment of extraterritoriality in Siam dates from the treaty of April 18, 1855 with Great Britain. The United States and Great Britain have enjoyed extraterritorial rights in Borneo since the middle of the last century. Before the Tonga Islands fell under the protection of Great Britain, various Powers obtained title to rights of jurisdiction in that country. The first treaty containing a specific grant of this nature was that with Great Britain, dated November 29, 1879. Finally, in Samoa, the United States, Germany, and Great Britain enjoyed extraterritorial rights before the islands were divided up between Germany and the United States in 1899." Liu, *Extraterritoriality*, 91–4. According to Harold Scott Quigley, the

origins of extraterritoriality in China can be traced to the ninth century, when Arab traders residing at Canfu (Canton or Haiyen) were permitted to govern themselves under their own laws. See Harold Scott Quigley, "Extraterritoriality in China," *The American Journal of International Law* 20:1 (1926): 48.

31 Kayaoğlu further claims that Western governments collaborated with each other to sustain extraterritoriality in non-Western countries. By contrast, non-Western powers never exercised extraterritoriality, with the exception of Japan, which, as a result, was considered a member in the exclusive club of "civilized sovereignty states." See Kayaoğlu, *Legal Imperialism*, 8.

32 Ibid., 9–12.

33 Cassel, *Grounds of Judgment*, 10.

34 Ibid., 12.

35 "From which it would necessarily follow that within a settlement or concession non-treaty foreigners when defendants would be under the jurisdiction of the mixed court." Quigley, "Extraterritoriality in China," 54.

36 Kavalam Madhava Panikkar, *Asia and Western Dominance: A Survey of the Vasco da Gama Epoch of Asian History, 1498–1945* (London: G. Allen & Unwin, 1953), 134–5. See also Jorgen Osterhammel, "Semi-Colonialism and Informal Empire in Twentieth-Century China: Towards a Framework of Analysis," in *Imperialism and After: Continuities and Discontinuities*, ed. Wolfgang Justin Mommsen (London: Allen & Unwin, 1986), 290–314.

37 "The Anglo-Chinese and American-Chinese treaties signed on January 1, 1943, which brought an end to British and American extraterritorial rights have been regarded as the "finale" which ended the old order and ushered in a new one in China." K. C. Chan, "The Abrogation of British Extraterritoriality in China 1942–43: A Study of Anglo-American-Chinese Relations," *Modern Asian Studies* 11:2 (1977): 260.

38 Council of Europe, *Convention for the Protection of Human Rights and Fundamental Freedoms*, 1950, accessed August 1, 2013, https://www.echr.coe. int/Documents/Convention_ENG.pdf. The treaty's relation to the application of exterritorial human rights has been described as highly important for two reasons. "First, the ECHR system is by far the strongest of all human rights regimes (if far from perfect) in its ability to effectively secure compliance and exercise a direct impact on state policy. The stakes are highest in Strasbourg because the Court is respected. Secondly, it is precisely because the stakes are highest in Strasbourg that the jurisprudence of the European Court of Human Rights on extraterritorial application is the most fully developed. At the same time, it is the most problematic, suffering from rampant casuistry and conceptual chaos. It is a jurisprudence of compromise, at times quite unprincipled, owing mostly to the Court's understandable desire to avoid the merits of legally and politically difficult cases by relying on the preliminary issue of extraterritorial application." See Marko

Milanovic, *Extraterritorial Application of Human Rights Treaties* (Oxford: Oxford University Press, 2011), 4.

39 Ibid.

40 See Eliav Lieblich, "Exterritory" (lecture, Exterritory Project Symposium, Haifa, December 20, 2013). In his talk, Lieblich further stressed how despite the fact that these processes were perceived as positive developments, they were also abused by Western states as pretexts for intervention and as instruments of neo-colonization.

41 Noura Erakat, *Justice for Some: Law and the Question of Palestine* (Redwood City, CA: Stanford University Press, 2019), 6–7.

42 Maarten Den Heijer, *Europe and Extraterritorial Asylum* (London: Bloomsbury Publishing, 2012), 29, 31; Milanovic, *Extraterritorial Application of Human Rights Treaties*, 35.

43 On Israel's legal assertions aimed at renouncing its status as an occupying power, see also Chapter 2, pp. 34–35.

44 For example, the increasing tendency of developed states to prefer exercising their immigration border control: "both decision-making and enforcement – prior to an individual's arrival on their territory." Bernard Ryan, "Extraterritorial Immigration Control: What Role for Legal Guarantees?" in *Extraterritorial Immigration Control: Legal Challenges*, ed. Bernard Ryan and Valsamis Mitsilegas (Leiden, The Netherlands: Brill/Nijhoff, 2010), 3.

45 According to political philosopher James C. Scott, Zomia, a border area in Southeast Asia, is the largest area in the world in which people were not fully incorporated into the state system until the 1950s. Scott (who uses the term "fully occupied world") identifies four eras of political-territorial organization: (1) the stateless era (which was by far the longest); (2) the era of small-scale states encircled by vast and easily accessed stateless peripheries; (3) a period in which stateless peripheries shrank and were beleaguered by the expansion of state power; and, finally, (4) the current era in which virtually the entire globe has become an "administered space," with stateless peripheries remaining "not much more than a folkloric remnant." James C. Scott, *The Art of Not Being Governed: An Anarchist History of Upland Southeast Asia* (New Haven, CT: Yale University Press, 2009), 324.

46 See, e.g., Eyal Weizman, *Hollow Land: Israel's Architecture of Occupation* (Brooklyn: Verso Books, 2012). See also Michel Agier, "Humanity as an Identity and Its Political Effect: A Note on Camps and Humanitarian Government," *Humanity: An International Journal of Human Rights, Humanitarianism and Development* 1:1 (2010): 29–45; Carl Levy, "Refugees, Europe, Camps/State of Exception: 'Into the Zone,' the European Union and Extraterritorial Processing of Migrants, Refugees, and Asylum-Seekers (Theories and Practice)," *Refugee Survey Quarterly* 29:1 (2010), 92–119; Sari Hanafi, *Governing Palestinian Refugees in the Arab East* (Beirut: Issam Fares Institute, American University of Beirut, 2010), 1–25; Adam Ramadan,

"Destroying Nahr el-Bared: Sovereignty and Urbicide in the Space of Exception," *Political Geography* 28:3 (2009): 153–63, among many others.

47 According to Agamben, the origins of the "state of exception" can be traced back to the German "state of necessity," and (following Schmitt), even earlier, to the Napoleonic "state of siege" which extended military power and suspended constitutional law. Agamben explores the history of the state of exception in the French constitution (where "the power to suspend the law can belong only to those who produce the laws"). In the anti-democratic, anti-constitutional European dictatorships between the two world wars. Following Carl Schmitt, he writes that the state of exception is "an exclusive legacy of the undemocratic tradition." Agamben, *Omnibus Homo Sacer* (Redwood City, CA: Stanford University Press, 2017), 176, 179. See also Giorgio Agamben, *Homo Sacer: Sovereign Power and Bare Life* (Redwood City, CA: Stanford University Press, 1998), 15–19.

48 Carl Schmitt, *Political Theology: Four Chapters on the Concept of Sovereignty* (Chicago: University of Chicago Press, 2005), 5.

49 Walter Benjamin, *Selected Writings, Vol. 1: 1913–1926*, eds. Marcus Bullock and Michael W. Jennings (Cambridge, MA: Belknap Press, 1996), 236–52.

50 Agamben, *Sovereign Power*, 64.

51 Agamben, *State of Exception*, 4, 16, 29, 38, 39, 40.

52 Ibid., 20. Cf. Agamben, *Means without End*, 14–24.

53 Agamben, *Sovereign Power*, 95–7.

54 Ibid., 175.

55 *Sacratio* arises out of the conjunction of two traits: the unpunishability of killing and the exclusion of sacrifice. Agamben claims that the structure of *Sacratio* is connected to the structure of sovereignty, which is based on a double exclusion: the sovereign sphere is the sphere in which it is permitted to kill without committing homicide and without celebrating sacrifice. Agamben further writes, "the sovereign is the one with respect to whom all men are potentially *homines sacri*, and homo *sacer* is the one with respect to whom all men act as sovereigns." Agamben, *Sovereign Power*, 84–5.

56 Agamben, *Means without End*, 3–15. Agamben quotes Schmitt to emphasize the relation between territory and the "state of exception" inscribed in sovereign law: "The 'ordering of space' that is, according to Schmitt, constitutive of the sovereign *nomos* is therefore not only a 'taking of land' (*Landesnahme*)—the determination of a juridical and a territorial ordering (of an *Ordnung* and an *Ortung*)—but above all a 'taking of the outside,' an exception (*Ausnahme*)." Agamben, *Sovereign Power*, 19.

57 Agamben, *Means without End*, 14–24.

58 As I noted earlier, some claim that extraterritoriality first emerged from jurisdictional conflicts. For this claim in relation to the "state of emergency," see Agamben, *State of Exception*, 10.

59 Ibid., 31.

60 On the concept of pure violence, see Walter Benjamin, "Critique of Violence" in *Reflections: Essays, Aphorisms, Autobiographical Writings*, ed. Peter Demetz, trans. Edmund Jephcott (New York: Schocken, 1986), 277–300.

61 In Lebanon, 463 of 664 refugees were registered with UNRWA (United Nations Relief and Works Agency for Palestinian Refugees in the Near East) as of January 1, 2017. Palestinian refugees are estimated to have made up ten per cent of Lebanon's population in 2017. UNRW, "In Figures," 2017, accessed April 2, 2020 https://www. unrwa.org/sites/default/files/content/resources/unrwa_in_figures_2017_english. pdf.

62 Sari Hanafi, "Palestinian Refugee Camps in Lebanon Laboratory of Indocile Identity Formation," in *Manifestations of Identity: The Lived Reality of Palestinian Refugees in Lebanon*, ed. Muhammad Ali Khalidi (Beirut: Institute of Palestine Studies, 2010), 51.

63 Sari Hanafi, "Palestinian Refugee Camps in Lebanon: Laboratories of State-in-the-Making, Discipline and Islamist Radicalism," in *Biopolitics and States of Exception*, ed. Ronit Lentin (London: Zed Books, 2008), 86.

64 Hanafi, "Laboratories," 89–90; Hanafi, "Indocile Identity Formation," 53. According to Hanfi, the camp's extraterritorial jurisdiction was an outcome of a burgeoning Palestinian nationalism. Later developments, however—the expulsion of the PLO and the horrific massacres at the camps Sabra and Shatila—bring to mind Agamben's view of the camp as a site for the production of political bare life, and thus a site of "de-nationalization." Agamben, *Sovereign Power*, 175–6.

65 See interview with Sari Hanafi (himself a Palestinian refugee): Ursula Biemann, *Mission Reports: Artistic Practice in the Field* (Umeå, Sweden: Bildmuseet, Umeå University, 2008), 97: "For Sari Hanafi … Nahr el Bared is the epitome of how the Lebanese authorities conceive of such extraterritorial space: 'The camp is located outside the city of Tripoli but they allow no infrastructure to connect the camp to the city; they marginalize it, govern it by emergency law and then abandon it. This is the very condition under which the refugee camps in Lebanon are turned into a place where other extraterritorial elements, like al-Qaeda, can come and establish their microcosm.'" A legal discussion of extraterritoriality in relation to non-state actors begins with the basic question of how non-state actors (e.g. al-Qaeda) ought to be classified. Noam Lubell writes, " … it is certainly plausible to argue that initially Al-Qaeda was a non-state actor, and may have remained as such at the time the US began its military operations in Afghanistan, but that at some point during the hostilities, when it appeared that some of the Al-Qaeda members were fighting within the structure and chain of command of the Taliban—the then

de facto government—those individuals and any hostilities they were involved in at that time and place would have been part of an international armed conflict. ... If, following the US invasion and the commencement of battle, Al-Qaeda fighters became integrated within the organizational structure of the Taliban forces, it could be argued that they too were then part of an international armed conflict." Noam Lubell, *Extraterritorial Use of Force against Non-State Actors* (Oxford: Oxford University Press, 2010), 98.

66 Hanafi, "Indocile Identity Formation," 58.

67 According to UNRWA, as of January 1, 2018, there were eight camps in the Gaza Strip and nineteen in the West Bank, with nearly 1.4 million registered refugees in Gaza, and 828, 328 in the West Bank. See UNRWA, "Where We Work," 2020, accessed September 24, 2020, https://www.unrwa.org/where-we-work.

68 Hanafi, *Governing Palestinian Refugees*, 22.

69 Michel Agier, "The Undesirables of the World and How Universality Changed Camp," *openDemocracy*, May 16, 2011, accessed April 2, 2020, https://www. opendemocracy.net/en/undesirables-of-world-and-how-universality-changed-camp/. In "Humanity as an Identity," Agier discusses extraterritoriality and the state of exception in the context of refugee camps in Asia and Africa, comparing them to retention centers in Europe: "[T]here is still a way to compare all these camps, if we consider the disorder that blurs the order presented above that is at once symbolic and social. This disorder takes two forms. On the one hand, it is the discretionary power that the extraterritoriality of camps gives to 'administrators' of spaces of exception. Moreover, the violence that takes place in a retention center in Europe can happen elsewhere by virtue of its invisibility—for example, in transit zones annexed to the most stable and monitored camps of the UNHCR in Africa ... What we can compare, in these cases, are practices in situations of exception." He goes on to claim that the three characteristics that identify the "space" of humanitarian apparatuses are extraterritoriality, religion, and exception. Agier, "Humanity as an Identity," 38. Additional examples can be found in Michel Agier and Françoise Bouchet-Saulnier, "Humanitarian Spaces: Spaces of Exception," in *The Shadow of Just Wars: Violence, Politics and Humanitarian Action*, ed. Fabrice Weissman (Ithaca, NY: *Medecins Sans Frontieres*, 2004), 228–46.

70 Agier, "Undesirables." Extraterritorial jurisdiction is administratively applied as a legal tool that enables states to withhold accesses to asylum seekers and in other varied ways. Additional examples mentioned by Agier are the use of coastal islands as detention centers in Europe and Australia, converted to retention centers for foreigners in order to circumvent the law of asylum. In another example, the US government has claimed not to be responsible for the actions of its own officials. US coast guards who apprehended Haitian asylum seekers outside of American jurisdiction and forced them to return to Haiti. More relevant to our discussion

are French laws which seem to challenge the very relation between space and the application of extraterritoriality. See also Vladislava Stoyanova, "The Principle of Non-Refoulement and The Right of Asylum-Seekers of Enter State Territory," *Interdisciplinary Journal of Human Rights Law* 3:1 (2008): 1–11.

71 Ibid.

72 Kal Raustiala, "The Geography of Justice," *Fordham Law Review* 73:6 (2005): 2501–60.

73 Ibid. The Guantánamo Bay Naval Base has been under US control since 1903. Despite the century-long American presence, the official position of the US government is that Guantánamo is not American territory. An unusual agreement declares that Cuba retains "ultimate sovereignty" over Guantánamo. The United States, however, exercises "complete jurisdiction and control." Raustiala describes the legal status of the camp as a form of US occupation, similar to the status of US bases in Iraq.

74 Eyal Weizman, Ines Geisler, and Anselm Franke, "'Islands': The Geography of Extraterritoriality," repr. in *Extraterritorialities in Occupied Worlds*, eds. Maayan Amir and Ruti Sela (Santa Barbara, CA: Punctum Books, 2016), 117–22. Cf. Primo Levi's description of the figure of the Muselmann as deprived of "all consciousness and all personality as to make him absolutely apathetic ... All his instincts are cancelled along with his reason." See Agamben, *Sovereign Power*, 184–5.

75 Interestingly, in Weizman's earlier work *Hollow Land,* he does implicitly ascribe extraterritoriality to the physical body itself, however, to that of the Jewish Settler in the West bank, he writes "This meant that a settler caught in crime within a Palestinian town would be subjected to Israeli law while a Palestinian at the same place would be subjected to military rule. The body of the settler has been legally understood to be an extraterritorial embodiment of the state. Its violation has thus become akin to a territorial violation." Weizman, *Hollow Land*, 286.

76 Agamben notes the debate among historians about the origins of the camp, with some dating the first camps to Spanish colonialism in Cuba, others to the South African concentration camps in which the English imprisoned the Boers. What is important, Agamben writes, is that in these camps "a state of emergency linked to a colonial war [was] extended to an entire civil population ... the camps [were] thus born out of a state of exception and martial law." Agamben, *Sovereign Power*, 166–7. Agamben adds, "The state of exception echoes the law at standstill[,]" ... "the production of juridical void," or "the state of exception is not defined as fullness of powers, a pleromatic state of law, as in the dictatorial model, but as a kenomatic state, an emptiness and standstill of the law." Agamben, *State of Exception*, 41–2, 48.

77 In contemporary times, extraterritoriality is claimed in varying degrees of legality, in many cases (according to some) unlawfully. Discussions of these issues received great public attention in the case of the camp at Guantánamo. Yet, as both Gregory and Weizman, Geisler, and Franke note, other camps with similar conditions have operated in Afghanistan and Iraq (receiving, as Derek Gregory writes, some of the detainees from Camp X-Ray when the latter was closed). See Derek Gregory, "The Black Flag: Guantánamo Bay and the Space of Exception," *Geografiska Annaler* 88:4 (2006): 405–27.

78 Ibid.

79 Boaventura de Sousa Santos, "Beyond Abyssal Thinking: From Global Lines to Ecologies of Knowledges," *Review* 30:1 (2007): 45–89.

80 Walter Benjamin writes, "The tradition of the oppressed tells us that the state of emergency in which we live in is not an exception but a rule. We must attain to a conception of history that is keeping with this insight ... This amazement is not the beginning of knowledge—unless it is the knowledge that the view of history which gives rise to it is untenable." Walter Benjamin, *Illumination* (New York: Schocken Books, 1968), 257. Santos himself recommends "that struggles for global social justice be based on a very broad conception of power and oppression." See Santos, "Beyond Abyssal Thinking," 45. Santos, *The Rise of the Global Left: The World Social Forum and Beyond* (London: Zed Books, 2006), 36–7. Cf. Agamben, *Means without End*, 8.

81 In "Beyond Abyssal Thinking," 67, Santos suggests replacing the dialectical notion with an "ecological" one: "As an ecology of knowledges, post-abyssal thinking is premised upon idea of the epistemological diversity of the world, the recognition of the existence of a plurality of knowledges beyond scientific knowledge."

82 Ibid., 48.

83 Ibid., 49.

84 Ibid., 53.

85 Ibid., 53.

86 Ibid., 66.

87 On exception and "justice without law," see, e.g., Giorgio Agamben, *The Time that Remains: A Commentary on the Letter to the Romans* (Redwood City, CA: Stanford University Press, 2005), 107.

88 Emmanuel Levinas, *Outside the Subject*, trans. Michael B. Smith (Redwood City, CA: Stanford University Press, 1993), 116–25.

89 Ibid., 123. Also see Robert Bernasconi, "Extra-Territoriality: Outside the State, Outside the Subject," *Levinas Studies* 3 (2008): 61–77.

90 Zygmunt Bauman, "The World Inhospitable to Levinas," *Philosophy Today* 43:2 (1999): 151–67, repr. in *Extraterritorialities in Occupied Worlds*, eds. Maayan Amir and Ruti Sela (Santa Barbara, CA: Punctum Books), 59–88.

91   Zygmunt Bauman, *Liquid Modernity* (Malden, MA: Polity Press, 2000).

92   Ibid., 10.

93   Ibid.

94   Ibid., 11.

95   Ibid., 121.

96   Ibid., 11.

97   Ibid., 13.

98   Keller Easterling, "Zone: The Spatial Software of Extrastatecraft," *Places Journal* (2012), accessed April 6, 2020, https://placesjournal.org/article/zone-the-spatial-softwares-of-extrastatecraft/?cn-reloaded=1#0.

99   Ibid.

100 Ibid.

101 At least not in his major books dedicated to these issues: *Sovereign Power, State of Exception*, and *Means without End*.

102 Agamben, *Means without End*, 23.

103 Ibid., 23.

104 Sari Hanafi, "New Models for the Nation-State," in *Solution 196–213: United States of Palestine-Israel*. ed. Joshua Simon (New York: Sternberg Press, 2011), 17–22.

105 Ibid., 18. See also Sari Hanafi, "The Broken Boundaries of Statehood and Citizenship," *Borderlands e-journal*, 2:3 (2003), accessed April 6, 2020, http://www.borderlands.net.au/vol2no3_2003/hanafi_boundaries.htm.

Chapter 2

1   Turkel Commission, Part 1, pp. 25–112.

2   Alan Levine, "The Status of Sovereignty in East Jerusalem and the West Bank," *New York University Journal of International Law and Politics* 5:3 (1972): 485.

3   Antony Anghie, "Colonialism and the Birth of International Institutions: Sovereignty, Economy, and the Mandate System of the League of Nations," *New York University Journal of International Law and Politics* 34 (2001): 513–14.

4   Avalon Project, The Covenant of the League of Nations: Article 22, Yale Law School, accessed January 31, 2020, https://avalon.law.yale.edu/20th_century/leagcov.asp.

5   John Quigley, *The Statehood of Palestine: International Law in the Middle East Conflict* (Cambridge, UK: Cambridge University Press, 2010), 20–31.

6   Avalon Project, The Covenant of the League of Nations: Article 22.

7   Shira Robinson, *Citizen Strangers: Palestinians and the Birth of Israel's Liberal Settler State* (Redwood City, CA: Stanford University Press, 2013), 7.

8   Levine, "Status of Sovereignty," 489.

9   Jack Donnelly, "Human Rights: A New Standard of Civilization?," *International Affairs* 74:1 (1998): 1–2, 9.

10 For example, the local judicial subservience is reflected in the fact the foreigners involved in a case could have requested to be tried by a British judge, while capitulations of "protected" subjects of European states remained in force. See Ellery C. Stowell, "Extraterritoriality—A Vanishing Institution: Part Two: Syria and Palestine," *Cumulative Digest of International Law and Relations* 3 (1934), 85.

11 On the obligation to sign international treaties as a condition for the mandate system termination, see Quigley, *Statehood of Palestine*, 52–65. Shira Robinson adds that the deployment of "non-self-governing territories was not surprising, as the imperial powers involved in drafting the UN Charter had signed off on this language only because they had banked on the exemption of their territories from eligibility. Indeed, the Charter failed to specify what constituted a non-self-governing territory, much less a 'people' with national rights. It also declined to list the criteria by which to measure if and when self-rule had been achieved, or to impose any enforcement obligations on the UN or the administering powers." Robinson, *Citizen Strangers*, 7.

12 Levine, "Status of Sovereignty," 488, note 19.

13 Quigley, *Statehood of Palestine*, 92.

14 Virginia Tilley, *Beyond Occupation: Apartheid, Colonialism and International Law in the Occupied Palestinian Territories* (London: Pluto Press, 2012), 27.

15 Ibid., 31–2.

16 Robinson, *Citizen Strangers*, 67.

17 Benny Morris, *The Birth of the Palestinian Refugee Problem Revisited*, Vol. 18 (Cambridge, UK: Cambridge University Press, 2004), 1. On the conceptualization of the condition of the Palestinian refugee through extraterritoriality, see Sandi Hilal, Alessandro Petti, and Eyal Weizman, *Architecture after Revolution* (Berlin: Sternberg Press, 2013), 39. See also the aforementioned discussion of the refugee camps in Lebanon, Chapter 1, pp. 22–23.

18 Benny Morris, *Israel's Border Wars, 1949–1956: Arab Infiltration, Israeli Retaliation, and the Countdown to the Suez War* (Oxford: Oxford University Press, 1997), 2.

19 Ibid., 116.

20 Ibid., 29–32. Morris notes that at first, between 1948 and 1949, infiltration was in most cases unarmed, however, in response to "free fire" policy, increasingly turned infiltrators armed and violent, *Israel's Border Wars*, 97.

21 Though diverse in scope and character, Israel has repeatedly carried out retaliatory and other military operations beyond its national borders, targeting Palestinians along with select individuals and groups allied to foreign militaries and militias, but also certain civilians it either considered a direct threat or unavoidable collateral damage in defense of its security. Operations were conducted from and carried out in neighboring countries both near and far, in the Middle East and elsewhere, more than often in clear violation of the territorial sovereignty of the states in question. For instance, Israel carried out assassination operations against prominent Palestinian militia members and official Palestinian leaders exiled in Beirut (1973), Malta (1995),

and Tunis (1988), among others: Victoria Brittain, "They Had to Die: Assassination against Liberation," *Race & Class* 48:1 (2006): 71. Israel also adheres to the so-called doctrine of "preventive war," conducting strikes against facilities identified as strategic enemy assets used for developing a capability for a future attack; these include for example the bombardment of the Osirak nuclear installation at Tuwaitha, Iraq (1981), and the attack on the alleged Syrian nuclear facility in Al-Kibar, Syria (2007): Joshua Kirschenbaum, "Operation Opera: An Ambiguous Success," *Journal of Strategic Security* 3:4 (2010): 49; Andrew Garwood-Gowers, "Israel's Airstrike on Syria's Al-Kibar Facility: A Test Case for the Doctrine of Pre-Emptive Self-Defence?," *Journal of Conflict & Security Law* 16:2 (2011): 263. Furthermore, since the late 2000s Israel resorted to a policy of targeted killings of Palestinians in the Occupied Territories and Gaza. While the Israeli military claims the practice is legal (for reasons of self-defense and counter-terrorism against "unlawful combatant," a claim largely enjoyed at first by the Israeli Supreme Court view of the practice "non-justiciability" and later in its 2006 ruling that despite raising objections to the term, expanded the definition of "direct participation" and did confirm the legality of preventive strikes), it is widely perceived as an extra-judicial practice in grave violation of international law: Adam Stahl, "The Evolution of Israeli Targeted Operations: Consequences of the Thabet Thabet Operation," *Studies in Conflict & Terrorism* 33:2 (2010): 121; Gal Luft, "The Logic of Israel's Targeted Killing," *Middle East Quarterly* 10:1 (2003). Orna Ben-Naftali and Keren R, Michaeli, "Justice Ability: A Critique of the Alleged Non Justiciability of Israel's Policy of Targeted Killings," *Journal of International Criminal Justice* 1:2 (2003): 369, supra note 2; Kristen E. Eichensehr, "On Target? The Israeli Supreme Court and the Expansion of Targeted Killings," *The Yale Law Journal* 116:8 (2007): 1873–81. Another method that contributed to pushing the local conflict outside of the state territory is Israel's continual deportations of Palestinians, since 1967, mostly as a punitive measure against individuals; however, in some cases it has affected entire groups, for example, in December 1992 there was a mass-deportation of hundreds of Palestinian activists, mostly members of Hamas, to Lebanon, following the kidnapping and murder of Israeli police officer Nissim Toledano: Elad Ben-Dror, "The Poets of Marj al-Zuhur: Poetry as the Psychological, Political, and Ideological Weapons of the Hamas Members Deported to Lebanon in 1992," *Terrorism and Political Violence* 28:1 (2016): 157–8; Elad Ben-Dror, "'We Were Getting Close to God, Not Deportees': The Expulsion to Marj al-Zuhur in 1992 as a Milestone in the Rise of Hamas," *The Middle East Journal* 74: 3 (2020): 399. It should be noted that the Palestinian resistance to the State of Israel has also been responsible for various attacks in many other countries. There have been different instances of plane hijackings or hijacking attempts by the Popular Front for the Liberation of Palestine (PFLP), such as the 1968 El Al plane en-route from Rome to Tel Aviv that was commandeered and taken to Algeria; the

1969 attempted hijack of an El Al flight from Zurich to Tel Aviv; and the Dawson's Field Attacks in 1970, in which four hijackings were attempted: three (Swissair, TWA, and Pan Am) were successful, and one (El Al) failed. In addition, there have been terror attacks on various Israeli embassies, as well as assaults on Jewish and Israeli civilians around the world that have been linked various Palestinian resistance groups. For example, the Munich Olympic Games Massacre of 1972, in which Israel's representatives were kidnapped and murdered; the PLO attempted assassination of Israeli ambassador to the United Kingdom, Shlomo Argov, in 1982: Paul G. Pierpaoli Jr., "Black September Organization," in *The Encyclopedia of the Arab-Israeli Conflict: A Political, Social, and Military History*, eds. Spencer C. Tucker and Priscilla Roberts (Santa Barbara, CA: ABC-CLIO, 2008), 225; Moshe Terdiman, "Civil War in Lebanon," in *The Encyclopedia of the Arab-Israeli Conflict: A Political, Social, and Military History*, eds. Spencer C. Tucker and Priscilla Roberts (Santa Barbara, CA: ABC-CLIO, 2008), 621; Brian Parkinson and Spencer C. Tucker, "Israeli Invasion of Lebanon," in *The Encyclopedia of the Arab-Israeli Conflict: A Political, Social, and Military History*, eds. Spencer C. Tucker and Priscilla Roberts (Santa Barbara, CA: ABC-CLIO, 2008), 623. See also Israeli Ministry of Foreign Affairs, "Shlomo Argov," February 23, 2003, https://mfa.gov.il/MFA/MFA-Archive/2003/Pages/Shlomo%20 Argov.aspx. These selected examples manifest how from its inception violent exchange over the unsettled territory of Palestine was borderless, also in the sense of challenging the idea of territorial sovereignty, not only in the local context but also infringing that of other states in the region and beyond.

22 Morris, *Israel's Border Wars*, 186; Derek Varble, *The Suez Crisis* (New York: The Rosen Publishing Group, 2008), 86.

23 Adekeye Adebajo, *UN Peacekeeping in Africa: From the Suez Crisis to the Sudan Conflicts* (Boulder, CO: Lynne Rienner Publishers, 2011), 26; Alexander Bligh, "The United Nations Emergency Force (UNEF), 1956–67: Past Experience, Current Lessons," *Middle Eastern Studies* 50:5 (2014): 803.

24 Arnon Yehuda Degani, "The Decline and Fall of the Israeli Military Government, 1948–1966: A Case of Settler-Colonial Consolidation?," *Settler Colonial Studies* 5:1 (2015): 87. These rules that enabled the military to declare "closed areas" and restricted "security zones," also facilitated an extensive process of confiscation of Arab lands in the post 1948-war era, exemplified by the village of al-Ghabisiya. We can observe that, more generally speaking, in order to pursue the seizure of Arab lands after 1948, Israel had made use of the legal category of the "absentee," first enacted through emergency regulations and later enshrined as the 1950 Absentees Property Law. As a fairly inclusive legal construct, the "absentee" clause involved not only the refugees who fled the war (or were expelled to other countries) in the expropriation of their property back home, but also affected a substantial number of Arabs who were still residing in Israel (e.g., those who

were nationals of other Arab states, individual who traveled to other Arab states during, etc.; see page 86). After 1967 the State extended the Absentees Property clause to cover other land legislations to the Occupied Territories. The repercussions of this law are vast, and some are still being contended—specifically as regards the annexation of East Jerusalem—were due to the Jordanian and other Arab state citizenship held by the majority of the population, the law of Absentees Property risked turning their entire property subject to expropriation. See Sabri Jiryis, "The Legal Structure for the Expropriation and Absorption of Arab Lands in Israel," *Journal of Palestine Studies* 2:4 (1973): 93–5; Robert Home, "An 'Irreversible Conquest'? Colonial and Postcolonial Land Law in Israel/Palestine," *Social & Legal Studies* 12:3 (2003): 301.

25 Ibid., 87. For archival material on the Military Government, see Israel State Archive File No. 17005/6, October 1969, accessed July 31, 2020, https://www.akevot.org.il/wp-content/uploads/2019/05/ISA-File-GL-17005-6.pdf.

26 Robinson, *Citizen Strangers*, 3.

27 Michael B. Oren, *Six Days of War: June 1967 and the Making of the Modern Middle East* (Oxford: Oxford University Press, 2002), 305, 307.

28 Levine, "Status of Sovereignty," 485–502.

29 Eyal Benvenisti and Eyal Zamir, "Private Claims to Property Rights in the Future Israeli-Palestinian Settlement," *The American Journal of International Law* 89:2 (1995): 299; Neve Gordon, *Israel's Occupation* (Oakland, CA: University of California Press, 2008), 49–50; Alice M. Panepinto, "The Annexation of Palestine," in *The Extraterritoriality of Law: History, Theory, Politics*, ed. Daniel S. Margolies et al. (London: Routledge, 2019), 200–14.

30 In the first year Israel did apply this law however, it was advised by the military advocate to reject its applicability. Panepinto, "The Annexation of Palestine," 202–3. On the commitment to apply extraterritorial jurisdiction in cases of effective control and Israel rejection of such obligations, see Orna Ben-Naftali, "The Extraterritorial Application of Human Rights to Occupied Territories." *Proceedings of the ASIL Annual Meeting,* vol. 100, 90–95. Cambridge University Press, 2006.

31 Tilley, *Beyond Occupation*, 34.

32 Ibid., 36; Gordon, *Israel's Occupation*, 26–7. See also B'Tselem, "Land Grab: Israel Settlement Policy in the West Bank," May, 2002, accessed February 27, 2020, https://www.btselem.org/publications/summaries/200205_land_grab.

33 Gordon, *Israel's Occupation*, 4; Eyal Benvenisti, *Legal Dualism: The Absorption of the Occupied Territories into Israel* (London: Routledge, 2018), 1–8.

34 B'Tselem, "Land Grab." Attempts to settle in the occupied area preceded this period, but for the most part met with government resistance. Idith Zertal and Akiva Eldar, *Lords of the Land: The War over Israel's Settlements in the Occupied Territories,*

1967–2007 (Or Yehuda, Israel: Kinneret, Zmora-Bitan, Dvir, 2004), 453–62. See also Karen Tenenbaum and Ehud Eiran, "Israeli Settlement Activity in the West Bank and Gaza: A Brief History," *Negotiation Journal* 21:2 (2005): 172.

35 Benvenisti, *Legal Dualism*, 3–32.

36 Gordon, *Israel's Occupation*, 28.

37 Ibid., 28. See also *B'Tselem*, "Land Grab."

38 Weizman, *Hollow Land*, 7.

39 Ibid., 15.

40 *B'Tselem*, "Land Grab."

41 Weizman, *Hollow Land*, 121.

42 Benvenisti, *Legal Dualism*, 59, supra note 2.

43 Ibid., 23; Panepinto, "The Annexation of Palestine," 200.

44 Especially significant are the 1978 Camp David Accords, which paved the way for the 1979 Israel Egyptian Peace Treaty that included Israeli consent to retreat from the Sinai Peninsula. See, e.g., United Nations Peacekeepers, *Framework for Peace in the Middle East Agreed at Camp David*, June 14, 1979, accessed February 16, 2020, https://peacemaker.un.org/sites/peacemaker.un.org/files/EG%20IL_780917_Framework%20for%20peace%20in%20the%20MiddleEast%20agreed%20at%20Camp%20David.pdf.

45 Idem, United Nations Peacekeepers, *Separation of Forces between Israel and Syria*, May 31, 1974, accessed February 16, 2020, https://peacemaker.un.org/sites/peacemaker.un.org/files/IL%20SY_740531_Separation%20of%20Forces%20between%20Israel%20and%20Syria.pdf; United Nation Security Council, *Egyptian-Israeli Agreement on Disengagement of Forces in Pursuance of the Geneva Peace Conference*, January 18, 1974, accessed February 16, 2020, https://peacemaker.un.org/egyptisrael-disengagementforces.

46 Israeli Ministry of Foreign Affairs, Israel-Egypt Peace Treaty, March 26, 1979, accessed June 25, 2020, https://mfa.gov.il/mfa/foreignpolicy/peace/guide/pages/israel-egypt%20peace%20treaty.aspx; Moshe Hirsch, "Treaty-Making Power: Approval of the Israel-Egypt Philadelphia Accord by the Knesset," *Israel Law Review* 39 (2006): 229–37.

47 UN, *Security Council Report, Lebanon/Israel (UNIFIL) January 2006 Monthly Forecast*, December 22, 2005, accessed February 18, 2020, https://www.securitycouncilreport.org/monthly-forecast/2006-01/lookup_c_glkwlemtisg_b_1313235.php.

48 UN, "Unanimously Adopting Resolution 2433, Security Council Extends Mandate of United Nations Force in Lebanon, Calls on Government to Increase Naval Capacity," August 30, 2018, accessed February 16, 2020, https://www.un.org/press/en/2018/sc13481.doc.htm; UN, General Assembly, *Fifth Committee*, August 26, 2019, accessed February 16, 2020, https://digitallibrary.un.org/record/3833933?ln=en#record-files-collapse-header.

49 See Annex in United Nations Peacemakers, *Declaration of Principles on Interim Self-Government Arrangements (Oslo Accords)*, October 11, 1993, accessed February 20,

2020, https://peacemaker.un.org/sites/peacemaker.un.org/files/IL%20PS_930913_
DeclarationPrinciplesnterimSelf-Government%28Oslo%20Accords%29.pdf, 6.

50 Economic Cooperation Foundation, Cairo Agreement—on the Gaza Strip and
the Jericho Area, May 4, 1994, accessed February 2020, https://ecf.org.il/media_
items/618, 1–4.

51 Ibid., 4.

52 Idem., 4.

53 Israel Ministry of Foreign Affairs, Israeli-Palestinian Interim Agreements, September
28, 1995, accessed February 20, 2020, https://mfa.gov.il/mfa/foreignpolicy/peace/
guide/pages/the%20israeli-palestinian%20interim%20agreement.aspx, esp. Chapter
2, Section 4; United Nations Peacemakers, *Israeli-Palestinian Interim Agreement on
the West Bank and the Gaza Strip (Oslo II)*, September 28, 1995, accessed February 20,
2020, https://peacemaker.un.org/israelopt-osloII95, 17.

54 Israel Ministry of Foreign Affairs, "The Israeli-Palestinian Interim Agreement –
Main Points," September 28, 1995, accessed February 20, 2020, https://mfa.gov.il/
mfa/foreignpolicy/peace/guide/pages/the%20israeli-palestinian%20interim%20
agreement%20-%20main%20p.aspx.

55 Ibid.

56 Ibid.

57 United Nations Peacemakers, *Protocol Concerning the Redeployment in Hebron*,
September 28, 1995, accessed February 20, 2020, https://peacemaker.un.org/
israelopt-redeploymenthebron97.

58 Tilley, *Beyond Occupation*, 41.

59 See, e.g., Dan Rothem, "How to Connect the West Bank and the Gaza Strip," *The
Atlantic*, October 27, 2011, accessed February 20, 2020, https://www.theatlantic.
com/international/archive/2011/10/how-to-connect-the-west-bank-and-gaza-
strip/247475/. See also Friends of the Arc.org, "On the Arc Project: Friends of the
Arc, What's the Arc," accessed February 20, 2020, http://friendsofthearc.org/.

60 "Will ICC Membership Help or Hinder the Palestinians' Cause?" *BBC World
News*, April 1, 2015, accessed February 25, 2020, https://www.bbc.com/news/
world-middle-east-30744701; Fadwa Hodali, "Report: Abbas Peace Plan Calls
for Israeli Withdrawal from West Bank," *The Philadelphia Inquirer*, September 4,
2014, accessed February 25, 2020, https://www.inquirer.com/philly/news/nation_
world/20140904_Report__Abbas_peace_plan_calls_for_Israeli_withdrawal_from_
West_Bank.html; ICC, "Statement of the Prosecutor of the International Criminal
Court, Fatou Bensouda."

61 The ICCPR; the ICESCR; the Convention on the Elimination of All Forms of
Discrimination Against Women (CEDAW); the Convention Against Torture and
Other Forms of Cruel, Inhuman or Degrading Treatment or Punishment (CAT) 10;

and the Convention on the Rights of the Child (CRC). See Orna Ben-Naftali and Yuval Shany, "Living in Denial: The Application of Human Rights in the Occupied Territories," *Israel Law Review* 37:1 (2003): 17–118; United Nations, Office for the Coordination of Humanitarian Affairs Occupied Palestinian Territory, *Barrier Update, Special Focus*, July 2011, accessed February 16, 2020, https://www.ochaopt. org/sites/default/files/ocha_opt_barrier_update_july_2011_english.pdf, 25. It was claimed that the state objection was overruled in some cases by the Supreme Court. Tilley, *Beyond Occupation*, 12.

62 United Nations, *Barrier Update, Special Focus*, 3–5.

63 Ibid.

64 Ibid., 5.

65 It should be noted that legally, the extraterritorial status of these areas remains to be negotiated, Hilal, Petti, and Weizman, *Architecture after Revolution*, 155, 157, 164–9.

66 Weizman, *Hollow Land*, 178.

67 Weizman, *Hollow Land*, 258. Perhaps in legal terms, this assertion demands further clarification.

68 Ibid., 12.

69 For Plasticity in terms of Eyal Weizman's description of the Political Plastic, see Weizman, *Hollow Land*, 5.

70 Jean-Pierre Filiu, *Gaza: A History* (Oxford: Oxford University Press, 2014), 26, 37, 40, 65–6.

71 Morris, *Israel's Border Wars*, 1, 186.

72 Ibid.

73 Ibid.

74 Ibid.

75 Varble, *The Suez Crisis*.

76 Ilana Feldman, "Ad Hoc Humanity: UN Peacekeeping and the Limits of International Community in Gaza," *American Anthropologist* 112:3 (2010): 418.

77 Ibid., 418, 420.

78 Ibid., 422.

79 Bligh, "The United Nations Emergency Force", 797. This force, made up of soldiers from various countries, was approximately 6,000 soldiers strong at the time of deployment, though their numbered dwindled to around 3,400 by 1967, at which time Egypt demanded that UNEF forces withdraw from their territory. See Adebajo, *UN Peacekeeping in Africa*, 37.

80 Zertal and Eldar, *Lords of the Land*, 453–62.

81 Moshe Horwitz, "The Border between Israel and Egypt," 2006, accessed June 26, 2020, https://lib.cet.ac.il/pages/item.asp?item=14913.

82 Filiu, *Gaza: A History*, 225–8.

83 On the Occupation of the Gaza Strip and its ramifications, see, e.g., *B'Tselem*, "The Gaza Strip," November 11, 2017, accessed June 20, 2020, https://www.btselem.org/gaza_strip.

84 Israel Ministry of Foreign Affairs, "Israel's Disengagement Plan: Renewing the Peace Process," 2005, accessed April 10, 2020, https://mfa.gov.il/mfa/foreignpolicy/peace/guide/pages/israeli%20disengagement%20plan%2020-jan-2005.aspx.

85 Yaacov Bar Siman-Tov, ed., *The Disengagement Plan: The Dream and Its Break*, Jerusalem: The Israel Institute for Advanced Studies (IIAS) of Jerusalem, 2009, https://jerusaleminstitute.org.il/wp-content/uploads/2019/05/PUB_diseng2009_heb.pdf, 11.

86 Graham Usher, "The Democratic Resistance: Hamas, Fatah, and the Palestinian Elections," *Journal of Palestine Studies* 35:3 (2006): 20–2.

87 *B'Tselem*, "Reality Check."

88 Turkel Commission, Part 1, p. 15.

89 *B'Tselem*, "The Siege on the Gaza Strip: 1.5 Million People Imprisoned," May 31, 2010, accessed June 21, 2020, https://www.btselem.org/gaza_strip/20100531_the_siege_on_gaza.

90 In 2009, Gaza was not yet officially recognized as a "non-member observer state," a status received from the UN on November 29, 2012, with the approval of Resolution 67/19. United Nations General Assembly GA/11317, "General Assembly Votes Overwhelmingly to Accord to Palestine 'Non-Member Observer State' Status in United Nations," November 29, 2012, accessed August 2, 2020, https://www.un.org/press/en/2012/ga11317.doc.htm. For the Turkish claim that Israel holds effective control over Gaza, see Turkish National Committee of Inquiry, *Report on the Israeli Attack*, 82.

91 Turkish National Commission of Inquiry, *Report on the Israeli Attack*; *B'Tselem*, "Reality Check."

92 A publication by the IHH Research Department notes at different points that the flotilla set sail in order to "end an ongoing embargo on Gaza." A press release dated April 3, 2010, included in the same publication, states that the flotilla is "a coalition bringing together a number of organisations and movements working to break Israel's illegal blockade." According to the same publication, the Free Gaza Movement stated that the initiative was launched by "an umbrella organisation established by pro-Palestinian groups and human rights advocates to increase public awareness of the blockade on the Gaza Strip … [in order] to break the siege of Gaza." IHH, "*Mavi Marmara:* Gaza Freedom Flotilla," 8, 12, 33.

93 This tendency emerges from the responses offered by the passengers of the freedom flotilla to the questions "Why did you join the freedom flotilla? What was your motivation?" Forty interviews with flotilla passengers were collected in

Zahide Tuba Kor, ed., *Witnesses of the Freedom Flotilla: Interviews with Passengers* (Istanbul: IHH Kitap, 2011).

94 Turkish National Commission of Inquiry, *Report on the Israeli Attack*, 66, 76–7.

95 Ibid., 76. The Turkish National Commission report claims that both blockades have economic purposes and that "the humanitarian flotilla was set up in 2008 as a direct consequence of Israel's increasingly severe economic blockade on Gaza," 75.

96 Ibid., 75.

97 Both Turkey and Israel stress the importance of this issue in their reports. See Turkel Commission Report, Part 1, pp. 25–60; Turkish National Commission of Inquiry, *Report on the Israeli Attack*, 60–98. See also UN, *Report of the Secretary-General's Panel of Inquiry*, 38–44; and Migdalovitz, *Israel's Blockade of Gaza.*

98 Turkel Commission, Part 1, pp. 38–54. See also Turkish National Commission of Inquiry, *Report on the Israeli Attack*, 99: "Israel's claim that it was entitled to interdict the vessels in the humanitarian aid convoy rests on its argument that it was acting in self-defence to enforce a legitimately established blockade."

99 The Israeli armed forces boarded the *Mavi Marmara* and the other flotilla vessels in international waters, 70–100 nm from Gaza. Israel's Turkel Commission, Part 1, p. 220, claims that according to the US Commander's Handbook on Naval Operations, customary international law stipulates that a ship that is aware of a naval blockade and is sailing toward the blockaded port is "*subject to capture wherever it is located.*" The UN, *Report of the Secretary-General's Panel of Inquiry* 52, 80, agrees that a blockade can be legally extended to the high seas. For "Israel to maintain the blockade, it had to be effective, so it must be enforced. Such enforcement may take place on the high seas." The Turkish National Commission of Inquiry, *Report on the Israeli Attack*, 56, asserts, however, that international law does not recognize a general right to visit or seize a foreign ship in the high seas, except in limited situations which do not apply to the flotilla.

100 Turkel Commission, Part 1, p. 38.

101 Ibid., 39.

102 According to Elizabeth Spelman, blockades were originally regarded as strictly naval measures, and were only later extended to encompass land, aerial, and technological blockades. See Elizabeth Spelman, "The Legality of the Israeli Naval Blockade of the Gaza Strip," *Web Journal of Current Legal Issues* (2013) accessed March 12, 2013, http://ojs.qub.ac.uk/index.php/webjcli/article/view/207/277.

103 *B'Tselem*, "Siege on the Gaza Strip."

104 Ibid. Following the implementation of the disengagement plan, Israel cited various legal sources to ban maritime movement off the Gaza coast. As it could no longer invoke the law of occupation, it justified this control as "security restrictions

on fishing areas off the Gaza Strip." See Gisha—Legal Center for Freedom of Movement, *Scale of Control: Israel's Continued Responsibility in the Gaza Strip*, 2012, accessed June 2, 2012, http://www.gisha.org/UserFiles/File/scaleofcontrol/scaleofcontrol_en.pdf.

105 Gisha—Legal Center for Freedom of Movement, *Disengaged Occupiers: The Legal Status of Gaza*, 2006, accessed January 4, 2013, http://www.gisha.org/UserFiles/File/Report%20for%20the%20website.pdf.

106 Jeremy M. Sharp, "The Egypt-Gaza Border and Its Effect on Israeli-Egyptian Relations," Foreign Press Center, US Department of State, 2008, accessed April 10, 2020, http://www.vfp143.org/lit/Gaza/RL34346.pdf, 8–10.

107 On the extensive deployment of cameras at the Rafah crossing, see Gisha – Legal Center for Freedom of Movement, *Rafah Crossing: Who Holds the Keys?*, 2009, accessed April 1, 2015, http://www.gisha.org/userfiles/File/publications/Rafah_Report_Eng.pdf.

108 Sharp, "The Egypt-Gaza Border," 3.

109 Israel, *The 2014 Gaza Conflict 7 July—26 August 2014 Factual and Legal Aspects*, May 2015, accessed June 26, 2020, https://mfa.gov.il/ProtectiveEdge/Documents/2014GazaConflictFullReport.pdf, 40.

110 Ibid., 42.

111 The last border crossing, Erez, was closed on January 25, 2006, the day of the Palestinian elections. See Sharat G. Lin, "Gaza's Shrinking Borders: 16 Years of the Oslo Process," *Dissident Voice*, December 26, 2009, accessed March 26, 2013, http://dissidentvoice.org/2009/12/gaza_s-shrinking-borders-16-years-of-the-oslo-process. An Israeli government resolution of February 19, 2006, stipulated that due to security concerns, "control at border crossings will increase." Turkel Commission, Part 1, p. 29, n. 46.

112 Turkel Commission, Part 1, p. 29.

113 Daphné Richemond-Barak, *Underground Warfare* (Oxford: Oxford University Press, 2017), 60.

114 In response, Israel plans to dig a 40-mile-deep underground barrier that will include seismic sensors and cameras with the aim of recording and thus controlling this invisible activity. See Ilan Zion, "Israel Digs Deep to Thwart Tunnel Threat from Gaza Strip," *AP*, January 18, 2018, accessed January 24, 2018, https://apnews.com/322f1f35210d47bfa78647fa5f4a226d; Yossi Melman, "How Will Hamas React to Israel's Major Gaza Border Project?," *The Jerusalem Post*, June 23, 2017, accessed June 24, 2017, https://www.jpost.com/jerusalem-report/hamass-dilemma-492146.

115 Turkish National Commission of Inquiry, *Report on the Israeli Attack*, 75.

116 Turkel Commission, Part 1, pp. 29–30.

117 Sharp, "Egypt-Gaza Border," 8–9.

118 *B'Tselem*, "Lift the Restrictions on the Gaza Fishing Range," March 24, 2013, accessed April 1, 2013, http://www.btselem.org/gaza_strip/20130324_restrictions_on_fishing_should_be_lifted.

119 Turkel Commission, Part 1, pp. 54–5.

120 Ibid., 35.

121 According to the Turkel Commission, Part 1, p. 59, these assertions are based on the US Commander's Handbook on Naval Operations and the San Remo Manual.

122 Ibid., 59.

123 Ibid., 59.

124 Ibid., 59–61.

125 Amnesty Interntational, "Israel/Gaza: Operation Cast Lead: 22 Days of Destruction," July 9, 2009, accessed April 10, 2020, 1, 51, https://www.amnesty.org/download/Documents/48000/mde150152009en.pdf. According to the Congressional Research Service, Israel's Operation Cast Lead in Gaza was conducted "in order to stop rocket fire into southern Israel and to weaken or overthrow Hamas." It resulted "in more than 1,000 Palestinian deaths and the destruction of much of the Gaza Strip's infrastructure and many buildings." It also led to a tighter blockade whose end was conditioned "on the release of IDF Sergeant Gilad Shalit, who had been captured in 2006." See Migdalovitz, *Israel's Blockade of Gaza*, 1.

126 Amnesty International, "Israel/Gaza: Operation Cast Lead: 22 Days of Destruction," 52.

127 Turkel Commission, Part 1, p. 36. See also State of Israel, Ministry of Transport and Road Safety, Notice to Mariners No. 1/2009 Blockade of the Gaza Strip, January 6, 2006, accessed April 2020, http://asp.mot.gov.il/en/shipping/notice2mariners/547-no12009.

128 Ibid., 37.

Chapter 3

1 Reports vary as to the precise time of the blackout—12:41 a.m. according to the Israeli report, and as late as 4:00 a.m. according to the Turkish report. Reports differ also as to the precise degree to which communications were blocked. See Turkel Commission, Part 1, p. 138; Turkish National Committee of Inquiry, *Report on the Israeli Attack*, 20; IBH/FOCA, *Timeline and Inconsistencies Report*, 30. Interestingly, the Israeli military and the activists chose different images to represent the launching of the electronic blackout. Whereas the IDF clip shows an image of a boat surrounded on all sides by moving red waves, the IHH clip shows a screenshot of a cellular phone announcing reception failure. The difference indicates a certain economy of vision: whereas the military views the event from an

external vantage point, the activists view it from within and individually, through the solitary signifier of the individual cellular device.

2   This aim is emphasized both on the organization level, as reflected in its overarching objective, as it appeared in an IHH publication where it was defined as "an umbrella organization established by pro-Palestinian groups and human rights advocates to increase public awareness against the blockade on Gaza Strip with the help of ships carrying humanitarian supplies," as well as specifically in regard to the 2010 initiative, as could be learned from the IHH press release published in April 2010, "Coalition to Break the Blockade on Gaza Announced," which stated that one of the organizers' goals was to "use this action to wake the world's consciousness about the crimes committed against Palestinians." See IHH, "*Mavi Marmara*: Gaza Freedom Flotilla," 13, 33. According to the Turkel Commission, an official announcement published on the IHH website indicated "the organizers' desire that the conflict with the navy would take place in daylight so that the media could document it, in order to make waves in the international media." Turkel Committee Report, Part 1, p. 119.

3   IHH (@MaviMarmaraCase), Twitter, May 26, 2014, accessed April 25, 2020, https://twitter.com/MaviMarmaraCase.

4   Testimony of Gülden Sönmez, *Mavi Marmara* Indictment, 2012, accessed February 1, 2013, https://www.dropbox.com/sh/l0zl7g242zi1bu9/r5EMPzTa6V/STATEMENT%20OF%20GULDEN%20SONMEZ%20%28IHH%20MEMBER%20OF%20BOARD%20LAWYER%29.pdf, 10.

5   TV crews broadcasting live from the ship included TRT, TV Net, HABERTÜRK TV, Press TV, al-Hivar, *Al-Jazeera*, the Kuwait News Agency, Telesur & Venezüela TV, *Burunei Times*, al-Aksa TV, *El Cezire Arabich*, and Gulf News Agency. See the testimony of Gülden Sönmez, *Mavi Marmara* Indictment, 9. The flotilla organizers' interest in media coverage was reflected in their investment in social media. According to Adi Kuntsman and Rebecca Stein, "[f]rom its inception, the journey of the Freedom Flotilla was a social media event. In the days leading up to the commando raid on the lead ship, *Mavi Marmara*, the activists' supporters 'tweeted and tweeted' so that the Flotilla might 'trend,' or become one of the highly popular discussion topics crawling across the top of the screen on Twitter's home page. ... The organizers used social media extensively, tweeting updates from the boats, webcasting live with cameras uplinked to the Internet and a satellite, enabling simultaneous rebroadcasting, employing Facebook, Flickr, YouTube, and other social networking websites to allow interested persons to see and hear them in real time, and using Google Maps to chart their location at sea ... A quarter of a million people watched the video feed on Livestream alone, while many more people consumed these images in abbreviated form on television news." See Adi Kuntsman

and Rebecca L. Stein, "Another War Zone: Social Media in the Israeli-Palestinian Conflict," *Middle East Report Online (MERIP)*, September 7, 2010, http://www.merip.org/mero/interventions/another-war-zone#.UBF0yo1TSiE.email.

6   IHH, "*Mavi Marmara*: Gaza Freedom Flotilla," 25.

7   IHH leased two frequencies from Turksat 3A, a communication satellite launched by Turkey in 2008, ibid.

8   Turkish National Committee of Inquiry, "*Report on the Israeli Attack*," 15–16. Israel's Turkel Commission reported 29 crew members and 561 passengers on board the *Mavi Marmara*, yet acknowledged that "the data submitted to the committee on this matter is not unambiguous." Turkel Commission, Part 1, pp. 15–16. See also Gilad Atzmon, "Shocking Testimonies from the *Mavi Marmara* Survivors and One Israeli Fembot," June 11, 2010, accessed April 11, 2020. https://gilad.online/writings/shocking-testimonials-from-the-mavi-marmara-survivors-and-on.html.

9   "Turkish Court Begins Trial of Israeli Officers on *Mavi Marmara* Raid," *Anadolu [News] Agency "AA*," November 6, 2012, accessed September 24, 2020, https://www.aa.com.tr/en/turkey/turkish-court-begins-trial-of-israeli-officers-on-mavi-marmara-raid/312215.

10   This policy is reflected, for example, in the Israeli military's extended preparations to block and electronically screen the flotilla's communication systems in order to thwart the activists' efforts to broadcast during the takeover. This was emphasized in a letter from the Adalah organization to the Israeli Attorney General, claiming that the electronic screening was meant to "prevent the broadcast of harsh images from the takeover of the flotilla vessels." See Turkel Commission, Part 1, pp. 126–7.

11   See Turkel Commission, Part 1, pp. 129, 176, 178. See also footnote 39 on page 114.

12   IHH, "Freedom: Last Destination—*Mavi Marmara*."

13   Kor, *Witnesses of the Freedom Flotilla*, 69.

14   Cihat Gökdemir, *Mavi Marmara* Indictment, 2012, accessed February 1, 2013, https://www.dropbox.com/sh/l0zl7g242zi1bu9/50rnIguSdl/STATEMENT%20 OF%20CIHAT%20GÖKDEMIR%20%28DIRECTOR%20OF%20 MAZLUMDER%20NGO%29.pdf. 4–5. Cihat Gökdemir is director of the human rights NGO, Mazlumder, and an attorney at the Elmadağ Hukuk law firm which represents the IHH. He is a signee of the firm's referral to the International Criminal Court accusing the IDF of war crimes and crimes against humanity. See ICC, "ICC Prosecutor Receives Referral."

15   Bayoumi, *Midnight on the Mavi Marmara*, 37. A slightly different version of this testimony appears in a BBC documentary, where O'Keefe states, "I was given the opportunity to either be a part of filming or witnessing or defending the ship and

I made a decision to defend it … " See also *BBC*, "Death in the Med," *Panorama*, Television Documentary, 30 mins., August 22, 2010, https://www.bbc.co.uk/programmes/b00thr24.

16   Philip Weiss, "UN: Two Men Killed on *Mavi Marmara* were Holding Cameras when They Were Shot," *Mondoweiss*, September 25, 2010, accessed April 6, 2020, https://mondoweiss.net/2010/09/un-two-men-killed-on-mavi-marmara-were-holding-cameras-when-they-were-shot/. See also IHH, Indictment Files, 106–8.

17   ICC, "ICC Prosecutor Receives Referral," 12: "He was shot while he was taking a photo, at the moment when his camera … flashed. He was shot in his forehead."

18   Cihat Gökdemir, *Mavi Marmara* Indictment, 7–8.

19   See soldiers' testimonies recorded in the Turkel Report, Part 1, pp. 21, 155: "I was surrounded by six people and another person who arrived a few seconds later. This person had a large camera tripod in his hand; he joined the terrorists and beat me with the tripod. My situation at that point was that I was surrounded by terrorists."

20   Ibid., 158.

21   Ibid., 160, 162.

22   Cihat Gökdemir, *Mavi Marmara* Indictment, 7. That the activists were unsure whether their cameras were working is reflected in an interview with Iara Lee, who stated, "Our connection to the world was cut off: we were sitting without knowing how many people were dead or wounded. We didn't know whether or not our reserve cameras were still functioning." See Kor, *Witnesses of the Freedom Flotilla*, 70.

23   Kor, *Witnesses of the Freedom Flotilla*, 162.

24   According to eyewitness testimony, the injured were treated right outside the press room lobby. See Kor, Witnesses *of the Freedom Flotilla*, 146. See also Turkel Commission, Part 1, pp. 173–4.

25   This figure is based on the estimates mentioned earlier in this chapter. See Atzmon, "Shocking Testimonies."

26   Turkel Commission, Part 1, p. 178, n. 605.

27   Colonel Shai Shtern, "Victory Consciousness Is More Valuable than the Outcome on the Field," *IDF* (blog), September 8, 2011, accessed March 30, 2015, http://www.idf.il/1133-13098-he/Dover.aspx.

28   This fact was strongly criticized in the Israeli State Comptroller's Report, *A Critical Review of the Application of the National Security Committee Law and the Handling of the Turkish Flotilla*, 112, 114, and in the Israeli Parliament. See Knesset State Control Committee.

29   I interviewed Colonel (in reserve) Oded Hershkovitz on Mach 13, 2019 in Israel. Hershkovitz was the highest-ranking commander of the operation on behalf of the IDF's Spokesperson Unit. The fact that the electronic screening inadvertently disrupted military communication is also indicated in the Turkel report, where it is noted that the last IDF warning call which was meant to reach the flotilla's captains before the takeover failed to reach them: "The recordings from the radio network

that were submitted to the Commission show that four communications were indeed transmitted in full, and according to the prepared text. The optional fifth communication was not transmitted." Turkel Commission, Part 1, p. 138.

30   Several activists claim to have filmed the entire attack. See, e.g., Kor, *Witnesses of the Freedom Flotilla*, 77, 81.

31   Turkel Commission, Part 1, p. 23, n. 421.

32   The Israeli Freedom of Information Law permits withholding information for reasons of national security. See Israeli Ministry of Justice, Israeli Law of Freedom of Information Law, 1988, accessed April 11, 2020, https://www.justice.gov.il/Units/YechidatChofeshHameyda/GlobalDocs/Law.pdf. On the IDF Spokesperson's use of national security reasoning, see Noam Sheizaf, "IDF Spokesperson Spins *Mavi Marmara* Video for Local Political Purposes," *The Promised Land* (blog), August 23, 2010, accessed April 12, 2020, https://www.972mag.com/idf-spokesperson-spins-mavi-marmara-video-for-local-political-purposes/.

33   The fact that hundreds of hours of videotaped evidence exist and were reviewed by the Turkel Commission is indicated at Turkel Commission, Part 1, pp. 11, 23.

34   Kor, *Witnesses of the Freedom Flotilla*, 212: "An Israeli [standing] next to me smashed the CCTV camera off the side of the ship and casually put it in his bag."

35   According to the indictment submitted to the criminal court at Istanbul, "[m]any journalists who were on board the flotilla in their professional capacity have subsequently submitted various complaints regarding the confiscation of their data and equipment and the non-payment of damages or compensation. An example of this is a letter on behalf of approximately 60 journalists that was sent to request action by the European Committee." See IHH, Indictment Files, 145.

36   The UN inquiry was based exclusively on the national investigations conducted separately by Israel and Turkey. The UN "obtained its information through diplomatic channels" and exercised "no coercive power to compel witnesses to provide evidence." Its task was merely "to unpack the events by ... looking at the two sides of the story." UN, *Report of the Secretary-General's Panel of Inquiry*, 8.

37   The fact that the confiscated materials constitute crucial evidence is emphasized in the Turkish report. See Turkish National Committee of Inquiry, *Report on the Israeli Attack*, 5. The importance of free access to the documentary footage was stressed in the United Nations Human Rights Council, *Report of the International Fact-Finding Mission*, 4, 58. See also IHH, Indictment Files, 39, 41, 56, 144–5.

38   The Turkel Commission describes reviewing hundreds of hours of audio and video footage of the forty-minute skirmish, representing multiple sources and perspectives. See Turkel Commission, Part 1, p. 11.

39   Presumably, the unreleased visual material can resolve some of the factually disputed issues, though probably not all the associated moral and political controversies.

40   IHH, "*Mavi Marmara*: Gaza Freedom Flotilla," 24.

41 That the army has used footage taken by the activists is indicated not only by the visual evidence but also in Turkel Commission, Part 1, p. 178, n. 605, in which an IDF official is quoted as saying that some of the magnetic media gathered on the ship was "transferred to Israel by helicopter to be used by the IDF Spokesperson and Advocacy Department." Some have claimed, however, that certain materials released by the IDF are inauthentic. See, e.g., IBH/FOCA, *Timeline and Inconsistencies Report*, 95–7.

42 IDF Habat—Unit of Technological Education and Training, "Timeline of the *Mavi Marmara* Incident," 21:17 mins. This clip was also viewed by the Turkel Commission. See Turkel Commission, "IDF's Response to the Flotilla Events (Part 1 of 2)," YouTube Video, 11:39 mins., 2011, accessed August 15, 2012, http://www.youtube.com/watch?v=Zy5SXWv8U0I.

43 The IHH pre-installed two Turksat frequencies in case the IDF jammed communications, yet few of the activists knew how to run and manage the additional frequency. See IHH, "*Mavi Marmara*: Gaza Freedom Flotilla," 25.

44 *Al-Jazeera English*, "Israeli Troops Storm Gaza Flotilla," YouTube Video, 1:28 mins., May 31, 2010, accessed October 10, 2012, http://www.youtube.com/watch?v=xFEBbDkyrqQ.

45 IHH, "Freedom: Last Destination—*Mavi Marmara*."

46 *CNN TURK*, "*Dakika, Dakika, Mavi Marmara ya Saldiri*," YouTube Video, 8:24 mins., June 1, 2010, accessed February 11, 2013, http://www.youtube.com/watch?v=INVT98698R8.

47 Ibid. See also "MGF—Millî Görüş Forum—IHH.flv", YouTube Video, 2:56 mins., May 31, 2010, accessed July 9, 2013, http://www.youtube.com/watch?v=bfFfK4CxUHM.

48 Channel 2 Israel and DHA, "The Flotilla Ship *Mavi Marmara*, Peace Activist Stabbing IDF Soldier," YouTube Video, 0:48 mins., 2011, accessed March 24, 2012, http://www.youtube.com/watch?v=o6MLJErSD2s. The clip was also shown on channel 10 news edition on June 1, 2010. Channel 10 and DHA, Channel 10 News Edition, "Nine Participants in Flotilla Killed," YouTube Video, 11:35 mins., June 1, 2010, accessed April 12, 2020, https://www.youtube.com/watch?v=eSeEtNHtCPI.

49 Channel 2 Israel and DHA, "The Flotilla Ship *Mavi Marmara*, Peace Activist Stabbing IDF Soldier"; IDF Habat—Unit of Technological Education and Training, "Timeline of the *Mavi Marmara* Incident."

50 IHH, "*Mavi Marmara* Truth: Israeli Soldiers Killing Furkan (The Freedom Flotilla)," YouTube Video, 0:22 mins., June 9, 2010, accessed June 30, 2013, http://www.youtube.com/watch?v=rdA6jJ8dOZQ.

51 IHH, Indictment Files, 38. See also UN, *Report of the Secretary-General's Panel of Inquiry*, 59.

52 IHH, "*Mavi Marmara* Truth: Israeli Soldiers Killing Furkan (The Freedom Flotilla)."

53 IDF, "*Mavi Marmara* Passengers Attack IDF before Soldiers Boarded Ship," YouTube Video, 1:10 mins, May 31, 2010, accessed November 6, 2012, http://www.youtube.com/watch?v=B6sAEYpHF24.

54 Turkel Commission, Part 1, p. 143.

55 IHH, "Freedom: Last Destination—*Mavi Marmara.*"

56 Ibid.

57 No shooting is heard in the clips released by the Israeli military, despite their own admission that its soldiers shot 659 bullets during the confrontation. See Turkel Commission, Part 1, p. 260.

58 Israel Defense Force, "Flotilla Rioters Prepare Rods, Slingshots, Broken Bottles and Metal Objects," YouTube Video, 2:24 mins., June 2, 2010, accessed December 4, 2012, http://www.youtube.com/watch?v=HZlSSaPT_OU.

59 IHH, "Freedom: Last Destination—*Mavi Marmara.*" The segments are shown at 28:25–28:32, 32:47–32:48, and 32:51–33:00 min.

60 See Idfnadesk, "Close Up Footage of *Mavi Marmara* Passengers Attacking IDF Soldiers (with sound)," YouTube Video, 1:01 mins., May 31, 2010, accessed June 1, 2010, https://www.youtube.com/watch?v=gYjkLUcbJWo; and Idfnadesk, "Demonstrators Use Violence against Israeli Navy Soldiers Attempting to Board the Ship," YouTube Video, 1:04 mins., May 31, 2010, accessed June 1, 2010, http://www.youtube.com/watch?v=bU12KW-XyZE.

61 IHH, "Freedom: Last Destination—*Mavi Marmara.*" The first segment is at 33:15–33:16 min. An audio clip released by the Israeli military purportedly documents a radio exchange in which the army addressed the flotilla ships with the request to change route prior to the takeover. Also heard in the clip are a series of responses which, according to the IDF, originated from the flotilla boats, including, "Shut up, Israeli navy, shut up!" "Shut up, go back to Auschwitz," and "We're helping Arabs to go and get the US, don't forget 9/11, guys!" The alleged responses drew controversy when bloggers such as Max Blumenthal disputed their authenticity. See Max Blumenthal, "Israeli Army Admits It Doctored Gaza Freedom Flotilla Audio Clip," *Global Research News*, June 10, 2010, accessed April 14, 2020, https://www.globalresearch.ca/israel-military-admits-it-doctored-gaza-freedom-flotilla-audio-clip/19646. The Turkel Commission was indecisive: "Since the radio was operated on channel 16 which is an international frequency, it is impossible to determine which of the vessels issued these responses." Turkel Commission, Part 1, p. 140. Interestingly, this issue did not come up in the Palmer Report.

62 In an interview for Kor's book, *Witnesses of the Freedom Flotilla*, when asked how she managed to smuggle video footage of the ship, Lee answered, "Before the Israeli commandos boarded our ship, I had asked my cameraman [Srdjan Stojilkovic] to switch to small SD cards since I could anticipate that the Israeli Navy would

confiscate our gear, hard drive, memory cards. He did, and to avoid getting the SD taken, he hid them behind the stitches of his underwear. I instructed him to tell that he was requested by me to hide them and that he was just doing his job. Since Israelis at the jail facility had to body search hundreds of people and were focusing on Muslim men with long beards, my white cameraman was searched in a less meticulous manner." Kor, *Witnesses for the Freedom Flotilla*, 63.

63 See Cultures of Resistance Films, "Israeli Attack on the *Mavi Marmara* (1 Hour Raw Footage)," YouTube Video, 62 mins., June 11, 2010, accessed March 19, 2012, http://www.youtube.com/watch?v=vwsMJmvS0AY. See especially 37:06–44:00 min. See also *Culture of Resistance*, 2010, feature documentary, directed by Iara Lee, produced by George Gund, USA, 73 min.

64 The characteristics of the sound of shooting that are heard remain indistinctive to the ears of the ordinary viewer on the backdrop of the IDF claim to have used paintball guns at that stage of the interception. See Turkel Commission, Part 1, p. 143.

65 Cultures of Resistance Films, "Israeli Attack on the *Mavi Marmara* (1 Hour Raw Footage)," 38:26–39:06. The footage shows an onboard exchange in which a passenger holding a camera claims that the red stains are actually paint. Pertinent to this is the IDF's decision to use red paintballs. Whether the stains were blood or not remains unclear. The Turkel Commission Report takes special note of the army's problematic choice of color. According to the committee, this use of color was exploited by "advocates" as "evidence that IDF soldiers used excessive force, when, in fact, just the opposite was the case." Turkel Commission, Part 1, p. 259. It should be emphasized that from an ethical point of view, other testimonies which describe the deployment of paintballs shot at close range, leading to severe wounds, contradict the notion that the practice has only "symbolic" value. International Criminal Court, Pre-Trial Chambers, 1, ICC-O1/13, January 29, 2015, accessed April 15, 2020, https://www.icc-cpi.int/CourtRecords/CR2015_00576.PDF, 54.

66 A description matching this account appears in the indictment submitted to the criminal court in Istanbul: "One passenger standing just inside the door was shot through the broken porthole in the door by a soldier standing a few meters away on the bridge deck outside." This description may also imply, however, that the specific segment was included in the video evidence submitted to the court, though the list of materials was not published. See IHH, Indictment Files, 2012, 104. See also Cultures of Resistance Films, "Israeli Attack on the *Mavi Marmara* (1 Hour Raw Footage)," 41:30–42:44, (soldier rappelling down the rope, passenger shoots with slingshot), 50:29–53:00, (group of men defending the door).

67 Still images from the ship, mostly showing injured soldiers, were also published after the event. Photos reportedly taken by journalist Adem Özköse and recovered from smuggled memory cards were acquired by the Turkish daily *Hürriyet*.

Additional still images, concealed at the time of the takeover and smuggled through army censorship, were published by reporter Şefik M. Dinç. For both groups of photos, see Robert Mackey, "Photographs of Battered Israeli Commandos Show New Side of Raid," *The Lede* (blog), *The New York Times*, June 7, 2010, accessed April 5, 2012, http://thelede.blogs.nytimes.com/2010/06/07/photographs-of-battered-israeli-commandos-show-new-side-of-raid. Photos taken by Canadian activist Kevin Neish were reportedly disseminated on June 6. See Meagan Perry, "Kevin Neish's Photos of *Mavi Marmara* Attack Published Plus Full Interview," *Rabble.Ca*, June 9, 2010, accessed August 5, 2012, http://rabble.ca/news/2010/06/do-not-publish-yet-kevin-neishs-photos-mavi-maramara-attack-published. In the media, the same still images were often used in support of conflicting claims, though in contrast to the use of video footage, this was usually facilitated by deceptive efforts to manipulate the contents of the images, e.g. by cropping. In one instance, an American blogger charged *Reuters* with deceptive cropping and image editing: "Reuters' photo service edited out knives and blood traces from pictures taken aboard the activist ship *Mavi Marmara*. ... The pictures of the fight were released by IHH, the Turkish-based group that sponsored the six-ship fleet that tried to break Israel's blockade of Gaza. In one photo, an Israeli commando is shown lying on the deck of the ship, surrounded by activists. The uncut photo released by IHH shows the hand of an unidentified activist holding a knife. But in the *Reuters* photo, the hand is visible but the knife has been edited out." Reuters eventually admitted to the allegation. See Ed Barnes, "Reuters Admits Cropping Photos of Ship Clash, Denies Political Motive," *Fox News*, June 8, 2010, accessed March 9, 2012, http://www.foxnews.com/world/2010/06/08/reuters-fake-photos-ihh-gaza-blockade-commandos.

68 See "Cultures of Resistance Films, Israeli Attack on the *Mavi Marmara* (1 Hour Raw Footage)," 59:49–59:52, 1:02:10–1:02:13.

69 It may be interesting to note here that in her careful study of cases of Israeli military looting of Palestinian archives, focusing on operations conducted beyond the state borders—especially after the Israeli invasion of Lebanon in 1982 and the expropriation of the Palestinian Film Archive and the Palestine Research Center archive seized by the Israeli military from the offices of the PLO in West Beirut—curator Rona Sela has identified similarities to parallel cases of colonial sequestering of indigenous archives as a means to control and curtail knowledge and evidence that does not align with State interests or confirm its authority. Employing the approach proposed by anthropologist Ann Laura Stoler, which sees colonial use of such archives "not as sites of knowledge retrieval, but of knowledge production," Sela emphasizes that by taking command of these archives, Israel systematically concealed the history of Palestinian resistance as well as State's self-incriminating evidence by legally using national security restrictions. Ann

Laura Stoler, "Colonial Archives and the Arts of Governance: On the Content in the Form" in *Refiguring the Archive*, eds. Carolyn Hamilton et al. (New York, NY: Springer Publishing, 2002), 83–102; Rona Sela, "The Genealogy of Colonial Plunder and Erasure: Israel's Control over Palestinian Archives," *Social Semiotics* 28:2 (2008): 206, 202, 224.

70   Access to the archives in which the extraterritorial images are held is deliberately restricted by the Israeli authorities. Although this publication focuses on the inaccessible extraterritorial images and not on the archives themselves, for further discussion on the extraterritorial image and the archive, see Maayan Amir, "The Visual Side of Privacy: State-Incriminating, Coproduced Archives," *Public Culture* 32:1 (2020): 185–213.

Chapter 4

1   Tina Shaughnessy and Ellen Tobin, "Flags of Convenience: Freedom and Insecurity on the High Seas," *Journal of International Law & Policy* 5 (2006–7): 1–31.

2   "Turkish Rights Group's Cargo Ship to Set Sail with Gaza Aid," *Hürriyet Daily News*, April 13, 2010, accessed July 1, 2013, http://www.hurriyetdailynews.com/default. aspx?pageid=438&n=cargo-ship-will-set-out-to-gaza-to-deliver-aid-2010-04-13. See also IHH, "Ship Purchased for Gaza Campaign," March 29, 2010, accessed July 1, 2013, http://mavi-marmara.ihh.org.tr/en/main/news/0/ship-purchased-for-gaza-campaign/231. Commenting on the proximity between the IHH and the Turkish government led by the AKP party, *The New York Times* mentioned that at the time of the purchase of the vessel, Ali Yandir, a trustee of the IHH charity and a former AKP party candidate for the mayor's office in Istanbul's Esenler District in 2004, was also a senior manager at the Istanbul City Municipality Transportation Corporation from which the *Marmara* was bought for the sum of 1.2 million dollars. Dan Bilefsky, and Sebnem Arsu, "Sponsor of Flotilla Tied to Elite of Turkey," *The New York Times*, July 16, 2010, accessed April 16, 2020, https://www.nytimes. com/2010/07/16/world/middleeast/16turkey.html?auth=login-email&login=email.

3   International Transport Workers Federation, "What Are Flags of Convenience?," accessed April 19, 2020, https://www.itfglobal.org/en/sector/civil-aviation/flags-of-convenience.

4   International Criminal Court, "Registered Vessels of Comoros, Greece and Cambodia," November 29, 2017, accessed April 16, 2020, https://www.icc-cpi.int/ comoros. See also International Criminal Court, Pre-Trial Chamber, ICC-01/13.

5   International Criminal Court, Pre-Trial Chamber, ICC-01/13, p. 3.

6   "*Mavi Marmara*: Why Did Israel Stop the Gaza Flotilla?" *BBC News*, June 27, 2016, accessed April 16, 2020, https://www.bbc.com/news/10203726.

7   "*Mavi Marmara* was registered in the Turkish International Ship Registry (TUGS) and was sold on April 27, 2010. It was then registered under TUGS on the same date. Based on this fact, the ship *Mavi Marmara* is considered a Turkish marine vessel according to the Maritime Trade Laws, and the crimes committed in and by this ship will be deemed as committed in Turkey based on the principle of territoriality. Turkish Penal Code applies in this incident." IHH, Indictment Files, 2012, 153. See also Turkish Criminal Code (2009), Article 15/1, p. 32.

8   On the status of the defenders as fugitives, see IHH, *The Mavi Marmara Case: Legal Actions Taken against Israeli Attack on the Gaza Freedom Flotilla on 31.05.2010*, 2012, accessed April 23, 2020, https://www.ihh.org.tr/public/publish/0/126/the-mavi-marmara-case.pdf, 13.

9   Tuğrul Ansay and Don Wallace, Jr., eds., *Introduction to Turkish Law* (The Hague, The Netherlands: Kluwer Law International, 2005), 182. In justifying the legal posture of the proceedings, the IHH claims that it was the application of universal jurisdiction that made possible the inclusion of non-Turkish victims in the prosecution: "foreign citizens [who were] within the vessel may be included in the case filed in Turkey, even if they are not able to file a complaint regarding the event in their own country." See IHH, *Legal Actions Taken against Israeli Attack*, 6.

10   An investigation of General Tal Russo was also initiated; He was accused of planning and carrying out the attack on the *Mavi Marmara*. Meir Amit Intelligence and Terrorism Information Center, 2012, *Overview* (blog), November 13, 2012, accessed April 19, 2020, https://www.terrorism-info.org.il/en/20422/. See also "IHH's Mehmet Kaya on *Mavi Marmara* Court Case," *Today in Gaza*, November 4, 2012, accessed April 18, 2014, http://todayingaza.wordpress.com/2012/11/04/ihhs-mehmet-kaya-on-mavi-marmara-court-case/.

11   See IHH, Indictment Files, 37.

12   Ibid., 158. Turkish law allows trials *in absentia* in several circumstances, for example, "when the accused is a fugitive and a decision to that effect is rendered by the trial court." See Articles 194 (2) and 247 (h) TCCP. Sezen Gökan, *A Study on the Turkish Criminal Trial System* (Istanbul: The Ankara Bar Association, 2010), 64–6.

13   IHH, "*Mavi Marmara* Trial Continues with the 4th Hearing," October 3, 2013, accessed April 17, 2020, https://www.ihh.org.tr/en/news/mavi-marmara-trial-continues-with-4th-hearing-1891. On the issuing of arrest warrants, see also Sönmez, Z., "Arrest Warrants Issued for Israeli Commanders over the Fatal Attack on *Mavi Marmara*," IHH press release, April 26, 2014, accessed June 7, 2014, http://www.ihh.org.tr/en/main/news/0/arrest-warrants-in-mavi-marmara-case/2341.

14   According to Turkish law, procedure trials are usually held in the presence of the parties. See, e.g., Gökan, *A Study on the Turkish Criminal Trial System*, 62.

15 "Turkey Tries IDF Commanders over *Marmara* Killings," *The Jerusalem Post*, May 11, 2012, accessed February 8, 2013, http://www.jpost.com/International/Article. aspx?id=290587; "Turkey Tries Israeli Commanders over *Mavi Marmara* Raid," *BBC World News*, November 6, 2012, accessed February 8, 2013, http://www.bbc. co.uk/news/world-europe-20215991. These responses immediately provoked reporters and bloggers to invoke Israel's past support for, and the use of trials *in absentia*, including the Nuremberg trials. See, e.g., "Turkey Begins Nuremberg Trials against Israel," *Global Research News*, November 6, 2012, accessed April 17, 2020, https://www.globalresearch.ca/turkey-begins-nuremberg-trials-against-israel/5310854.

16 IHH, "Witness Account of the Israeli Attack and Rights Violations," December 10, 2012, accessed January 26, 2013, http://www.ihh.org.tr/taniklar-israil-saldirisi-ve-sonrasindaki-ihlalleri-anlatti/en/.

17 IHH, *Legal Actions Taken against The Israeli Attack*, 8. The suggestion that witness testimony was an effective means of recapturing the lost footage, is also expressed in a Tweet transmitted by IHH during the court proceedings: "The trial at this stage is collecting evidence by hearing witnesses, to prevent [losing again what has been] lost" … "Media Members are giving their testimonies to the court. All their footage and reports have been confiscated." The missing images are often invoked in witness testimonies. See, e.g., IHH (@MaviMarmaraCase), Twitter, February 21, 2013, accessed March 31, 2014.

18 See, e.g., Jonathon Burch, "Turkey Tries Israeli Military over Gaza Ship Killings;" Jonathon Burch, "Turkey Tries Israeli Military over Gaza Strip Killings," *Reuters*, November 5, 2012, accessed March 18, 2013, http://mobile.reuters.com/article/idUSBRE8A415T20121105?irpc=932. It should be mentioned that the Turkish Criminal Procedure Code Article 196 prohibits external visual and audio recording inside the justice building. Turkish Criminal Code (2009), Article 183, p. 198.

19 An exception was made for photos smuggled from onboard the ship by human rights activist Kevin Neish, who is said to have handed them over to the court in Istanbul. See IHH (@MaviMarmaraCase), Twitter, November 6, 2012, accessed March 31, 2014.

20 See Article 285, Council of Europe, *European Commission for Democracy Through Law, Penal Code of Turkey*, February 15, 2016, accessed July 28, 2020, https://www.venice.coe.int/webforms/documents/default.aspx?pdffile=CDL-AD_2016_002-e, 23–4.

21 On May 19, 2014, I met the president of the İstanbul Seventh Aggravated Criminal Court (Cağlayan Adliyesi Court) in his office. I presented an official request to view the court documentation; He refused and referred me to the defendants' appointed advocates, stating that it is in their power to decide differently. I approached advocate Murat Bozkurt who adamantly refused my requests to receive a copy or

to view the documentation, declining to justify his refusal. When I approached advocate Alev Peken, she not only refused, but specified that she was furious at the Israeli commanders for what they did at sea. Advocate Uğur Kasapoğlu could not be reached. According to the Turkish Penal Code, the public can watch and follow trials, but cannot receive documents, images, or the like from the court. See Article 285, Council of Europe, *European Commission for Democracy Through Law*. It should be noted that one of the purposes of this enactment is to protect the privacy of the defendants, however, in the case of a public trial *in absentia*, extensively covered by the media, and terminated without any resolution, the withholding of visual recordings of the proceedings under the claim of protecting the privacy of the accused would seem to be beside the point, and, in this case, probably the result of the court president's decision to let the advocates be the arbiters of my request.

22   The extent to which the Turkish justice system should follow European practices has been a major issue in Turkey ever since the collapse of the Ottoman Empire and the establishment of the modern Turkish state by Atatürk in the aftermath of the First World War. In the 1920s a series of steps was taken to transform Turkey into a modern secular state, among them a major reorganization of the Turkish juridical system. Radical reforms abolished Islamic law in 1924, replacing it two years later with a civil code inspired by Swiss law and with a system of criminal law adopted from Italy. In 1926, new secular courts were introduced in place of the old Islamic *Shari'a* (or *Şeriat*) courts. Among the chief goals of the new judicial system was to implement the new values on nationalism, secularism, and gender equality. See Vakur Versan, "The Kemalist Reform of the Turkish Empire and Its Impact," in *Atatürk and the Modernization of Turkey*, ed. Jacob M. Landau (London: Routledge, 1984), 247–50. In 1929, Turkey adopted a German code of criminal procedures, further separating religion and state law. The Turkish justice system was thus modeled on European civil law, rules, and procedures. See M. Yasin Aslan, "Transformation of Turkish Criminal Law from the Ottoman-Islamic Law to the Civil Law Tradition," *Ankara Bar Review* 2:2 (2009): 96 and M. Üzeyir Karabiyik, "Turkish Juridical Reform: It Has Achieved Much but There Is Much to Be Done," *International Justice Monitor*, 2012, accessed March 28, 2014, http://www.judicialmonitor.org/ archive_summer2012/judicialreformreport.html. Despite later counter-reforms that reinstated Islamic legal codes and practices, the European influence remained strong in Turkey's legal system. The European influence persisted and intensified as a result of Turkey's long-term effort to join the European Union. Turkey first applied for full EU membership on April 14, 1987, and was granted official candidate status at the Helsinki Summit in December 1999 (a status formally ratified in 2005). See "Turkey's Application for Full Membership Was Filed Under the Treaty of Rome," in Embassy of the Republic of Turkey, "Turkey and the EU," September 27, 2007, accessed February 26, 2013, https://web.archive.org/web/20070927211417/ http://

www.turkishembassy.org/index.php?option=com_content&task=view&id=57 &Itemid=235. Political Islamic groups have been divided on the issue of EU membership, with positions ranging from strict resistance to outright support. See Ihsan Yilmaz, "State, Law, Civil Society and Islam in Contemporary Turkey," *The Muslim World* 95:3 (2005): 385–411; Pinar Tank, "Political Islam in Turkey: A State of Controlled Secularity," *Turkish Studies* 6:1 (2005): 3–19; Cengiz Erişen and Elif Erişen, "Attitudinal Ambivalence towards Turkey's EU Membership," *Journal of Common Market Studies* 52:2 (2013): 217–33.

23 Turkey had been taking steps in order to meet the Copenhagen criteria required for accession to the European Union. To comply with the European Council's standards, Turkey has been expected to undertake major reforms in its judicial system in general, and with respect to human rights specifically. A program of "harmonization" reforms started with constitutional amendments in 2001 and continued with the complete revision of the Turkish Criminal Code (TCA) and Turkish Criminal Procedure Act (TCPA), and the introduction of new institutions, practices, and codes. B. Demren Dönmez, "Cross-Examination in Turkish Criminal Procedure Law," *Ankara Law Review* 8:1 (2011): 54. These new codes added European- and US-inspired laws to the already existing Turkish system (which, as noted above, had been an amalgam of Swiss, German, Italian, French, and Roman codes). See Esin Örücü, "What Is a Mixed Legal System: Exclusion or Expansion?," *Electronic Journal of Comparative Law*, 12:1 (2008) accessed April 27, 2014, http:// www.ejcl.org/121/art121-15.pdf, 10.

24 Despite the ample legal reforms—some of which have even been seen as models for emulation by other countries—in effect most of the revisions and amendments have not been successfully implemented. See, e.g., United Nations Development Program [UNDP], *A Declaration on Judicial Transparency Endorsed by Asian Countries in Istanbul*, November 27, 2013, accessed April 18, 2020, https://www.tr.undp.org/content/turkey/en/home/presscenter/ pressreleases/2013/11/27/a-declaration-on-judicial-transparency-endorsed-by-asian-countries-in-istanbul.html, 1; Karabiyik, "Turkish Juridical Reform," Cf. "EU-Turkey Relations," *EurActive*, November 14, 2005, accessed February 27, 2013, http://www.euractiv.com/enlargement/eu-turkey-relations/article-129678; "EU Will Lose Turkey if It Hasn't Joined by 2023, Erodgan Says," *EurActive*, October 31, 2012, accessed February 26, 2013, http://www.euractiv.com/ enlargement/eu-lose-turkey-hasnt-joined-2023-news-515780. It has been noted that efforts to achieve the implementation of the reforms succeeded in holding workshops and training sessions for judges and prosecutors. Nevertheless, there has been substantial criticism of the fact that, in practice, the reform legislation has been executed inefficiently, or has not been implemented at all (as in the case of the Constitutional Court, the judicial police, freedom of speech, etc.).

See, e.g., European Commission, Staff Working Document [SWP], *Enlargement Strategy and Main Challenges 2012–2013*, October 10, 2012, accessed February 26, 2013, http://ec.europa.eu/enlargement/pdf/key_documents/2012/package/tr_rapport_2012_en.pdf. See also European Commission, Staff Working Document [SWP], *Turkey 2013 Progress Report*, October 16, 2013, accessed April 27, 2020, https://www.ab.gov.tr/files/2013%20ilerleme%20raporu/tr_rapport_2013_en.pdf, 44–47. This EU Commission criticism was intensified in the 2016 report that examined the measures taken by Turkey following the failed coup attempt of July 15, 2016. Under the declared state of emergency, the Turkish government enacted new laws by decree. It was reported that "Turkey notified the Council of Europe of a derogation from its obligation to secure a number of fundamental rights protected by the European Convention on Human Rights." Furthermore, it was claimed that the state of the judicial system had vastly deteriorated, referring to its independence. European Commission, *Turkey 2016 Report*, November 9, 2016, accessed July 5, 2018, https://ec.europa.eu/neighbourhood-enlargement/system/files/2018-12/20161109_report_turkey.pdf. Moreover, due to the measures taken by the Turkish government after the coup attempt—measures that involved violations of the rights of thousands of citizens, and a threat to re-impose capital punishment—on November 24, 2016, the European Parliament voted to suspend the Turkey accession process. "Turkey's EU Bid in Jeopardy After Council of Europe Vote," *EurActive*, April 25, 2017, accessed July 7, 2018, https://www.euractiv.com/section/global-europe/news/turkeys-eu-bid-in-jeopardy-after-council-of-europe-vote/.

25 See European Commission, *European Neighbourhood Policy and Enlargement Negotiations, Conditions for Membership*, November 28, 2013, accessed March 18, 2014, http://ec.europa.eu/enlargement/policy/conditions-membership/index_en.htm. The first product of legal reform was the constitutional amendment introduced in October 2001. To date, numerous "harmonization packages" have been introduced, most importantly an amendment made to Article 90 of the Constitution following international agreements in the area of fundamental rights and freedoms. Nevertheless, many jurists have stated that human rights norms are not taken into account in trials. See Suavi Aydin, Meryem Erdal, Mithat Sancar and Eylem Ümit Atilgan, *Just Expectations: A Compilation of TESEV Research Studies on the Judiciary in Turkey* (Istanbul: TESEV Publications, 2011), https://www.tesev.org.tr/wp-content/uploads/report_Just_Expectations_Compilation_Of_TESEV_Research_Studies_On_The_Judiciary_In_Turkey.pdf, 38, 42, 45. The backsliding of the judicial system after the 2016 attempted coup, and the subsequent measures taken by government, undermined the ability of the judicial system to secure human and civil rights and to maintain separation from the executive. In addition, various

emergency decrees enacted since 2016 "have notably curtailed certain civil and political rights, including freedom of expression, freedom of assembly and procedural rights." European Commission, *Turkey 2018 Report*, April 17, 2018, accessed July 5, 2018, https://ec.europa.eu/neighbourhood-enlargement/sites/near/files/20180417-turkey-report.pdf, 3.

26 The concept of "access to justice" was first introduced with the Treaty of Lisbon, which forms the constitutional basis of the EU. In the 1998 Aarhus Convention, "access to justice" was discussed together with access to information. In 2006, "access to justice" was enshrined in a UN convention. See FRA, The European Union Agency for Fundamental Rights, *Accesses to Justice in Europe: An Overview of Challenges and Opportunities*, 2011, accessed April 9, 2014, http://fra.europa.eu/sites/default/files/fra_uploads/1520-report-access-to-justice_EN.pdf, 14–20. On the important role the EU attributes to access to justice, see, e.g., FRA, *Access to Justice in Cases of Discrimination in the EU: Steps to Further Equality*, 2012, accessed April 2, 2014, https://fra.europa.eu/sites/default/files/fra-2012-access-to-justice-social.pdf. See also European Commission, "Better Access to Justice in Turkey."

27 Seda Kalem Berk, *'Access to Justice' in Turkey: Indicators and Recommendations*, (Istanbul: TESEV Publications, 2011), accessed March 3, 2014, https://www.tesev.org.tr/wp-content/uploads/report_Access_To_Justice_In_Turkey_Indicators_And_Recommendations.pdf, 32–5.

28 Fahrettin Özdemirci, "Government Records and Records Management: Law on the Right to Information in Turkey," *Government Information Quarterly* 25:2 (2008): 306.

29 Berk, *Access to Justice*, 11.

30 UN Development Program [UNDP], *Istanbul Declaration on Transparency in the Judicial Process*, November, 2013, accessed March 6, 2013, http://www.ge.undp.org/content/dam/turkey/docs/demgovdoc/%C4%B0stanbul%20Declaration.pdf, 1.

31 Ibid., 4, 7. Turkey has been cited as the nation with the largest number of imprisoned journalists, nearly all on terrorism or other anti-state charges. The state of freedom of the press and freedom of information has been described as a "stain on Ankara's democratic reputation, economic standing and diplomatic position." The reaction of the government to the accusations has been to insist that such allegations amount to "insulting language or terrorism." The wide interpretation of terrorism by the courts has been criticized for creating confusion between terrorism and acts of freedom of thought and expression. The status of freedom of expression has deteriorated since the failed coup on July 15, 2016. See also European Commission, Staff Working Document [SWP], *Enlargement Strategy and Main Challenges 2012–2013*, 10. See also Joel Simon, "For Turkey, World's Leading Jailer, a Path Forward," Committee to Protect Journalists, December 11, 2012,

accessed February 25, 2013, https://cpj.org/2012/12/for-turkey-worlds-leading-jailer-of-the-press-a-pa/.

32 See, e.g., Republic of Turkey, Turkey Law on the Right to Information, No. 4982, 2003, accessed April 22, 2020, https://publicofficialsfinancialdisclosure. worldbank.org/sites/fdl/files/assets/law-library-files/Turkey_Right%20to%20 Information%20Law_2004_en.pdf. Information and documents pertaining to state secrets, the economic interests of the state, state intelligence, administrative investigations, judicial investigations, and prosecutions are outside the scope of this law. "Access to Judicial Information Draft Report," Open Society Justice Initiative, March 2009, accessed September 15, 2020, 25–7. Any refusal to provide information based on the different exemption may be submitted to the "Turkish Right to Information Assessment Council," then to the courts. "Turkish Law on the Right to Information," No. 4982. Another example is provided by the laws governing media content in Turkey which contain restrictions based on principles of "national unity," "national security," and "territorial integrity". Dilek Kurban, and Ceren Sözeri, *Policy Suggestions for Free and Independent Media in Turkey* (Istanbul: TESEV Publication, 2013), accessed April 22, 2020, https://www. tesev.org.tr/wp-content/uploads/report_Policy_Suggestions_For_Free_And_ Independent_Media_In_Turkey.pdf, 1–2. The radical nature of the restrictions on freedom of the press in Turkey was emphasized in a report which was also set to explain the fact that the media failed to cover the major protests concerning Gezi Park in Istanbul. The protests took place in a substantial number of Turkish cities, mainly during May and June 2013. As a result of confrontations, six people lost their lives and more than 8,000 were injured. The inspections carried out by the Ministry of Interior concluded that police used disproportionate force against protesters. A large number of human rights defenders faced prosecution and legal proceeding on charges of promoting propaganda for terrorism during demonstrations and meetings and at a press conference. The prosecutions led to a number of convictions. See European Commission, *Turkey 2013 Progress Report*, 2–3, 50. As mentioned in the note above, reference to the status of freedom of the press and freedom of expression worsened after the coup attempt, including strong restrictions on criticizing the government, and placing the press under pressure to serve as mediator of the restrictions. European Commission, *Turkey 2018 Report*, 35.

33 Ibid., 44, 49.

34 See, e.g., "Lawyers on Trial: Abusive Prosecutions and Erosion of Fair Trial Rights in Turkey," Human Rights Watch, April 10, 2019, accessed April 22, 2020, https:// www.hrw.org/report/2019/04/10/lawyers-trial/abusive-prosecutions-and-erosion-fair-trial-rights-turkey.

35 See the report by Marc Pierini with Markus Mayr, *Freedom of the Press in Turkey*, Carnegie Europe, Carnegie Endowment for International Peace, Belgium & Open Society Foundation in Turkey, 2013, accessed February 25, 2013, http:// carnegieendowment.org/files/press_freedom_turkey.pdf, 1. See also Thomas Hammarberg, *Report on Administration of Justice and Protection of Human Rights in Turkey*, Commissioner for Human Rights of the Council of Europe, following his visit to Turkey from 10 to 14 October 2011, Strasbourg: Council of Europe, January 10, 2012, accessed February 26, 2013, http://www.europarl.europa.eu/ meetdocs/2009_2014/documents/d-tr/dv/0131_04/0131_04en.pdf, 4.

36 A judicial reform adopted in mid-2012 transferred jurisdiction over serious criminal offenses (including terrorism) to specialized regional courts. See Pierini, *Freedom of the Press in Turkey*, 8. It should be noted that prior to the 2016 Turkish Coup, the Turkish Journalists Union reported that more than 15,000 websites had been blocked by the state. For more than two years, YouTube was banned on the grounds that some YouTube videos insulted modern nation founder Mustafa Kemal Atatürk. Many of the media members accused were tried in the İstanbul Seventh Aggravated Criminal Court during the same period in which the *Mavi Marmara* trial was conducted. See Dan Bilefsky and Sebnem Arsu, "Charges against Journalists Dim the Democratic Glow in Turkey," *The New York Times*, January 5, 2012, accessed February 26, 2013, http://www.nytimes.com/2012/01/05/world/ europe/turkeys-glow-dims-as-government-limits-free-speech.html?pagewanted=all.

37 See Simon, "For Turkey, World's Leading Jailer," 7.

38 "EU Has Juridical Concerns with Turkey," *UPI.com*, January 15, 2014, accessed April 4, 2014, http://www.upi.com/Top_News/Special/2014/01/15/EU-has-judicial-concerns-with-Turkey/UPI-34421389798136.

39 European Commission, *Turkey 2016 Report*.

40 Ibid., 64; European Commission, *Turkey 2018 Report*. Laura Pitel, "Arrest of Turkish Judges Prompts Fears over Checks and Balances," *Financial Times*, July 17, 2016, accessed August 14, 2018, https://www.ft.com/content/79f72260-4c3c-11e6-88c5-db83e98a590a.

41 European Commission, *Turkey 2016 Report*, 17.

42 Ibid., 64.

43 Ibid., 17.

44 Kjell Björnberg and Ross Cranston, *The Functioning of the Judicial System in the Republic of Turkey: Report of an Advisory Visit*, European Commission Brussels, June 13–22, 2005, accessed April 5, 2014, http://www.deontologie-judiciaire. umontreal.ca/en/textes%20int/documents/TURQUIE_ENQUeTE.pdf, 52–3. According to amended Article 129 of the Criminal Court, "a record of the hearing should be drawn up and should be signed by the presiding judge and the court clerk." In addition, "If the actions taken during the hearing have been recorded by

means of technical equipment, written minutes of the recording shall be prepared without delay." See Law No. 5271, Code on Criminal Procedure, April 4, 2004.

45 The project was started in 2000 and completed by the end of 2007. See Ali Riza Cam, "EU Principles in Modernisation of Justice and the Turkish IT Project UYPA," *European Journal of ePractice*, 2008, accessed April 23, 2020, https://www.slideshare.net/epracticejournal/ali-riza-presentation.

46 See İsmail Aksel, "Turkish Judicial System – Bodies, Duties and Officials," The Ministry of Justice of Turkey, Department for Strategy Development, 2013, accessed April 21, 2020, https://rm.coe.int/turkish-judicial-system-bodies-duties-and-officials-by-ismail-aksel-ju/168078f25f, 19, esp. note 4.

47 European Commission, "Better Access to Justice in Turkey," 7, 8–14.

48 Ibid., 7.

49 Turkish Criminal Code (2009), 87.

50 The case was filed at the Seventh High Criminal Court on May 29, 2012. The first set of hearings was conducted on November 6–9, 2012, the second on February 21, 2013, the third on May 20–21, 2013, the fourth on October 10, 2013, the fifth on March 27, 2014, the sixth on May 26, 2014, and the seventh on March 11–12, 2015. Additional hearings were conducted on October 9, 2016, on December 2, 2016, and the last one on December 9, 2016. IHH reported on a total of fourteen hearings. For general information about the hearings dates, see IHH, "The *Mavi Marmara* Trials: Legal Actions Taken against Israeli Attack on the Gaza Freedom Flotilla on May 31, 2010," December 12, 2012, accessed April 23, 2020, https://www.ihh. org.tr/public/publish/0/126/the-mavi-marmara-case.pdf. In the media, see, e.g., Jon Sharman, "Turkey Halts Case over Israeli Raid on Gaza Flotilla That Killed 10 People," *The Independent*, December 9, 2016, accessed July 16, 2018, https://www. independent.co.uk/news/world/middle-east/turkey-halt-court-case-israel-mavi-marmara-raid-victims-a7466311.html.

51 IHH (@MaviMarmaraCase), posted by Izzet Şahin, Twitter, November 3, 2012, accessed March 31, 2014.

52 I attended the hearings between 2012 and 2014.

53 Richard Folk, "Israel on the Felons Dock: Double Standards in International Law," Lecture at the Foundation for Human Rights, Freedom and Humanitarian Relief [IHH], University of Istanbul, accessed April 15, 2014, http://eski.ihh.org.tr/falk-uluslararasi-hukuk-cifte-standartli/en/.

54 Republic of Turkey, Ministry of Justice, Judicial Reforms Strategy, 2009, accessed April 28, 2014, http://www.sgb.adalet.gov.tr/yrs/Judicial%20Reform%20Strategy. pdf, 29. See also Alp Aziz Bacak, *Adiuelerinn Fiziksel ve Mimari Koşullari Bağlaminda Yargisal*, 2015, accessed May 20, 2016, http://tbbdergisi.barobirlik.org. tr/m2015-120-1514, 261–88.

55 "Europe's Largest Palace of Justice in Istanbul," *Turkish Diary*, August 1, 2011, accessed March 19, 2013, http://www.buyuyenturkiye.com/turkishdiary/

haber/europes-largest-palace-of-justice-in-istanbul. According to the Center for Legal and Court Technology, the court infrastructure demands raised floors, cabling infrastructure, special location for the racks with adequate ventilation, etc. See also Martin E. Gruen, "The World of Courtroom Technology," Center for Legal and Court Technology, 2003, accessed June 24, 2014, http://www.legaltechcenter.net/download/whitepapers/The%20World%20Of%20Courtroom%20Technology.pdf.

56　The extent to which the Turkish justice system should emulate European ways has been a major issue in recent years. The issue has roots in the Ottoman Empire long before the current Turkish state and in its relationship with Europe—a relationship largely marked by perceptions of superiority and inferiority. For claims regarding Ottoman superiority, and parallel assertions regarding Western superiority and more advanced technology, see, e.g., June Starr, *Law as a Metaphor: From Islamic Courts to the Palace of Justice* (Albany, NY: State University of New York Press, 1991). See also Suraiya Faroqhi, Bruce McGowan, Donald Quataert, Sevket Pamuk, and Halil Inalcik, *An Economic and Social History of the Ottoman Empire*, Vol. 2: 1600–1914 (Cambridge, UK: Cambridge University Press 1995).

57　In her statement to the court, Gülden Sönmez complained about the size of the courtroom: "You know there are more than 700 victims. Some of them are abroad. Unfortunately, they cannot come here and testify at the court because the courtroom is too small and the hearing is only one day long." See IHH, "Second Hearing of *Mavi Marmara* Trial Held," February 21, 2013, accessed April 23, 2020, https://www.ihh.org.tr/en/news/second-hearing-of-mavi-marmara-trial-held-1593. The insufficient capacity of the court was blamed for triggering violence at the final hearings in 2016, when it was reported that plaintiffs' lawyers and victims' families were unable to enter the court. After a protest erupted, it was quashed by riot police. Sharman, "Turkey Halts Case over Israeli Raid."

58　UN Development Program [UNDP], *Istanbul Declaration on Transparency in the Judicial Process*, 2.

59　According to a survey on the application of digital technologies in courtrooms, as early as 2011, more than 30,000 courthouses had adopted digital audio and video recording technology to capture court proceedings, a process that began at the end of the 1990s: "[M]ost digital recording systems today are comprised of at least four components: recording, note-taking, playback, and storage. For the best quality, and to facilitate the creation of verbatim transcripts, typical courtroom venues require four independent audio channels (from a minimum of 4 microphones, one each for the judge, prosecution, defense and witness) are recorded." See Philip M. Langbroek, "Digital Technology Leading the Way in Court Recording," *International Journal for Court Administration*, 3:2 (2011): 21–30.

60　Republic of Turkey, Second Chapter-Essence of Criminal Responsibility, Article 20 (2004), Turkish Criminal Code, Law No. 5327. Legislation Online, September 26,

2004, accessed April 1, 2014, http://legislationline.org/documents/action/popup/id/6872/preview. During the hearings I attended, one witness testified to having seen former Israeli chief of staff Gabi Ashkenazi on board the *Mavi Marmara*. This remark failed to elicit any questions from the judge or the defendants' lawyer.

61 See also e.g., IHH, "About the Trial: Israel on the Felon's Dock!," 2012, accessed February 5, 2013, http://www.ihh.org.tr/dava-hakkinda/en.

62 Resmi Derneği, "Second Hearing Held in Historic Trial," The Freedom and Solidarity Association *Mavi Marmara*, 2013, accessed April 15, 2014, http://www.mavimarmara.org/en/?p=105.

63 Ibid.

64 IHH, "About the Trial: Israel on the Felon's Dock!," 9.

65 IHH, "Second Hearing of *Mavi Marmara* Trial Held."

66 IHH (@MaviMarmaraCase), Twitter, February 21, 2013.

67 Sarah Colborne, "Three Years On, the *Mavi Marmara* Is Still Making Waves," Palestinian Solidarity Campaign, May 31, 2013, accessed April 16, 2020, https://www.palestinecampaign.org/three-years-on-the-mavi-marmara-is-still-making-waves/.

68 IHH (@MaviMarmaraCase), Twitter, February 21, 2013.

69 "Israel Must Be Held Accountable," *Veterans News Now*, March 28, 2014, accessed April 20, 2014, http://www.veteransnewsnow.com/2014/03/28/israel-must-be-held-accountable. See also "Israel Must Be Held Accountable," *Altahrir, News of Islam, Muslims, Arab Spring and Special Palestine*, March 29, 2014, accessed April 25, 2020, https://altahrir.wordpress.com/2014/03/29/israel-must-be-held-accountable/.

70 Colborne, "*Mavi Marmara* Still Making Waves."

71 IHH (@MaviMarmaraCase), Twitter, February 21, 2013.

72 Aksel, "Turkish Judicial System," 14.

73 Hammarberg, *Report on Administration of Justice and Protection of Human Rights in Turkey*, 2. This accusation pales in comparison to the utter lack of independence of the judiciary described in 2016, the last year of the trial after the coup attempt.

74 Ibid., 19.

75 Turkish Criminal Code (2009), 208, 236–7.

76 See also Yonah Jeremy Bob, "Turkey Resumes Gaza Flotilla Trial for ex-IDF Heads," *The Jerusalem Post*, February 21, 2013, accessed April 16, 2013, http://www.jpost.com/Diplomacy-and-Politics/Turkey-resumes-Gaza-flotilla-trial-for-ex-IDF-heads.

77 It is worth noting, however, that in the Turkish legal system, the judge's task of reiterating the testimonies and dictating them to the court clerk is highly redactive in nature, often involving substantial editing of the witnesses' statements, choice of words, tone, etc.

78 Gökan, *Study on the Turkish Criminal Trial System*, 70.

79 It should be noted that according to the Turkish legal system, there are some cases in which defendants must be represented by counsel, but these advocates are paid extremely low wages (e.g., 561 Turkish Liras in 2013). See *Resmi Gazete*, Republic of Turkey, Ministry of Justice, December 29, 2012, accessed July 28, 2020, https://www.barobirlik.org.tr/dosyalar/belgeler/CMKUcretTarifesi/tarife2013.pdf.

80 Hammarberg, *Report on Administration of Justice and Protection of Human Rights in Turkey*, 19. See also Dönmez, "Cross-Examination in Turkish Criminal Procedure Law," 53–69.

81 Ibid.

82 Ibid., 20.

83 Berk, *Access to Justice*, 32–5.

84 Ibid., 34.

85 Ibid., 35.

86 The invitation to foreign citizens to participate and testify at court was legally justified based upon a claim that in accordance with the Turkish law in cases in which "inhuman treatment and torture was applied to defenseless people, it is subject to the provisions of the Turkish law as a result of the application of universal jurisdiction principle." IHH, *The Mavi Marmara Case: Legal Actions*.

87 Republic of Turkey, Constitution of 1982 with Amendments through 2011, constituteproject.com, July 27, 2018, accessed July 15, 2018, https://www.constituteproject.org/constitution/Turkey_2011.pdf?lang=en, 11.

88 Ibid., 12. On theater of justice, see Shoshana Felman, *The Scandal of the Speaking Body: Don Juan with JL Austin, or Seduction in Two Languages* (Redwood City, CA: Stanford University Press, 2003). On judges' lack of independency, see, e.g., Aydin et al., "Just Expectations," 38, 42, 45. On lawyers' arrests, see, "*Çağlayan Adliyesi'nde Polis Müdahalesi Cascade Police Intervention*," YouTube video, 2011, accessed September 7, 2014, https://www.youtube.com/watch?v=x0yyQaNb5cU.

89 Yifa Yaakov, "Netanyahu: Syrian Chaos Necessitated My Apology to Turkey," *The Times of Israel*, March 23, 2013, accessed July 17, 2018, https://www.timesofisrael.com/netanyahu-syria-major-factor-in-turkey-normalization-decision/; Thomas Seibert, "US Worries over Syria, Iran Behind Push for Israel's Apology to Turkey," *The National*, March 24, 2013, https://www.thenational.ae/world/mena/us-worries-over-syria-iran-behind-push-for-israel-s-apology-to-turkey-1.656300.

90 Herb Keinon, "Netanyahu Apologizes to Turkey over Gaza Flotilla," *The Jerusalem Post*, March 22, 2013, accessed July 17, 2018, https://www.jpost.com/International/Obama-Netanyahu-Erdoğan-speak-by-phone-307423.

91 The content of the agreement was denounced by IHH: "Israel's arrogant attitude as if to say 'I kill people and pay in cash whatever is the cost' is unacceptable." IHH added a Palestinian saying, "Whoever covers up with Israel will remain naked." Mustafa Özbek, IHH Media Press Release, June 27, 2016.

92   The event that is considered to have marked the beginning of the deterioration
     of the ties between the two countries was the failure of Israel-Syria peace talks
     which were mediated by Erdoğan. Presumably, these talks ended when Israel
     launched "Operation Cast Lead" in 2008. However, it was not until after the flotilla
     incident that the diplomatic relations were downgraded. After the publication of
     the 2011 UN Palmer Report, Turkey expelled Israel's ambassador. See Selin Nasi,
     "Turkey-Israel Deal: A Key to Long-Term Reconciliation?," *Global Political Trends
     Center Policy Briefs*, January 2017, accessed July 17, 2018, http://fes-org-il-wp.
     s3.eu-central-1.amazonaws.com/wp-content/uploads/2017/01/10110901/Turkey-
     Israel-Deal.pdf; Hay Eytan Cohen Yanarocak "Turkish–Israeli Reconciliation: The
     End of 'Precious Loneliness?,'" The Moshe Dayan Center, Tel Aviv University, June
     26, 2016, accessed September 16, 2020, https://dayan.org/content/turkish-israeli-
     reconciliation-end-precious-loneliness. A day after the agreement signature, it was
     reported that ISIS carried out a terror attack at Atatürk Airport, killing 45 people,
     and injuring more than 230. In response to the attack, which took place in the
     airport international zone, the Turkish government ordered an immediate media
     blackout across the country, not unlike the tactic Israel deployed in extraterritorial
     waters in reaction to the flotilla's approach. See, e.g., Oren Dorell, "Istanbul Airport:
     A Scene of Gunfire, Bombs and Sirens," *USA Today*, June 28, 2016, accessed July 25,
     2018, https://www.usatoday.com/story/news/world/2016/06/28/istanbul-airport-
     scene-gunfire-bombs-and-sirens/86498648/. See also "Procedural Agreement of
     Compensation between the Republic of Turkey and the State of Israel."
93   "Report: Israel Paid $20M to Turkey as Compensation for *Mavi Marmara*."
94   Eran Lerman, "The Rapprochement Deal between Israel and Turkey: Intermediate
     Summary" *BESA Perspectives*, July 6, 2016, accessed July 2018, https://besacenter.
     org/wp-content/uploads/2016/07/Lerman-Eran-Turkey-Israel-deal-PP-348-
     HEBREW-6-July-2016.pdf.
95   IHH, "International Panel Held in LSE about *Mavi Marmara*."
96   Özbek, IHH Media Press Release, October 19, 2016.
97   Özbek, IHH Media Press Release, December 8, 2016.
98   In December 2017, it was reported that as the Turkish Government was still
     reluctant to transfer the compensation to the victims' families, the IHH filed a
     petition in court on the families' behalf. It was further reported that the dispute
     was about the total sum each family should receive. The Turkish Finance Ministry
     responded to the lawsuit, stating that while the government "can never aim
     to upset or offend the families of citizens who lost their lives," [it nevertheless
     rejected] "the exorbitant amount of material and moral compensation asked
     by the plaintiff." The Turkish nationals aboard the *Mavi Marmara*, the ministry
     said, "should have foreseen that they may be subject to such an attack because
     the problems between the Israeli state and Gaza are well-known. They took the
     risk of any attack or intervention. These elements should be considered when

determining the amount of compensation to be paid." Smadar Perry, "Turkish Gov't Delays Compensation Payment to *Marmara* Families," *YNET News. com*, December 6, 2017, accessed July 25, 2018, https://www.ynetnews.com/articles/0,7340,L-4974635,00.html.

99　It may be interesting to note that in Israel, following publication that Israel had reached an accord with Turkey, soldiers from the commando unit which raided the *Mavi Marmara* filed a petition in the Israeli Supreme Court seeking to prevent the transfer of compensation to the victims' families. It was reported that the petition asserted an unwritten covenant between the state and its soldiers that committed Israel to vouch for its soldiers first and foremost: "this covenant is written in the blood of the fallen soldiers of Israel," the petitioners proclaimed. Thus, the efforts to legally contest the Israel-Turkey agreement seemed not only to resemble the reaction by Israel's adversaries, but to resemble their rhetoric. Disappointed with the actions of the sovereign, both sets of aggrieved parties turned to notions of primordial or pre-state "laws written with blood." Concerning the specific contents of the Israeli soldiers' petition, see Uzi Barch, "Commando Soldiers Field a Petition against the Rapprochement Deal," *Arutz-7*, June 30, 2016, accessed July 19, 2018, https://www.inn.co.il/News/News.aspx/325186.

100　Although Erdoğan claimed to be an advocate of the flotilla initiative, he responded to IHH criticism by asking, "Did you ask me (for my opinion/permission) when you were leaving (for Gaza)?" He also implied that the initiative was to "show-off." According to Yanarocak, "This, incidentally, briefly became a slogan used to ridicule the president for his alleged abandonment of the Palestinian struggle." See BIA, "Erdoğan Changes Opinion over the *Marmara* Case," *Bianet News Desk*, June 30, 2016, accessed July 25, 2018, https://bianet.org/english/politics/176388-Erdoğan-changes-opinion-on-mavi-marmara-crisis; Hay Eytan Cohen Yanarock, "Turkey's Long Month: Agreements to Normalize Relations, Terror, and a Failed Coup," *Turekyscope* 4:7 (2016), accessed September 16, 2020, https://dayan.org/content/turkeys-long-month-agreements-normalize-relations-terror-and-failed-coup. The imposition of an electronic blockade for reasons of "national security" is not unique to the Israeli military. The Erdoğan regime exercises a strict and consistent policy of information blocking. Turkish courts often demand mass online censorship and social media blackouts, not only of sites that publish secret information such as Wikileaks, but also of the video-sharing platform, YouTube, the message-exchange platform, WhatsApp, social, news, and media networks such as Twitter and Facebook, and even the free encyclopedia, Wikipedia. For a comprehensive list of digital censorship in Turkey, see "Turkey Blocks: Mapping Internet Freedom in Real Time," accessed July 15, 2018, https://turkeyblocks.org/.

101　Sharman, "Turkey Halts Case over Israeli Raid."

102　Commanding the entrance of the İstanbul 7th Aggravated Criminal Court entrance hall where the *Mavi Marmara* trial of the four Israeli senior commanders was held *in absentia* rises a monumental three-story high statue of the blindfolded goddess of Justice. At the time the *Mavi Marmara* hearings were conducted, around Istanbul's court's blind Justice statue, using its very pedestal at their support, an assortment of random gaudy illustrations were exhibited for sale, and for the visual consumption of court attendees seeking justice from the system. Symbolically, this anecdotal sight of the goddess of justice which was now blindly protecting a makeshift bazaar of ad-hoc images placed on display at the foot of the pedestal seemed to signal an ironic counterpoint to all the visual evidence that remained concealed from the proceedings unfolding within the courthouse, like a visual reminder of the implications of withholding images from the judicial system. Statue of the blindfolded goddess of justice, unable to see the images laid at its feet. İstanbul 7th Aggravated Criminal Court, Istanbul, October 10, 2013. Photo: Maayan Amir.

Chapter 5

1   While choosing to explore the legal history of the image as evidence especially under common law, one finds it important to note that every state may enforce its codes of evidence and the corresponding legal conceptualization of images as evidence. Common law systems have exerted enormous influence, including in Israel. Unlike Israel, Turkey has adopted the mixed system of criminal proceedings prevalent in Continental Europe. In fact, the Panel Code and Code of Criminal Procedure, which were in place until 2005, were derived from Italy and Germany, respectively. One of the main principles of the Turkish criminal justice system is that of "free evaluation of evidence," i.e. that anything may be used as evidence if it can help the judge resolve the dispute and assist the judge in coming to a determination, unless the evidence was unlawfully obtained. See, e.g., Article 217 CCP, 218, 296. In 2005, both panel codes were replaced, although the German influence remains strong. Critics claim that the new code adopts concepts from different countries and systems, with the result of incoherence and confusion, and misunderstandings among legal practitioners. In addition, in regard to cases that arose prior to 2005, the former codes still apply. One of the fundamental principles of the Turkish legal system is "providing evidence by documentation" (set forth by former Code of Civil Procedure No. 1086). Under the new Code No. 5271, some changes have been made concerning which evidence is deemed "written preliminary evidence," and which is merely "preliminary evidence." The previous requirement that preliminary evidence be in written form has been superseded by new provisions which permit other types of evidence to be considered "preliminary evidence." The new Code provides a new definition of "record," "written or printed

texts or documents, certificates, drawing, plans, sketches, photographs, films, visual or audio data and electronic data and other means of collection of information, which are convenient for proving facts related to the dispute, are records under this act." See Osman Doğru, *Mills that Grind Defendants: The Criminal Justice System in Turkey From a Human Rights Perspective*, (Istanbul: TESEV Publications, March 2012), accessed April 27, 2020, https://www.tesev.org.tr/wp-content/uploads/report_Mills_That_Grind_Defendants_Criminal_Justice_System_In_Turkey_From_A_Human_Rights_Perspective.pdf; Alper Uzun, "Evidence by Documentation and Its Exceptions under the Code of Civil Procedure," *Erdem & Erdem*, September 2013, accessed September 16, 2020, http://www.erdem-erdem.av.tr/publications/law-post/evidence-by-documentation-and-its-exceptions-under-the-code-of-civil-procedure/.

2   Timothy Thurston, "The Law and Science of Evidence," Roy Rosenzweig Center for History and New Media, accessed June 29, 2014, http://chnm.gmu.edu/aq/photos/frames/essay01.htm. "Hearsay" evidence is testimony or other forms of evidence derived from a source other than the person who is in court offering the testimony or other evidence. Its use raises questions of reliability and credibility, and impairs an opposing party's opportunity to conduct effective cross-examination since the source of the evidence is not present in court. Thus, the use of hearsay evidence may deprive an opposing party of the fundamental right to confront adverse witnesses. Jurisdictions vary concerning the extent to which hearsay evidence may be allowed, subjecting its admissibility to certain prerequisites. If it is admitted, fact-finders face the issue of whether they should attribute the same weight to it as to non-hearsay evidence. See also Piyel Haldar, "The Evidencer's Eye: Representations of Truth in the Laws of Evidence," *Law and Critique* 2 (1991): 171–89.

3   See Thurston, "Law and Science of Evidence"; Allan Sekula, "The Body and the Archive," *October*, 39 (1986): 3–64. See also Jonathan Cohen and Aaron Meskin, "Photographs as Evidence," in *Photography and Philosophy: Essays on the Pencil of Nature*, ed. Scott Walden (West Sussex, UK: Blackwell Publishing, 1986): 70–90; Rodney G. S. Carter, "Ocular Proof: Photographs as Legal Evidence," *Archivaria* 69 (2010): 23; Glenn Porter and Michael Kennedy, "Photographic Truth and Evidence," *Australian Journal of Forensic Sciences* 44:2 (2012): 183–92.

4   Jay A. Siegel and Pekka Saukko, eds., *Encyclopedia of Forensic Science*, 2nd edition (San Diego: Academic Press, 2013), 335–41. Similar uses of photography by the police have been employed in the US. See Thurston, "Law and Science of Evidence."

5   Mnookin provides an example of an early use of photography that appeared in an American photographic journal. According to the journal, French lawyers in 1852 used daguerreotype evidence "as a means of convincing the judge and jury that it is more eloquent than their words." According to Mnookin, photographs

were considered by the US Supreme Court as early as in 1864. According to Guilshan, photographs were admitted as evidence by US courts even earlier, in 1860. Carter claims that in the US, photographs were admitted in evidence in late 1850, and adds that in France, a report suggests the use of daguerreotypes in 1852. See Jennifer L. Mnookin, "The Image of Truth: Photographic Evidence and the Power of Analogy," *Yale Journal of Law & Humanities* 10:1 (1998): 8–9; Carter, "Ocular Proof," 23, 26–7; Christine A. Guilshan, "A Picture is Worth a Thousand Lies: Electronic Imaging and the Future of the Admissibility of Photographs into Evidence," *Rutgers Computer & Technology Law Journal* 1 (1992): 365.

6   Mnookin, "Photographic Evidence," 12, 13, 66.

7   Ibid., 20.

8   Ibid.

9   Brain, "Demonstrative Evidence," 972.

10 Ibid., 986–7.

11 Jeremy Bentham, *The Works of Jeremy Bentham*, Vol. 7, ed. John Bowring (Edinburgh: William Tait, 1838–43), 8, and also Brain, "Demonstrative Evidence," 989–91.

12 Bentham, *Works of Jeremy Bentham,* 10.

13 Brain, "Demonstrative Evidence," 988. Brain mentioned that England, "The first genuine treatise on the law of evidence was written by Lord Chief Baron Gilbert sometimes prior to 1754."

14 This preference may be for various reasons, including the ability to vocally claim an assertion as well as to support it with an oath, which is consistent with a medieval hierarchy of the living over the dead, in that the witness can be seen and heard. Another reason is that adversarial trials focus on cross-examination of the witness. Piyel Haldar, "The Return of the Evidencer's Eye: Rhetoric and the Visual Technologies of Proof," *Griffith Law Review* 8:1 (1999): 91–3.

15 Mnookin, "Photographic Evidence," 60; Brain, "Demonstrative Evidence," 997.

16 Mnookin, "Photographic Evidence," 64; Carter, "Ocular Proof," 23.

17 Brain, "Demonstrative Evidence," 995.

18 Mnookin, "Photographic Evidence," 67.

19 See, respectively, James F. Lucas, "Props: An Overview of Demonstrative Evidence," *American Journal of Trial Advocacy* 13 (1990): 1097–139, and David S. Santee, "More than Words: Rethinking the Role of Modern Demonstrative Evidence," *Santa Clara Law Review* 52:1 (2012): 105–44; Mnookin, "Photographic Evidence," 69–70.

20 It has been asserted that in Roman law, the concept of "proof" is indistinguishable from the word "rhetoric." Furthermore, some believe that this ontological approach has influenced the development of the modern law of evidence. Haldar, "Return of the Evidencer's Eye," 86–101.

21 Mnookin, "Photographic Evidence," 40. See also Thurston, "Law of Science and Evidence."

22 Mnookin, "Photographic Evidence," 44.

23 By the 1870s, photographs were frequently used in criminal cases in the US as a way to prove identity, either of the victim or the accused. Mnookin, "Photographic Evidence," 11–13. On reliability of photographs in court, See also Glenn Porter, "A New Theoretical Framework regarding the Application and Reliability of Photographic Evidence," *International Journal of Evidence and Proof* 15:1 (2011): 26–61.

24 John Henry Wigmore, *A Supplement to a Treatise on the Anglo-American System of Evidence in Trials at Common Law* (Boston: Little, Brown & Company, 1915).

25 Brain, "Demonstrative Evidence," 1002.

26 Ibid., 998–9.

27 Ibid., 1009.

28 Santee, "More than Words," 123–4.

29 Mnookin, "Photographic Evidence," 47. See also Jessica M. Silbey, "Judges as Film Critics: New Approaches to Filmic Evidence," *University of Michigan Journal of Law Reform*, 37:2 (2004): 499.

30 Tal Golan, "The Emergence of the Silent Witness: The Legal and Medical Reception of X-rays in the USA," *Social Studies of Science* 34:4 (2004): 476.

31 Mnookin, "Photographic Evidence," 64; Carter, "Ocular Proof," 23. Joan M. Schwartz, "Records of Simple Truth and Precision: Photography, Archives, and the Illusion of Control," in *Archives, Documentation, and Institutions of Social Memory: Essays from the Sawyer Seminar*, ed. Francis X. Blouin and William G. Rosenberg. (Ann Arbor: University of Michigan Press, 2006), 71.

32 Brain, "Demonstrative Evidence," 1002, 1013.

33 Due to the incoherence of common law, US courts have applied three different judicial approaches to filmic evidence. See Silbey, "Judges as Film Critics," 493; Golan, "Silent Witness," 490.

34 This change has motivated a shift of focus among experts on witness testimony from "interpretation" to "verification." Radiologists were asked to concentrate on affirming the validity of the production process rather than sharing their opinion and interpretation of the meaning of the images. See Tal Golan, *Laws of Men and Laws of Nature* (Cambridge, MA: Harvard University Press, 2004), 490, 469–99. See also Benjamin V. Madison III, "Seeing Can Be Deceiving: Photographic Evidence in a Visual Age—How Much Weight Does It Deserve?," *William and Mary Law Review* 25:4 (1984): 705.

35 Golan, *Laws of Men and Laws of Nature*, 490.

36 Ibid., 201.

37 Steven I. Bergel, "Evidence—Silent Witness Theory Adopted to Admit Photographs without Percipient Witness Testimony," *Suffolk University Law Review* 19 (1985): 353–9. In tandem with the introduction of surveillance cameras, police deployed the new technology as a monitoring tool to reduce crime, having installed CCTV in certain American cities for the purpose of public surveillance as early as 1956. See Chris A. Williams, "Police Surveillance and the Emergence of CCTV in the 1960s," *Crime Prevention and Community Safety* 5:3 (2003): 27–37.

38 Bergel, "Silent Witness Theory," 379.

39 Ibid., 369.

40 Ibid., 379–80.

41 Lucas, "Props: An Overview," 1101. It was further argued that while demonstrative evidence helped initiate photography into the realm of evidence, its legal status is less explanatory of the status of films in courts. See Silbey, "Judges as Film Critics," 506–7.

42 Lucas, "Props: An Overview," 1134. Of course, there are also differences between the technologies, which may create different criteria for admissibility and authentication processes. Some of the aspects with respect to which technologies may differ are the scale of resolution, the process of production of the image, etc. Different states may use different standards; in the US, criteria may even be determined by individual judges.

43 Carter, "Ocular Proof," 41. It is also worth noting that according to US law, whether evidence is recorded manually or automatically is not a relevant factor to the question of admissibility. Haldar, "The Evidencer's Eye," 179.

44 Paul Mason, "Lights, Camera, Justice? Cameras in the Courtroom: An Outline of the Issues," *Crime Prevention and Community Safety* 2:3 (2000): 23–34.

45 For example, enactments prohibiting courtroom photography in England and Wales date back to 1925. In 1989, a debate on the subject was conducted at the General Council Bar, and resulted in a proposed experiment enabling judges of all courts to allow photography and recording of proceedings according to their judgment, subject to principles of conducting a fair trial for a period of two years. Despite the full support of the bar, legislation offered to permit such an experiment did not pass. In the US, the 1946 Federal Rule banning photography and radio broadcasting of criminal proceedings in federal courts was enforced until 1981. Daniel Stepniak, "Technology and Public Access to Audio-Visual Coverage and Recordings of Court Proceedings: Implications for Common Law Jurisdiction," *William and Mary Bill of Rights Journal* 12:3 (2004): 797, 802, 795.

46 Robert K. L. Collins and David M. Skover, "Paratexts," *Stanford Law Review* 44:3 (1992): 509–52.

47 On the audio-visual recording court proceedings, see, e.g., Paul Lambert, *Courting Publicity: Twitter and Television Cameras in Court* (West Sussex, UK: Bloomsbury Professional, 2011) and Stepniak, "Technology and Public Access."

48 Collins and Skover, "Paratexts," 509.

49 Ibid., 529.

50 Ibid., 532.

51 Ibid., 533.

52 On the diverse approaches of temporary international criminal courts to the issue, see, e.g., Trudy H. Peterson, "Temporary Courts, Permanent Records," Woodrow Wilson Center, March 24, 2014, accessed September 17, 2020, https://www.wilsoncenter.org/publication/temporary-courts-permanent-records.

53 Some have expressed criticism regarding the role of international tribunals "as authors of history," claiming that "it is not a burden that should be placed on the shoulders of the judiciary." See, e.g., Christian Delage and Peter Goodrich, eds., *The Scene of the Mass Crime: History, Film and International Tribunals* (London: Routledge, 2013), 28.

54 The chief prosecutor, US Supreme Court justice Robert H. Jackson, made the decision. He was determined both to document the trial and to use film as evidence, viewing it as a tool of conviction. Although all the trials were sound recorded, the military filming crew (Army Signal Corps) filmed only 25 hours over the course of ten and half months. Interestingly, Jackson's preference for documentary evidence rather than calling a large number of victims to testify has been explained as follows: "he feared that they would not be able to control their emotions." Christian Delage, "The Place of the Filmed Witness from Nuremberg to the Khmer Rouge Trial," *Cardozo Law Review* 31 (2009): 1092.

55 The testimonial power of images has been the subject of a debate since at least the mid-twentieth century. The debate is mapped out in a book by Libby Saxton, which examines some prominent views concerning the ability of documentary images to bear witness to the Holocaust, as well as the ability of cinema to represent traumas and atrocities. On the one hand, Saxton posits Gérard Wajcman's claim that the Holocaust is an event without an image (60), and his emphasis is on every image being "a sort of denial of absence" (59). Saxton cites Slavoj Žižek's assertion that the image of atrocity can shield or veil us from the event itself (60). Others, however, including film director Jean-Luc Godard, differ, pointing to the images' power of resurrection through cinema (49). Didi Huberman claims, "images have just as important a role to play as words in bearing witness to the Holocaust" (58). While this debate has certainly been prominent in recent decades, Saxton writes that "the focus of critical discussion and artistic intervention has shifted from the question of whether the event could be or should be represented to the question of how it might be adequately

or responsibly represented" (2). My own point of departure here is that any discussion regarding the limits of visual representation is first conditioned upon access to the images themselves; To judge the images' testimonial value, we must first see them. Libby Saxton, *Haunted Images: Film, Ethics, Testimony and the Holocaust* (London and New York: Wallflower Press, 2008).

56 Delage and Goodrich, *History, Film and International Tribunals*, 3. These arguments do not claim that the application of CCTV is a simple mirror of reality. Nevertheless, CCTV is often considered more objective because it is not controlled at the time of filming by human intervention defined as "an observation mode of physical evidence." Porter, "Reliability of Photographic Evidence," 58. CCTV produces static shots, and it presents records of the image through a stable set framing and a scheduled time. "Furthermore, some CCTV cameras are controlled by remote security staff by panning, tilting and zooming the camera." Nevertheless, it may be that "In the US early constitutional discussions over the use of CCTV were connected to the issue of right of confrontation in cases in which the accused was excluded from the courtroom, and was allowed access only via CCTV." Porter and Kennedy, "Photographic Truth and Evidence," 189.

57 According to the Israeli Courts Act (section 70 (b)), no filming is allowed in the courtroom. Also forbidden is the publication of photographs taken inside the courtroom, except when court permission is granted. In only a very few cases have Israeli courts permitted broadcasting of their proceedings. The exceptional cases include the above-discussed Adolf Eichmann trial, and the trial of John (Ivan) Demjanjuk, the Ukrainian prisoner of war who was convicted of war crimes for being an accessory to the murder of thousands of Jews during World War II. In both cases, the court proceedings were broadcast on radio and television. In 1996, television and radio broadcasted live the reading of the verdict in the trial of Yigal Amir, the assassin of late Israeli Prime Minister Yitzhak Rabin. In 1999, the District Court in Jerusalem permitted live radio broadcast of the summary of the verdict in the trial of Aryeh Deri, leader of ultra-orthodox political party, *Shas*. Following the introduction of a Knesset private bill to amend the old prohibition in 2000, a commission headed by Supreme Court President Dorit Beinisch was established to examine the issue. In 2004, the commission recommended exercising restraint with respect to the expansion of electronic coverage of court proceedings. It suggested that a controlled small-scale experiment should take place only within the framework of the High Court of Justice. Other than that, the use of cameras to film or videotape court proceedings remains an issue of debate, and the above limited rule is exercised. However, there seems to be greater openness to the possibility of filming proceedings, with all parties entitled to submit a request. In the event the request is granted, the party who requested it would bear the costs of production. At times, the judge is empowered with discretion to order that proceedings be recorded, such as when a typed transcript might not be sufficient. See Committee to Examine Opening

Courts in Israel to the Electronic Media, The State of Israel, Jerusalem, 2004, accessed August 15, 2015, http://elyon1.court.gov.il/heb/doch%20electroni.pdf, 19–20.

58   Amit Pinchevski and Tamar Liebes, "Served Voices: Radio and Mediation of Trauma in the Eichmann Trial," *Public Culture* 22:2 (2010): 265.

59   Amit Pinchevski, Tamar Liebes, and Ora Herman, "Eichmann on the Air: Radio and the Making of an Historic Trial," *Historical Journal of Film, Radio and Television* 27:1 (2007): 8.

60   Ibid. Hava Yablonka, quoted in Pinchevski, Liebes and Herman, "Eichmann on the Air," 1.

61   The trial was partially broadcast, including some sessions and other coverage as part of the radio program, *Yoman Ha'mishpat*. See Pinchevski and Liebes, "Mediation of Trauma," 19.

62   Judge quoted in Christian Delage, *Caught on Camera: Film in the Courtroom from the Nuremberg Trials to the Trials of the Khmer Rouge*, ed. and trans. Ralph Schoolcraft and Mary Byrd Kelly (Philadelphia: University of Pennsylvania Press, 2006), 170.

63   Pinchevski, Liebes and Herman, "Eichmann on the Air," 2.

64   Zinder to Landor, June 15, 1960, ISA, Prime Minister's Office, G/6384 I/3657. Cited in: Pinchevski, Liebes and Herman, "Eichmann on the Air," 7.

65   Israel Ministry of Justice, *Adolf Eichmann Trial, Records of the Attorney General Against Adolf Eichmann, Vol. A*, 2002, accessed August 15, 2014, http://index. justice.gov.il/Subjects/EichmannWritten/volume/vol1_shaar.pdf, 14. The decision to allow filming and broadcasting of the trial met with resistance from all sides, but mainly by the judiciary. Minister of Justice Pinchas Rosen expressed concern about the novelty of such an innovation in the nation's legal affairs, and expressed the fear that the defense might try to discredit the judicial process. Defense lawyer Servatius also objected, but was overruled by the court. Pinchevski, Liebes and Herman, "Eichmann on the Air," 7–8.

66   The Nuremberg trials were also the first legal proceedings to extensively utilize film as evidence. Pursuant to Article 19, the tribunal declared that it was not bound by technical rules of evidence. One of the films which served as visual proof was "The Nazi Plan," a documentary commissioned by US counsel. Later, the same film would be shown in the Eichmann trial. Additional films were shown as well. See Wayne Morrison, "Visualising Atrocity: Arendt, Evil, and the Optics of Thoughtlessness: The Scene of the Mass Crime: History, Film, and International Tribunals," Book review, *Theoretical Criminology* 18:2 (2014): 252–6, 253. The Tokyo War Crimes Trial, "Japan in Time of Emergency," was also partially documented at the behest of the court, which also authorized the use of film as evidence. See Mayfield S. Bray and William T. Murphy, "Audiovisual Records in the National Archives Relating to World War I," Preliminary Draft, National Archives

and Records Service (GSA), Washington, D.C. 1972, accessed August 11, 2014, http://files.eric.ed.gov/fulltext/ED081239.pdf, 37.

67 UN ICTY, *Report on the Audiovisual Coverage of the ICTY's Proceedings Finds that Cameras Contribute to a Proper Administration of Justice*, The Hague, April 19, 2000, accessed March 24, 2014, http://www.icty.org/sid/7869. See also Peterson, "Temporary Courts, Permanent Records."

68 See UN ICTY, Courtroom Technology, 2014, accessed September 2, 2014, http://www.icty.org/sid/167. See also Paul Mason, "Court on Camera: Broadcast Coverage of The Legal Proceedings," 2020, accessed August 30, 2020, https://cap-press.com/sites/pj/camera-mason.htm.

69 See Delage, "The Place of the Filmed Witness," 1111. See also Extraordinary Chambers in the Courts of Cambodia (ECCC), "Introduction to the ECCC," accessed March 24, 2014, http://www.eccc.gov.kh/en/about-eccc/introduction.

70 Tom A. Adami, "'Who Will Be Left to Tell the Tale?' Recordkeeping and International Criminal Jurisprudence," *Archival Science* 7:3 (2007): 219.

71 In 1996, audio recordings of the floor proceedings and of the translations were introduced. In 1999, video recording was added. The soundtracks of the video recordings are duplicates of the audio. In an anecdotal note, one might add that the ICTY and the ICTR do not use electronic systems of recording, and future discussion should explore different recording cultures. See Peterson, "Temporary Courts, Permanent Records," 14–15.

72 Richard May and Marieke Wierda, "Trends in International Criminal Evidence: Nuremberg, Tokyo, The Hague, and Arusha." *Colum. J. Transnat'l L.* 37 (1998): 765.

73 Haldar, "The Return of the Evidencer's Eye," 88.

74 International Criminal Court, *Regulation of the Court*, May 26, 2004, accessed August 27, 2014, http://www.icc-cpi.int/NR/rdonlyres/B920AD62-DF49-4010-8907-E0D8CC61EBA4/277527/Regulations_of_the_Court_170604EN.pdf, 11–12. See, e.g., International Criminal Tribunal for the former Yugoslavia, *Rules of Procedure and Evidence, UN Doc. IT/32/Rev. 7*, Entered into Force March 14, 1994, Amendments Adopted January 8, 1996, accessed September 2, 2014, http://www1.umn.edu/humanrts/icty/ct-rules7.html, 25–6, 37, 47; International Criminal Tribunal of Rwanda, *Rules of Procedure of Evidence*, July 5, 1996, accessed April 30, 2020, http://hrlibrary.umn.edu/africa/RWANDA1.htm, Rule 81. See also Special Court for Sierra Leone, Rules of Procedure and Evidence, 2003, accessed September 2, 2014, https://www1.umn.edu/humanrts/instree/SCSL/Rules-of-proced-SCSL.pdf, Rule 81, p. 43. At the ECCC, judges may invoke disclosure, yet this ability does not appear to be explicitly grounded in considerations of national security. It may or may not be related to the fact that the tribunal is a governmental court and thus the protection of such interests is a given. See Extraordinary Chambers in The Courts of Cambodia (ECCC), Internal Rules (Rev. 8), Rule 97, as revised on August 3, 2011, accessed September 2, 2014, http://www.eccc.gov.kh/sites/default/

files/legal-documents/ECCC%20Internal%20Rules%20(Rev.8)%20English.pdf, 68; Special Court for Sierra Leone, Rules of Procedure and Evidence.

Chapter 6

1 Guy Peleg, "Commando Unit Warrior Is Prosecuting."
2 Ibid.
3 See also Maayan Amir and Ruti Sela, "Representing Extraterritorial Images," *Utrecht Law Review* 13:2 (2017): 7–12.
4 Nicholas Schmidle, "Getting bin Laden," *The New Yorker*, August 8, 2011, accessed February 6, 2019, https://www.thomasweibel.ch/artikel/110808_new_yorker_getting_bin_laden.pdf. See also Phillips, "Osama bin Laden Dead."
5 Phillips, "Osama bin Laden Dead."
6 Ibid.
7 Ibid.
8 "'Osama bin Laden, al-Qaeda Leader, dead'—Barack Obama," *BBC World News*, May 2, 2011, accessed January 31, 2019, https://www.bbc.com/news/world-us-canada-13256676; See also Schmidle, "Getting bin Laden."
9 Chris Lawrence, "'No Land Alternative' Prompts bin Laden Sea Burial," *CNN World*, May 3, 2011, accessed February 6, 2019, http://edition.cnn.com/2011/WORLD/asiapcf/05/02/bin.laden.burial.at.sea/index.html.
10 Adrian Brown, "Osama bin Laden's Death: How it Happened," *BBC*, September 10, 2012, accessed January 31, 2019, https://www.bbc.com/news/world-south-asia-13257330. See also "'Osama bin Laden, al-Qaeda Leader, dead'—Barack Obama."
11 Liam Kennedy, "Seeing and Believing: On Photography and the War on Terror," *Public Culture* 24:2–67 (2012): 267.
12 Jothie Rajah, "Law as Record: The Death of Osama bin Laden," *No Foundations* 13 (2012): 58.
13 Kennedy, "Seeing and Believing," 269.
14 Ibid., 273.
15 Rajah, "Law as Record," 50. The debates around the legality of the killings were not confined to scholarly writings, but also appeared in the general media. See, e.g., Rajah, "Law as Record: The Death of Osama bin Laden," 58; Aidan Lewis, "Osama bin Laden: Legality of Killing Questioned," *BBC World News*, May 12, 2011, accessed January 31, 2019, https://www.bbc.com/news/world-south-asia-13318372.
16 "Re: Freedom of Information Act Request," *Judicialwatch.org*, May 2, 2011, accessed September 16, 2020, http://www.judicialwatch.org/wp-content/uploads/2014/02/DOD-Osama-Op-FOIA-Request-5-13-2011.pdf.

17 *Judicial Watch,* "Judicial Watch Sues Department of Defense for Records of
    Communications Relating to May 2011 FOIA Request for bin Laden Death
    Photos," *Judicialwatch.org,* July 24, 2014, accessed February 5, 2019, https://www.
    judicialwatch.org/press-room/press-releases/judicial-watch-sues-department-
    defense-records-communications-relating-may-2011-foia-request-bin-laden-
    death-photos/.

18 Josh Gerstein, "CIA Finds Seven More Photos of Dead bin Laden," *Politico,*
    February 15, 2013, accessed June 11, 2020, https://www.politico.com/blogs/under-
    the-radar/2013/02/cia-finds-seven-more-photos-of-dead-bin-laden-157185.

19 *GlobeNewswire,* "Judicial Watch Asks Supreme Court to Review Lawsuit Against
    CIA and DoD to Force Release of bin Laden Death Images," *GlobeNewsWire.com,*
    August 19, 2013, accessed June 11, 2020, https://www.globenewswire.com/news-
    release/2013/08/19/1046449/0/en/Judicial-Watch-Asks-Supreme-Court-to-Review-
    Lawsuit-Against-CIA-and-DOD-to-Force-Release-of-bin-Laden-Death-Images.html.

20 *Judicial Watch,* "Judicial Watch Uncovers Email Revealing Top Pentagon Leader
    Ordered Destruction of bin Laden Death Photos," *Judicialwatch.org,* February
    10, 2014, accessed June 11, 2020, https://www.judicialwatch.org/press-releases/
    pentagon-destruction-of-bin-laden-death-photos/.

21 Kim Geiger, "Officials Helped Makers of Osama bin Laden Film, Documents
    Show," *Los Angeles Times,* May 24, 2012, accessed March 6, 2019, http://articles.
    latimes.com/2012/may/24/nation/la-na-cia-hollywood-20120524. For an extended
    report of the capture, see Schmidle, "Getting bin Laden." This tactic is not new; It
    was reported that while the CIA has collaborated with Hollywood directors since
    1947 in order to improve the agency's image, it was not until the 1990s that "the
    agency formally hired an entertainment industry liaison and began openly courting
    favorable treatment in films and television." Nicholas Schou, "How the CIA
    Hoodwinked Hollywood," *The Atlantic,* July 14, 2014, accessed February 5, 2019,
    https://www.theatlantic.com/entertainment/archive/2016/07/operation-tinseltown-
    how-the-cia-manipulates-hollywood/491138/.

22 James Der Derian, *Virtuous War: Mapping the Military-Industrial-Media-
    Entertainment Network* (London: Routledge, 2009), 163; Roger Stahl, *Militainment,
    Inc.: War, Media, and Popular Culture* (London: Routledge, 2009), 7.

23 "Notice of Defense Motion to Compel Production of Communications Between
    Government and Filmmakers of Zero Dark Thirty," The United States of America,
    AE195(AAA), July 31, 2013, accessed June 11, 2020, https://www.mc.mil/Portals/0/
    pdfs/KSM2/KSM%20II%20(AE195(AAA))_Part1.pdf.

24 Ibid., 4.

25 Ibid., 5. See also Rajah, "Law as Record," 53–5.

26 Eliav Lieblich, "Show Us the Films: Transparency, National Security and Disclosure
    of Information Collected by Advanced Weapon Systems Under International Law,"
    Israel Law Review 45:3 (2012): 459–91, 460. See also Jack M. Beard, "Law and

War in the Virtual Era," *The American Journal of International Law* 103:3 (2009): 415–16.

27　"Chapter 3, Counterinsurgency Operations," Global Security.org, accessed June 1, 2020, https://www.globalsecurity.org/military/library/policy/army/fm/3-07-22/ch3-iii.htm.

Bibliography

Adalah.org. "Legal Center for Arab Minority Rights in Israel, Supreme Court Rejects Far-Right-Wing Politicians' Petition against Decision to Close Investigation of MK Haneen Zoabi and Sheikh Raed Salah for Participating in Gaza Flotilla." December 24, 2012, accessed August 9, 2020. https://www.adalah.org/en/content/view/8232.

Adami, Tom A. "'Who Will Be Left to Tell the Tale?' Recordkeeping and International Criminal Jurisprudence." *Archival Science* 7:3 (2007): 213–22.

Adebajo, Adekeye. *UN Peacekeeping in Africa: From the Suez Crisis to the Sudan Conflicts*. Boulder, CO: Lynne Rienner Publishers, 2011.

Agamben, Giorgio. *Homo Sacer: Sovereign Power and Bare Life*. Redwood City, CA: Stanford University Press, 1998.

_____. *Means without End*. Minneapolis: University of Minnesota Press, 2000.

_____. *State of Exception*. Chicago: University of Chicago Press, 2005.

_____. *The Time that Remains: A Commentary on the Letter to the Romans*. Redwood City, CA: Stanford University Press, 2005.

_____. *Omnibus Homo Sacer*. Redwood City, CA: Stanford University Press, 2017.

Agier, Michel. "Humanity as an Identity and Its Political Effect: A Note on Camps and Humanitarian Government." *Humanity: An International Journal of Human Rights, Humanitarianism and Development* 1:1 (2010): 29–45.

_____. "The Undesirables of the World and How Universality Changed Camp." *openDemocracy*, May 16, 2011, accessed April 2, 2020. https://www.opendemocracy.net/en/undesirables-of-world-and-how-universality-changed-camp/.

Agier, Michel, and Françoise Bouchet-Saulnier. "Humanitarian Spaces: Spaces of Exception." In *Shadow of Just Wars: Violence, Politics and Humanitarian Action*, edited by Fabrice Weissman. Ithaca, NY: *Medecins Sans Frontieres*, 2004: 228–46.

Aksel, İsmail. "Turkish Judicial System—Bodies, Duties and Officials." Ministry of Justice of Turkey, Department for Strategy Development. 2013, accessed April 21, 2020. https://rm.coe.int/turkish-judicial-system-bodies-duties-and-officials-by-ismail-aksel-ju/168078f25f.

Al-Jazeera English. "Israeli Troops Storm Gaza Flotilla." YouTube Video, 1:28 mins. May 31, 2010, accessed October 10, 2012. http://www.youtube.com/watch?v=xFEBbDkyrqQ. Television Broadcast.

Altahrir, News of Islam, Muslims, Arab Spring and Special Palestine. "Israel Must Be Held Accountable." March 29, 2014, accessed April 25, 2020. https://altahrir.wordpress.com/2014/03/29/israel-must-be-held-accountable/.

Amir, Maayan. "The Visual Side of Privacy: State-Incriminating, Coproduced Archives." *Public Culture* 32:1 (2020): 185–213.

Amir, Maayan, and Ruti Sela, eds. *Extraterritorialities in Occupied Worlds*. Santa
    Barbara, CA: Punctum Books, 2016.

Amir, Maayan and Ruti Sela. "Representing Extraterritorial Images". *Utrecht Law Review*
    13:2 (2017): 7–12.

Amnesty International. "Israel/Gaza: Operation Cast Lead: 22 Days of Destruction."
    July 9, 2009, accessed April 10, 2020. https://www.amnesty.org/download/
    Documents/48000/mde150152009en.pdf.

Anadolu [News] Agency 'AA.' "Turkish Court Begins Trial of Israeli Officers on *Mavi*
    Marmara Raid." November 6, 2012, accessed September 24, 2020. https://www.
    aa.com.tr/en/turkey/turkish-court-begins-trial-of-israeli-officers-on-mavi-
    marmara-raid/312215.

Anghie, Antony. "Colonialism and the Birth of International Institutions: Sovereignty,
    Economy, and the Mandate System of the League of Nations." *New York University*
    Journal of International Law and Politics 34 (2001): 513–634.

Ansay, Tuğrul, and Don Wallace, Jr., eds. *Introduction to Turkish Law*. The Hague, The
    Netherlands: Kluwer Law International, 2005.

Aslan, M. Yasin. "Transformation of Turkish Criminal Law from the Ottoman-Islamic
    Law to the Civil Law Tradition". *Ankara Bar Review* 2:2 (2009): 92–8.

Atzmon, Gilad. "Shocking Testimonies from the *Mavi Marmara* Survivors and One
    Israeli Fembot." June 11, 2010, accessed April 11, 2020. https://gilad.online/writings/
    shocking-testimonials-from-the-mavi-marmara-survivors-and-on.html.

Augusti, Eliana. "From Capitulations to Unequal Treaties: The Matter of an Extraterritorial
    Jurisdiction in the Ottoman Empire." *Journal of Civil Law Studies* 4:2 (2011): 285–307.

Avalon Project. Covenant of the League of Nations: Article 22. Yale Law School. 2008,
    accessed January 31, 2020. https://avalon.law.yale.edu/20th_century/leagcov.asp.

Aydin, Suavi, Meryem Erdal, Mithat Sancar and Eylem Ümit Atilgan. *Just Expectations:*
    A Compilation of TESEV Research Studies on the Judiciary in Turkey. Istanbul:
    TESEV Publications, 2011. https://www.tesev.org.tr/wp-content/uploads/report_
    Just_Expectations_Compilation_Of_TESEV_Research_Studies_On_The_Judiciary_
    In_Turkey.pdf.

B'Tselem: Israeli Information Center for Human Rights in the Occupied Territories.
    "Land Grab: Israel Settlement Policy in the West Bank." May 2002, accessed February
    27, 2020. https://www.btselem.org/publications/summaries/200205_land_grab.

B'Tselem. "The Siege on the Gaza Strip: 1.5 Million People Imprisoned." May 31, 2010, accessed
    June 21, 2020. https://www.btselem.org/gaza_strip/20100531_the_siege_on_gaza.

B'Tselem. "Lift the Restrictions on the Gaza Fishing Range." March 24, 2013, accessed
    April 1, 2013. http://www.btselem.org/gaza_strip/20130324_restrictions_on_
    fishing_should_be_lifted.

B'Tselem. "Reality Check: Almost Fifty Years of Occupation." June 5, 2016, accessed
    April 9, 2020. https://www.btselem.org/sites/default/files/sites/default/files2/201606_
    reality_check_eng_0.pdf.

B'Tselem. "The Gaza Strip." November 11, 2017, accessed June 20, 2020. https://www.
    btselem.org/gaza_strip.

Bacak, Alp Aziz. *Adiuelerinn Fiziksel ve Mimari Koşullari Bağlaminda Yargisal.* 2015. http://tbbdergisi.barobirlik.org.tr/m2015-120-1514.

Bar Siman-Tov, Yaacov, ed. *The Disengagement Plan: The Dream and Its Break.* Jerusalem: The Israel Institute for Advanced Studies (IIAS) of Jerusalem, 2009. https://jerusaleminstitute.org.il/wp-content/uploads/2019/05/PUB_diseng2009_heb.pdf.

Barch, Uzi. "Commando Soldiers Field a Petition against the Rapprochement Deal." *Arutz-7.* June 30, 2016, accessed July 19, 2018. https://www.inn.co.il/News/News.aspx/325186.

Barnes, Ed. "Reuters Admits Cropping Photos of Ship Clash, Denies Political Motive." *Fox News.* June 8, 2010, accessed March 9, 2012. http://www.foxnews.com/world/2010/06/08/reuters-fake-photos-ihh-gaza-blockade-commandos.

Bassam, Tibi. "Europeanising Islam or the Islamization of Europe: Political Democracy vs. Cultural." In *Religion in an Expanding Europe.* Edited by Timothy A. Byrnes and Peter J. Katzenstein. Cambridge, UK: Cambridge University Press, 2006: 204–224.

Bauman, Zygmunt. "The World Inhospitable to Levinas." *Philosophy Today* 43:2 (1999): 151–67. Reprinted in "*Extraterritorialities in Occupied Worlds*," edited by Maayan Amir and Ruti Sela. Santa Barbara, CA: Punctum Books, 2016: 59–88.

———. *Liquid Modernity.* Malden, MA: Polity Press, 2000.

Bayoumi, Moustafa, ed. *Midnight on the Mavi Marmara: The Attack on the Gaza Freedom Flotilla and How It Changed the Course of the Israel/Palestine Conflict.* New York: Or Books, 2010.

BBC. "Death in the Med." *Panorama.* Television Documentary, 30 mins. August 22, 2010. https://www.bbc.co.uk/programmes/b00thr24.

BBC. "'Osama bin Laden, al-Qaeda Leader, dead'—Barack Obama." *BBC World News.* May 2, 2011, accessed January 31, 2019. https://www.bbc.com/news/world-us-canada-13256676.

BBC. "Turkey Tries Israeli Commanders over *Mavi Marmara* Raid." *BBC World News.* November 6, 2012, accessed February 8, 2013. http://www.bbc.co.uk/news/world-europe-20215991.

BBC. "Will ICC Membership Help or Hinder the Palestinians' Cause?" *BBC World News.* April 1, 2015, accessed February 25, 2020. https://www.bbc.com/news/world-middle-east-30744701.

BBC. "*Mavi Marmara*: Why Did Israel Stop the Gaza Flotilla?" *BBC News.* June 27, 2016, accessed April 16, 2020. https://www.bbc.com/news/10203726.

Beard, Jack M. "Law and War in the Virtual Era." *American Journal of International Law* 103:3 (2009): 409–45.

Ben-Dror, Elad. "The Poets of Marj al-Zuhur: Poetry as the Psychological, Political, and Ideological Weapon of the Hamas Members Deported to Lebanon in 1992." *Terrorism and Political Violence* 28:1 (2016): 157–179.

———. "'We Were Getting Close to God, Not Deportees': The Expulsion to Marj al-Zuhur in 1992 as a Milestone in the Rise of Hamas." *The Middle East Journal* 74:3 (2020): 399–416.

Ben-Naftali, Orna. "The Extraterritorial Application of Human Rights to Occupied Territories". *Proceedings of the ASIL Annual Meeting,* vol. 100, pp. 90–95. Cambridge University Press, 2006.

Ben-Naftali, Orna, and Keren R. Michaeli. "Justice Ability: A Critique of the Alleged Non Justiciability of Israel's Policy of Targeted Killings." *Journal of International Criminal Justice* 1:2 (2003): 368–405.

Ben-Naftali, Orna and Yuval Shany. "Living in Denial: The Application of Human Rights in the Occupied Territories." *Israel Law Review* 37:1 (2003): 17–118.

Benjamin, Walter. *Illumination*. New York: Schocken Books, 1986.

———. "Critique of Violence." In *Reflections: Essays, Aphorisms, Autobiographical Writings*. Edited by Peter Demetz. Translated by Edmund Jephcott. New York: Schocken, 1986: 277–300.

———. *Selected Writings, Vol. 1: 1913–1926*. Edited by Marcus Bullock and Michael W. Jennings Cambridge, MA: Belknap Press, 1996.

Bentham, Jeremy. *Works of Jeremy Bentham*, Vol. 7. Edited by John Bowring. Edinburgh: William Tait, 1838–43.

Benvenisti, Eyal. *Legal Dualism: The Absorption of the Occupied Territories into Israel.* London: Routledge, 2018.

Benvenisti, Eyal, and Eyal Zamir. "Private Claims to Property Rights in the Future Israeli-Palestinian Settlement." *American Journal of International Law* 89:2 (1995): 295–340.

Bergel, Steven I. "Evidence—Silent Witness Theory Adopted to Admit Photographs without Percipient Witness Testimony." *Suffolk University Law Review* 19 (1985): 353–9.

Berk, Seda Kalem. *'Access to Justice' in Turkey: Indicators and Recommendations* Istanbul: TESEV Publications, 2011, accessed March 3, 2014. https://www.tesev. org.tr/wp-content/uploads/report_Access_To_Justice_In_Turkey_Indicators_And_ Recommendations.pdf.

Bernasconi, Robert. "Extra-Territoriality: Outside the State, Outside the Subject." *Levinas Studies* 3 (2008): 61–77.

BIA. "Erdoğan Changes Opinion over the Marmara Case." *Bianet News Desk*. June 30, 2016, accessed July 25, 2018. https://bianet.org/english/politics/176388-Erdoğan-changes-opinion-on-mavi-marmara-crisis.

Biemann, Ursula. *Mission Reports: Artistic Practice in the Field*. Umeå, Sweden: Bildmuseet, Umeå University, 2008.

Bilefsky, Dan, and Sebnem Arsu. "Sponsor of Flotilla Tied to Elite of Turkey." *The New York Times*. July 16, 2010, accessed April 16, 2020. https://www.nytimes. com/2010/07/16/world/middleeast/16turkey.html?auth=login-email&login=email.

———. "Charges against Journalists Dim the Democratic Glow in Turkey." *The New York Times*. January 5, 2012, accessed February 26, 2013. http://www.nytimes. com/2012/01/05/world/europe/turkeys-glow-dims-as-government-limits-free-speech. html?pagewanted=all.

Björnberg, Kjell, and Ross Cranston. *The Functioning of the Judicial System in the Republic of Turkey: Report of an Advisory Visit.* European Commission Brussels. June 13–22, 2005, accessed April 5, 2014. http://www.deontologie-judiciaire.umontreal. ca/en/textes%20int/documents/TURQUIE_ENQUeTE.pdf.

Bligh, Alexander. "The United Nations Emergency Force (UNEF), 1956–67: Past Experience, Current Lessons." *Middle Eastern Studies* 50:5 (2014): 796–809.

Blumenthal, Max. "Israeli Army Admits It Doctored Gaza Freedom Flotilla Audio Clip." *Global Research News*. June 10, 2010, accessed April 14, 2020. https://www.globalresearch.ca/israel-military-admits-it-doctored-gaza-freedom-flotilla-audio-clip/19646.

Bob, Yonah Jeremy. "Turkey Resumes Gaza Flotilla Trial for ex-IDF Heads." *The Jerusalem Post*. February 21, 2013, accessed April 16, 2013. http://www.jpost.com/Diplomacy-and-Politics/Turkey-resumes-Gaza-flotilla-trial-for-ex-IDF-heads.

Brain, Robert D. "The Derivative Relevance of Demonstrative Evidence: Charting Its Proper Evidentiary Status." *UC Davis Law Review* 25:4 (1992): 957–1027.

Bray, Mayfield. S., and William T. Murphy. "Audiovisual Records in the National Archives Relating to World War I." Preliminary Draft, National Archives and Records Service (GSA). Washington, DC. 1972, accessed August 11, 2014. http://files.eric.ed.gov/fulltext/ED081239.pdf.

Brittain, Victoria. "They Had to Die: Assassination against Liberation." *Race & Class* 48:1 (2006): 60–74.

Brown, Adrian. "Osama bin Laden's Death: How it Happened." *BBC*. September 10, 2012, accessed January 31, 2019. https://www.bbc.com/news/world-south-asia-13257330.

Burch, Jonathon. "Turkey Tries Israeli Military over Gaza Ship Killings." *Reuters*. November 5, 2012, accessed March 18, 2013. http://mobile.reuters.com/article/idUS BRE8A415T20121105?irpc=932.

———. "Turkey Tries Israeli Military over Gaza Ship Killings." *Daily Star*. November 5, 2012, accessed January 15, 2013. http://www.dailystar.com.lb/News/Middle-East/2012/Nov-05/193962-turkey-to-try-israeli-top-brass-in-deadly-flotilla-raid.ashx#axzz2IRZw5noP.

"*Çağlayan Adliyesi'nde Polis Müdahalesi Cascade Police Intervention*." YouTube Video. (No longer available), accessed September 7, 2014. https://www.youtube.com/watch?v=x0yyQaNb5cU.

Cam, Ali Riza. "EU Principles in Modernisation of Justice and the Turkish IT Project UYPA." *European Journal of ePractice*. 2008, accessed April 23, 2020. https://www.slideshare.net/epracticejournal/ali-riza-presentation.

Carter, Rodney G. S. "Ocular Proof: Photographs as Legal Evidence." *Archivaria* 69 (2010): 23–47.

Cassel, Pär Kristoffer. *Grounds of Judgment: Extraterritoriality and Imperial Power in Nineteenth-Century China and Japan*. Oxford: Oxford University Press, 2012.

Chan, K. C. "The Abrogation of British Extraterritoriality in China 1942–43: A Study of Anglo-American-Chinese Relations." *Modern Asian Studies* 11:2 (1977): 257–91.

Channel 2 Israel and DHA. "The Flotilla Ship *Mavi Marmara*, Peace Activists Stabbing Israeli Soldier." YouTube Video. 0:48 mins. May 31, 2010, accessed March 24, 2012. https://www.youtube.com/watch?v=o6MLJErSD2s.

Channel 10 and DHA. Channel 10 News Edition. "Nine Participants in Flotilla Killed." YouTube Video. 11:35 mins. June 1, 2010, accessed April 12, 2020. https://www.youtube.com/watch?v=eSeEtNHtCPI.

Chatterjee, Nandini. "Reflections on Religious Difference and Permissive Inclusion on Mughal Law." *Journal of Law and Religion* 29:3 (2014): 369–415.

Chowdhury, M.L. Roy. "Principles of Law in the Mughal Empire." *Proceedings of the Indian History Congress* 10 (1947): 367–70.

CNN TURK. "*Dakika, Dakika, Mavi Marmara ya Saldiri.*" YouTube Video. 8:24 mins. June 1, 2010, accessed February 11, 2013. http://www.youtube.com/watch?v=INVT98698R8.

Cohen, Gilly. "IDF Unit Whose Role is to Make a Headache for the Enemy." *Haaretz.* November 30, 2012, accessed July 6, 2020. https://www.haaretz.co.il/news/politics/1.1876589.

Cohen, Jonathan, and Aaron Meskin. "Photographs as Evidence." In *Photography and Philosophy: Essays on the Pencil of Nature.* Edited by Scott Walden. West Sussex, UK: Blackwell Publishing, 1986: 70–90.

Cohn, Bernard S. "Some Notes on Law and Change in North India." *Economic Development and Cultural Change* 8:1 (1959): 79–93.

Colborne, Sarah. "Three Years On, the *Mavi Marmara* Is Still Making Waves." Palestine Solidarity Campaign. May 31, 2013, accessed April 16, 2014. http://www.palestinecampaign.org/three-years-on-the-mavi-marmara-is-still-making-waves/.

Collins, Robert. K. L., and David M. Skover. "Paratexts." *Stanford Law Review* 44:3 (1992): 509–52.

Council of Europe. *Convention for the Protection of Human Rights and Fundamental Freedoms.* 1950. https://www.echr.coe.int/Documents/Convention_ENG.pdf.

Council of Europe. *European Commission for Democracy Through Law, Penal Code of Turkey.* February 15, 2016, accessed July 28, 2020. https://www.venice.coe.int/webforms/documents/default.aspx?pdffile=CDL-AD_2016_002-e.

Cultures of Resistance Films. "Israeli Attack on the *Mavi Marmara* (1 Hour Raw Footage)." YouTube Video. 62 mins. June 11, 2010, accessed March 19, 2012. http://www.youtube.com/watch?v=vwsMJmvS0AY.

Degani, Arnon Yehuda. "The Decline and Fall of the Israeli Military Government, 1948–1966: A Case of Settler-Colonial Consolidation?" *Settler Colonial Studies* 5:1 (2015): 84–99.

Delage, Christian. *Caught on Camera: Film in the Courtroom from the Nuremberg Trials to the Trials of the Khmer Rouge.* Translated and edited by Ralph Schoolcraft and Mary Byrd Kelly. Philadelphia: University of Pennsylvania Press, 2006.

———. "The Place of the Filmed Witness: From Nuremberg to the Khmer Rouge Trial." *Cardozo Law Review* 31 (2009): 1087–112.

Delage, Christian, and Peter Goodrich, eds. *The Scene of the Mass Crime: History, Film and International Tribunals.* London: Routledge, 2013.

Den Heijer, Maarten. *Europe and Extraterritorial Asylum.* London: Bloomsbury Publishing, 2012.

Der Derian, James. *Virtuous War: Mapping the Military-Industrial-Media-Entertainment Network.* London: Routledge, 2009.

Dinç, M Şefik. *Kanili Mavi Marmara*. Istanbul: Kalkedon, 2010.

Doğru, Osman. "Mills That Grind Defendants: The Criminal Justice System in Turkey from a Human Rights Perspective." Istanbul: TESEV Publications, March 2012, accessed April 27, 2020. https://www.tesev.org.tr/wp-content/uploads/report_Mills_That_Grind_Defendants_Criminal_Justice_System_In_Turkey_From_A_Human_Rights_Perspective.pdf.

Dollinger, André. "Herodotus on Proteus." *An Introduction to the History and Culture of Pharaonic Egypt*. 2000, accessed August 7, 2013. http://www.reshafim.org.il/ad/egypt/herodotus/proteus.htm (no longer available).

Dönmez, B. Demren. "Cross-Examination in Turkish Criminal Procedure Law." *Ankara Law Review* 8:1 (2011): 53–69.

Donnelly, Jack. "Human Rights: A New Standard of Civilization?" *International Affairs*, 74:1 (1998): 1–23.

Dorell, Oren. "Istanbul Airport: A Scene of Gunfire, Bombs and Sirens." *USA Today*. June 28, 2016, accessed July 25, 2018. https://www.usatoday.com/story/news/world/2016/06/28/istanbul-airport-scene-gunfire-bombs-and-sirens/86498648/.

Easterling, Keller. "Zone: The Spatial Software of Extrastatecraft." *Places Journal* (2012), accessed April 6, 2020. https://placesjournal.org/article/zone-the-spatial-softwares-of-extrastatecraft/?cn-reloaded=1#0.

Economic Cooperation Foundation. Cairo Agreement—On the Gaza Strip and the Jericho Area. May 4, 1994, accessed February 20, 2020. https://ecf.org.il/media_items/618.

Eichensehr, Kristen E. "On Target? The Israeli Supreme Court and the Expansion of Targeted Killings." *The Yale Law Journal* 116:8 (2007): 1873–81.

Electronic Intifada. "Spain Prosecutor Requests ICC Referral of Case against Israel's Netanyahu for 2010 Flotilla Attack." January 17, 2013, accessed June 18, 2014. http://electronicintifada.net/blogs/ali-abunimah/spain-prosecutor-requests-icc-referral-case-against-israels-netanyahu-2010.

Erakat, Noura. *Justice for Some: Law and the Question of Palestine*. Redwood City, CA: Stanford University Press, 2019.

Erdem Law Office. "Key Notes on Legal Development of September 2011," accessed March 3, 2014. http://www.erdem-erdem.com/en/articles/key-notes-on-legal-developments-of-september-2011.

Erişen, Cengiz, and Elif Erişen. "Attitudinal Ambivalence towards Turkey's EU Membership." *Journal of Common Market Studies* 52:2 (2013): 217–33.

EurActive. "EU-Turkey Relations." November 14, 2005, accessed February 27, 2013. http://www.euractiv.com/enlargement/eu-turkey-relations/article-129678.

EurActive. "EU Will Lose Turkey if It Hasn't Joined by 2023, Erodgan Says." October 31, 2012, accessed February 26, 2013. http://www.euractiv.com/enlargement/eu-lose-turkey-hasnt-joined-2023-news-515780.

EurActive. "Turkey's EU Bid in Jeopardy After Council of Europe Vote." April 25,
2017, accessed July 7, 2018. https://www.euractiv.com/section/global-europe/news/
turkeys-eu-bid-in-jeopardy-after-council-of-europe-vote/.

European Commission. "Standard Summary Project Fiche Project Number: TR 05
01.01 Better Access to Justice in Turkey." January 1, 2005, accessed April 20, 2020.
https://ec.europa.eu/neighborhood-enlargement/sites/near/files/pdf/fiche-projet/
turkey/2005/pf-2005-01.01-better-access-to-justice-in-turkey.pdf.

European Commission. Staff Working Document [SWP]. *Enlargement Strategy and Main
Challenges 2012–2013.* October 10, 2012, accessed February 26, 2013. http://ec.europa.
eu/enlargement/pdf/key_documents/2012/package/tr_rapport_2012_en.pdf.

European Commission. Staff Working Document [SWP]. *Turkey 2013 Progress Report.*
October 16, 2013, accessed April 27, 2020. https://www.ab.gov.tr/files/2013%20
ilerleme%20raporu/tr_rapport_2013_en.pdf.

European Commission. *European Neighbourhood Policy and Enlargement Negotiations,
Conditions for Membership.* November 28, 2013, accessed March 18, 2014. http://
ec.europa.eu/enlargement/policy/conditions-membership/index_en.htm.

European Commission. *Turkey 2016 Report.* November 9, 2016, accessed July 5, 2018.
https://ec.europa.eu/neighbourhood-enlargement/system/files/2018-12/20161109_
report_turkey.pdf.

European Commission. *Turkey 2018 Report.* April 17, 2018, accessed July 5, 2018.
https://ec.europa.eu/neighborhood-enlargement/sites/near/files/20180417-turkey-
report.pdf.

Extraordinary Chambers in the Courts of Cambodia (ECCC). "Introduction to
the ECCC." accessed March 24, 2014. http://www.eccc.gov.kh/en/about-eccc/
introduction.

Extraordinary Chambers in the Courts of Cambodia (ECCC). Internal Rules (Rev. 8),
as revised on August 3, 2011, accessed September 2, 2014. http://www.eccc.gov.kh/
sites/default/files/legal-documents/ECCC%20Internal%20Rules%20_Rev.8_%20
English.pdf.

Faroqhi, Suraiya, Bruce McGowan, Donald Quataert, Sevket Pamuk, and Halil
Inalcik. *An Economic and Social History of the Ottoman Empire, Vol. 2: 1600–1914.*
Cambridge, UK: Cambridge University Press, 1995.

Feldman, Ilana. "Ad Hoc Humanity: UN Peacekeeping and the Limits of International
Community in Gaza." *American Anthropologist* 112:3 (2010): 416–29.

Feldman, Tamar. "A Tale of Two Closures: Comments on the Palmer Report
Concerning the May 2010 Flotilla Incident." *European Journal of International Law*
(blog). September 20, 2011, accessed July 5, 2013. http://www.ejiltalk.org/a-tale-of-
two-closures-comments-on-the-palmer-report-concerning-the-may-2010-flotilla-
incident.

Felman, Shoshana. *The Scandal of the Speaking Body: Don Juan with JL Austin, or
Seduction in Two Languages.* Redwood City, CA: Stanford University Press, 2003.

Filiu, Jean-Pierre. *Gaza: A History*. Oxford: Oxford University Press, 2014.

Filosu, Özgürlük. *Mavi Marmara Gazze*. Istanbul: IHH Kitap, 2011.

Folk, Richard. "Israel on the Felons Dock: Double Standards in International Law." Lecture at the Foundation for Human Rights, Freedom and Humanitarian Relief [IHH]. University of Istanbul, accessed April 15, 2014. http://eski.ihh.org.tr/falk-uluslararasi-hukuk-cifte-standartli/en/.

FRA, The European Union Agency for Fundamental Rights. *Accesses to Justice in Europe: An Overview of Challenges and Opportunities*. 2011, accessed April 9, 2014. http://fra.europa.eu/sites/default/files/fra_uploads/1520-report-access-to-justice_EN.pdf.

FRA, The European Union Agency for Fundamental Human Rights. *Access to Justice in Cases of Discrimination in the EU: Steps to Further Equality*. 2012, accessed April 2, 2014. https://fra.europa.eu/sites/default/files/fra-2012-access-to-justice-social.pdf.

Friends of the Arc.org. "On the Arc Project: Friends of the Arc, What's the Arc," accessed February 20, 2020. http://friendsofthearc.org/.

Furet, François. *The Passing of an Illusion*. Translated by Deborah Furet. Chicago: University of Chicago Press, 1999. Originally published as *Le passé d'une illusion*. Paris: Éditions Robert Laffont, 1995.

Garwood-Gowers, Andrew. "Israel's Airstrike on Syria's Al-Kibar Facility: A Test Case for the Doctrine of Pre-Emptive Self-Defence?" *Journal of Conflict & Security Law* 16:2 (2011): 263–91.

Geiger, Kim. "Officials Helped Makers of Osama bin Laden Film, Documents Show." *Los Angeles Times*. May 24, 2012, accessed March 6, 2019. http://articles.latimes.com/2012/may/24/nation/la-na-cia-hollywood-20120524.

Gerstein, Josh. "CIA Finds Seven More Photos of Dead bin Laden." *Politico*. February 15, 2013, accessed June 11, 2020. https://www.politico.com/blogs/under-the-radar/2013/02/cia-finds-seven-more-photos-of-dead-bin-laden-157185.

Gisha—Legal Center for Freedom of Movement. *Disengaged Occupiers: The Legal Status of Gaza*. 2006, accessed January 4, 2013. http://www.gisha.org/UserFiles/File/Report%20for%20the%20website.pdf.

Gisha—Legal Center for Freedom of Movement. *Rafah Crossing: Who Holds the Keys?* 2009, accessed April 1, 2015. http://www.gisha.org/userfiles/File/publications/Rafah_Report_Eng.pdf.

Gisha—Legal Center for Freedom of Movement. *Scale of Control: Israel's Continued Responsibility in the Gaza Strip*. 2012, accessed June 2, 2012. http://www.gisha.org/UserFiles/File/scaleofcontrol/scaleofcontrol_en.pdf.

GlobeNewswire. "Judicial Watch Asks Supreme Court to Review Lawsuit against CIA and DoD to Force Release of bin Laden Death Images." *GlobeNewsWire.com*. August 19, 2013, accessed June 11, 2020. https://www.globenewswire.com/news-release/2013/08/19/1046449/0/en/Judicial-Watch-Asks-Supreme-Court-to-Review-Lawsuit-Against-CIA-and-DOD-to-Force-Release-of-bin-Laden-Death-Images.html.

Global Research News. "Turkey Begins Nuremberg Trials against Israel." November 6, 2012, accessed April 17, 2020. https://www.globalresearch.ca/turkey-begins-nuremberg-trials-against-israel/5310854.

Global Security.org. "Chapter 3, Counterinsurgency Operations," accessed June 1, 2020. https://www.globalsecurity.org/military/library/policy/army/fm/3-07-22/ch3-iii.htm.

Gökan, Sezer. *A Study on the Turkish Criminal Trial System.* Istanbul: Ankara Bar Association, 2010.

Gökdemir, Cihat. *Mavi Marmara* Indictment. 2012, accessed February 1, 2013. https://www.dropbox.com/sh/l0zl7g242zi1bu9/50rnIguSdl/STATEMENT%20OF%20CIHAT%20GÖKDEMIR%20%28DIRECTOR%20OF%20MAZLUMDER%20NGO%29.pdf.

Golan, Tal. *Laws of Men and Laws of Nature.* Cambridge, MA: Harvard University Press, 2004.

———. "The Emergence of the Silent Witness: The Legal and Medical Reception of X-rays in the USA." *Social Studies of Science* 34:4 (2004): 469–499.

Gordon, Neve. *Israel's Occupation.* Oakland, CA: University of California Press, 2008.

Gorgos, Keith A. "Lost in Transcription: Why the Video Record Is Actually Verbatim." *Buffalo Law Review* 57:3 (2009): 1057–1128.

Gregory, Derek. "The Black Flag: Guantánamo Bay and the Space of Exception." *Geografiska Annaler* 88:4 (2006): 405–27.

Gruen, Martin E. "The World of Courtroom Technology." Center for Legal and Court Technology. 2003, accessed June 24, 2014. http://www.legaltechcenter.net/download/whitepapers/The%20World%20Of%20Courtroom%20Technology.pdf.

Guilshan, Christine A. "A Picture Is Worth a Thousand Lies: Electronic Imaging and the Future of the Admissibility of Photographs into Evidence." *Rutgers Computer & Technology Law Journal* 1 (1992): 365–80.

Haldar, Piyel. "The Evidencer's Eye: Representations of Truth in the Laws of Evidence." *Law and Critique* 2 (1991): 171–89.

———. "The Return of the Evidencer's Eye: Rhetoric and the Visual Technologies of Proof." *Griffith Law Review* 8:1 (1999): 86–101.

Hammarberg, Thomas. *Report on the Administration of Justice and Protection of Human Rights in Turkey.* Commissioner for Human Rights of the Council of Europe, following his visit to Turkey from 10 to 14 October 2011. Strasbourg: Council of Europe, January 10, 2012, accessed February 26, 2013. http://www.europarl.europa.eu/meetdocs/2009_2014/documents/d-tr/dv/0131_04/0131_04en.pdf.

Hanafi, Sari. "The Broken Boundaries of Statehood and Citizenship." *Borderlands e-journal* 2:3 (2003), accessed April 6, 2020. http://www.borderlands.net.au/vol2no3_2003/hanafi_boundaries.htm.

———. "Palestinian Refugee Camps in Lebanon: Laboratories of State-in-the-Making, Discipline and Islamist Radicalism." In *Biopolitics and States of Exception.* Edited by Ronit Lentin. London: Zed Books, 2008: 82–100.

———. "Palestinian Refugee Camps in Lebanon Laboratory of Indocile Identity Formation." In *Manifestations of Identity: The Lived Reality of Palestinian Refugees in*

Lebanon. Edited by Muhammad Ali Khalidi. Beirut: Institute of Palestine Studies, 2010: 45–74.

———. *Governing Palestinian Refugees in the Arab East*. Beirut: Issam Fares Institute, American University of Beirut, 2010.

———. "New Models for the Nation-State." In *Solution 196–213: United States of Palestine-Israel. Edited* by Joshua Simon. New York: Sternberg Press, 2011.

Hashemi, Kamran. *Religious Legal Traditions, International Human Rights Law and Muslim States*. Leiden, The Netherlands: Brill Publishers, 2008.

Herodotus. *Histories*. Translated by A. D. Godley. Cambridge, MA: Harvard University Press, 1920.

Hildebrandt, Mireille. "Extraterritorial Jurisdiction to Enforce in Cyberspace? Bodin, Schmitt, Grotius in Cyberspace." *University of Toronto Law Journal* 63:2 (2013): 196–224.

Hilal, Sandi, Alessandro Petti, and Eyal Weizman. *Architecture after Revolution*. Berlin: Sternberg Press, 2013.

Hirsch, Moshe. "Treaty-Making Power: Approval the Israel-Egypt Philadelphia Accord by the Knesset." *Israel Law Review* 39 (2006): 229–37.

Hodali, Fadwa. "Report: Abbas Peace Plan Calls for Israeli Withdrawal from West Bank." *The Philadelphia Inquirer*. September 4, 2014, accessed February 25, 2020. https://www.inquirer.com/philly/news/nation_world/20140904_Report__Abbas_peace_plan_calls_for_Israeli_withdrawal_from_West_Bank.html.

Home, Robert. "An 'Irreversible Conquest'? Colonial and Postcolonial Land Law in Israel/Palestine." *Social & Legal Studies* 12:3 (2003): 291–310.

Horwitz, Moshe. "The Border between Israel and Egypt." 2006, accessed June 26, 2020. https://lib.cet.ac.il/pages/item.asp?item=14913.

Human Rights Watch. "Lawyers on Trial: Abusive Prosecutions and Erosion of Fair Trial Rights in Turkey." April 10, 2019, accessed April 22, 2020. https://www.hrw.org/report/2019/04/10/lawyers-trial/abusive-prosecutions-and-erosion-fair-trial-rights-turkey.

Hürriyet Daily News. "Turkish Rights Group's Cargo Ship to Set Sail with Gaza Aid." April 13, 2010, accessed July 1, 2013. http://www.hurriyetdailynews.com/default.aspx?pageid=438&n=cargo-ship-will-set-out-to-gaza-to-deliver-aid-2010-04-13.

IBH/FOCA, International Bureau of Humanitarian NGOs and Friends of Charities Association. *Timeline and Inconsistencies Report*. 2010, accessed January 15, 2013. https://www.globalresearch.ca/new-side-by-side-gaza-flotilla-timeline-report-discredits-israeli-version-of-events/21356 (no longer available).

IHH. Foundation for Human Rights and Freedoms and Humanitarian Relief. "Ship Purchased for Gaza Campaign." March 29, 2010, accessed July 1, 2013. http://mavi-marmara.ihh.org.tr/en/main/news/0/ship-purchased-for-gaza-campaign/231 (no longer available).

IHH. "*Mavi Marmara* Truth: Israeli Soldiers Killing Furkan. (The Freedom Flotilla)." YouTube Video. 0.22 mins. June 9, 2010, accessed June 30, 2013. http://www.youtube.com/watch?v=rdA6jJ8dOZQ.

IHH. *Palestine Our Route Humanitarian Aid Our Load Flotilla Campaign Summary Report.* May 30, 2010, accessed April 10, 2020. https://www.ihh.org.tr/arsiv/uploads/2010/insaniyardim-filosu-ozet-raporu_en.pdf.

IHH. "*Mavi Marmara* Art Exhibition Opens." August 4, 2010, accessed May 1, 2013. http://www.ihh.org.tr/en/main/news/0/mavi-marmara-art-exhibition-opens/220.

IHH. "*Mavi Marmara* is on the Stage!" February 7, 2011, accessed July 30, 2020. https://www.ihh.org.tr/en/news/mavi-marmara-is-on-the-stage-275.

IHH. "Aljazeera Begins 15th-year Celebrations with *Mavi Marmara* Play." November 16, 2011, accessed May 1, 2013. http://mavi-marmara.ihh.org.tr/fr/main/news/0/aljazeera-begins-15th-year-celebrations-with-/1179.

IHH. *The Mavi Marmara Case: Legal Actions Taken against the Israeli Attack on the Gaza Freedom Flotilla on 31.05.2010.* 2012, accessed April 29, 2014. https://www.ihh.org.tr/public/publish/0/126/the-mavi-marmara-case.pdf.

IHH. "About the Trial: Israel on the Felon's Dock!" 2012, accessed February 5, 2013. http://www.ihh.org.tr/dava-hakkinda/en.

IHH. "Fact Sheet: Palestine Our Route, Humanitarian Aid Our Load." December 10, 2012, accessed January 18, 2013. https://www.dropbox.com/sh/l0zl7g242zi1bu9/fHZgXPt16S/IHH%20Deliller%20Dosyası.pdf.

IHH. "Witness Account on the Israeli Attack and Rights Violations." December 10, 2012, accessed January 26, 2013. http://www.ihh.org.tr/taniklar-israil-saldirisi-ve-sonrasindaki-ihlalleri-anlatti/en.

IHH. "*Mavi Marmara*: Gaza Freedom Flotilla." 2012, accessed April 10, 2020. https://www.ihh.org.tr/public/publish/0/79/mavi-marmara-freedom-flotilla.pdf.

IHH. "Freedom: Last Destination—*Mavi Marmara*." Vimeo Video. 91 mins. October 5, 2012. http://vimeo.com/50824956.

IHH. Indictment Files. 2012, accessed January 14, 2013. https://www.dropbox.com/sh/l0zl7g242zi1bu9/qFM6mGnflj.

IHH. "Israel on the Felon's Dock: *Mavi Marmara* Trial Begins in Çağlayan on November 6, 2012," accessed April 12, 2014. http://www.ihh.org.tr/.

IHH. *Mavi Marmara* Case: @MaviMarmaraCase. Twitter, November 6, 2012, accessed March 31, 2014. https://twitter.com/MaviMarmaraCase.

IHH. "*Mavi Marmara* Trial Postponed to 21th Feb 2013." November 10, 2012, accessed April 5, 2014. http://www.ihh.org.tr/uploads/2012/ihh-press-release-on-mavi-marmara-trial-10-11.pdf.

IHH. "Emergency Aid for Gaza." 2013, accessed January 6, 2013. http://www.ihh.org.tr/mavi-marmaraya-saldirinin-delilleri-mahkemede/en.

IHH. "The Free Gaza Movement." 2013, accessed February 4, 2013. http://www.freegaza.org.

IHH. *Mavi Marmara* Case: @MaviMarmaraCase/. February 21, 2013, accessed March 31, 2014. https://twitter.com/MaviMarmaraCase.

IHH. "Second Hearing of the *Mavi Marmara* Trial Held." February 21, 2013, accessed April 23, 2020. https://www.ihh.org.tr/en/news/second-hearing-of-mavi-marmara-trial-held-1593.

IHH. "*Mavi Marmara* Trial Continues with the 4th Hearing." October 3, 2013, accessed April 17, 2020. https://www.ihh.org.tr/en/news/mavi-marmara-trial-continues-with-4th-hearing-1891.

IHH. *Mavi Marmara* Case: @MaviMarmaraCase, posted by: Izzet Şahin. Twitter. November 3, 2012, accessed March 31, 2014. https://twitter.com/MaviMarmaraCase.

IHH. *Mavi Marmara* Case: @MaviMarmaraCase, posted by: Izzet Şahin, Twitter. May 2014, accessed April 25, 2020. https://twitter.com/MaviMarmaraCase.

IHH. Media Press Release by spokesman Mustafa Özbek. June 27, 2016. "Whoever Covers up with Israel will Remain Naked."

IHH. Media Press Release by spokesman Mustafa Özbek. October 19, 2016. "Turkish Court Continues the Hearing to the 2nd of December."

IHH. "International Panel Held in LSE about *Mavi Marmara*." November 29, 2016, accessed October 10, 2017. https://www.ihh.org.tr/en/news/international-panel-held-in-lse-about-mavi-marmara.

IHH. Media Press Release by Spokesman Mustafa Özbek. December 8, 2016. "Turkish Judge Holds that the Case Should Be Abated on the Grounds of the Turkey-Israel Agreement."

IHH. "*Mavi Marmara* Trials," accessed April 23, 2020. https://www.ihh.org.tr/en/mavi-marmara.

International Criminal Court. "ICC Prosecutor Receives Referral by the Authorities of the Union of the Comoros in Relation to the Events of May 2010 on the Vessel *Mavi Marmara*." 2013, accessed May 15, 2013. http://www.icc-cpi.int/iccdocs/otp/Referral-from-Comoros.pdf.

International Criminal Court. *Regulation of the Court*. May 26, 2004, accessed August 27, 2014. http://www.icc-cpi.int/NR/rdonlyres/B920AD62-DF49-4010-8907-E0D8CC61EBA4/277527/Regulations_of_the_Court_170604EN.pdf.

International Criminal Court. "Statement of the Prosecutor of the International Criminal Court, Fatou Bensouda, on Concluding the Preliminary Examination of the Situation Referred by the Union of Comoros: 'Rome Statute Legal Requirements Have Not Been Met.'" November 6, 2014, accessed November 8, 2014. http://www.icc-cpi.int/en_menus/icc/press%20and%20media/press%20releases/Pages/otp-statement-06-11-2014.aspx.

International Criminal Court. Pre-Trial Chamber, ICC-01/13. January 29, 2015, accessed April 19, 2020. https://www.icc-cpi.int/CourtRecords/CR2015_00576.PDF.

International Criminal Court. "Registered Vessels of Comoros, Greece and Cambodia." November 29, 2017, accessed April 16, 2020. https://www.icc-cpi.int/comoros.

International Criminal Court. *Situation on the Registered Vessels of the Union of the Comoros, the Hellenic Republic, and the Kingdom of Cambodia (ICC-01/13)*. December 2, 2019, accessed July 29, 2020. https://www.icc-cpi.int/RelatedRecords/CR2019_07299.PDF.

International Criminal Tribunal for the Former Yugoslavia. *Rules of Procedure and Evidence. UN Doc. IT/32/Rev.7*. Entered Into Force March 14, 1994, Amendments Adopted January 8, 1996, accessed September 2, 2014. http://www1.umn.edu/humanrts/icty/ct-rules7.html.

International Criminal Tribunal of Rwanda. *Rules of Procedure of Evidence*. July 5, 1996, accessed April 30, 2020. http://hrlibrary.umn.edu/africa/RWANDA1.htm.

International Transport Workers Federation. "What Are Flags of Convenience?" accessed April 19, 2020. https://www.itfglobal.org/en/sector/civil-aviation/flags-of-convenience.

Interpol Red Notice Removal Lawyers. *Report: Turkish Prosecutor Seeks Interpol Notice for Flotilla Attackers*. October 13, 2011, accessed January 15, 2013. http://interpolnoticeremoval.com/tag/istanbul-public-prosecutor-mehmet-akif-ekinci.

Israel. State Archive. File No. 17005/6. October 1969, accessed July 31, 2020. https://www.akevot.org.il/wp-content/uploads/2019/05/ISA-File-GL-17005-6.pdf.

Israel. Ministry of Foreign Affairs. Israel-Egypt Peace Treaty. March 26, 1979, accessed June 25, 2020. https://mfa.gov.il/mfa/foreignpolicy/peace/guide/pages/israel-egypt%20peace%20treaty.aspx.

Israel. Ministry of Justice. Israeli Law of Freedom of Information Law. 1988, accessed April 11, 2020. https://www.justice.gov.il/Units/YechidatChofeshHameyda/GlobalDocs/Law.pdf.

Israel. Ministry of Foreign Affairs. Israeli-Palestinian Interim Agreements. September 28, 1995, accessed February 20, 2020. https://mfa.gov.il/mfa/foreignpolicy/peace/guide/pages/the%20israeli-palestinian%20interim%20agreement.aspx.

Israel. Ministry of Justice. *Adolf Eichmann Trial, Records of the Attorney General Against Adolf Eichmann, Vol. A*. 2002, accessed August 15, 2014. http://index.justice.gov.il/Subjects/EichmannWritten/volume/vol1_shaar.pdf.

Israel. Committee to Examine Opening Courts in Israel to the Electronic Media. Jerusalem. 2004, accessed August 15, 2015. http://elyon1.court.gov.il/heb/doch%20electroni.pdf.

Israel. Ministry of Foreign Affairs. "The Israeli-Palestinian Interim Agreement—Main Points." September 28, 1995, accessed February 20, 2020. https://mfa.gov.il/mfa/foreignpolicy/peace/guide/pages/the%20israeli-palestinian%20interim%20agreement%20-%20main%20p.aspx.

Israel. Ministry of Foreign Affairs. "Shlomo Argov." February 23, 2003, accessed June 20, 2021. https://mfa.gov.il/MFA/MFA-Archive/2003/Pages/Shlomo%20Argov.aspx.

Israel. Ministry of Foreign Affairs. "Israel's Disengagement Plan: Renewing the Peace Process." 2005, accessed April 11, 2020. https://mfa.gov.il/mfa/foreignpolicy/peace/guide/pages/israeli%20disengagement%20plan%2020-jan-2005.aspx.

Israel. Ministry of Transport and Road Safety. Notice to Mariners No. 1/2009 Blockade of the Gaza Strip. January 6, 2006, accessed April 11, 2020. http://asp.mot.gov.il/en/shipping/notice2mariners/547-no12009.

Israel. Idfnadesk. "Close Up Footage of *Mavi Marmara* Passengers Attacking IDF Soldiers" (with sound). YouTube Video. 1:01 mins. May 31, 2010, accessed June 1, 2010. https://www.youtube.com/watch?v=gYjkLUcbJWo.

Israel. Idfnadesk. "Demonstrators Use Violence against Israeli Navy Soldiers Attempting to Board the Ship." YouTube Video. 1:04 mins. May 31, 2010, accessed June 1, 2020. http://www.youtube.com/watch?v=bU12KW-XyZE.

Israel. Ministry of Foreign Affairs. "IDF Forces Met with Pre-Planned Violence When Attempting to Board the Flotilla." May 31, 2010, accessed July 30, 2020. https://mfa.gov.il/mfa/pressroom/2010/pages/israel_navy_warns_flotilla_31-may-2010.aspx.

Israel. IDF. "*Mavi Marmara* Passengers Attack IDF before Soldiers Boarded Ship." YouTube Video. 1:10 mins. May 31, 2010, accessed November 6, 2012. http://www.youtube.com/watch?v=B6sAEYpHF24.

Israel. IDF. "Flotilla Rioters Prepare Rods, Slingshots, Broken Battles and Metal Objects." YouTube Video. 2:24 mins. June 2, 2010, accessed December 4, 2012. http://www.youtube.com/watch?v=HZlSSaPT_OU.

Israel. IDF announcement. "Maj. Gen. (Res.) Eiland Submits Conclusions of Military Examination Team Regarding Mavi Marmara." July 12, 2010, accessed August 9, 2020. https://idfspokesperson.wordpress.com/tag/giora-eiland/.

Israel. IDF Habat—Unit of Technological Education and Training. "Timeline of the *Mavi Marmara* Incident." YouTube Video. 21:18 mins. 2011, accessed July 1, 2013. http://www.youtube.com/watch?v=z31GesVrBjc.

Israel. State Comptroller's Report. *A Critical Review of the Application of the National Security Committee Law and the Handling of the Turkish Flotilla.* June 13, 2012, accessed April 11, 2020. https://www.mevaker.gov.il/he/Reports/Pages/105.aspx?AspxAutoDetectCookieSupport=1.

Israel. Knesset State Control Committee. Protocol No. 263. June 14, 2012, accessed April 11, 2020. https://www.mevaker.gov.il/he/Reports/Report_105/8587988a-92b8-4bd3-849d-8cab24f2d527/7685.pdf.

Israel. *The 2014 Gaza Conflict 7 July—26 August 2014 Factual and Legal Aspects.* May 2015, accessed June 26, 2020. https://mfa.gov.il/ProtectiveEdge/Documents/2014GazaConflictFullReport.pdf.

Israel. Procedural Agreement of Compensation between the Republic of Turkey and the State of Israel. June 28, 2016, accessed August 9, 2020. https://www2.tbmm.gov.tr/d26/1/1-0754.pdf.

Jerusalem Post. "Turkey Tries IDF Commanders Over *Marmara* Killings." May 11, 2012, accessed February 8, 2013. http://www.jpost.com/International/Article.aspx?id=290587.

Jewish Press. "Report: Israel Paid $20M to Turkey as Compensation for *Mavi Marmara*." October 2, 2016, accessed July 2018. http://www.jewishpress.com/news/breaking-news/report-israel-paid-20m-to-turkey-as-compensation-for-mavi-marmara/2016/10/02/.

Jiryis, Sabri. "The Legal Structure for the Expropriation and Absorption of Arab Lands in Israel." *Journal of Palestine Studies* 2:4 (1973): 82–104.

Johnsson, Richard C. B. "Non-Territorial Governance, Mankind's Forgotten Legacy: A Review of Shin Shun Liu's *Extraterritoriality: Its Rise and Its Decline*." In *Panarchy: Political Theories of Non-territorial States*. Edited by Aviezer Tucker and Gian Piero De Bellis. London: Routledge, 2015: 188–213.

Judicial Watch. "Re: Freedom of Information Act Request." *Judicialwatch.org*. May 2, 2011, accessed September 16, 2020, http://www.judicialwatch.org/wp-content/uploads/2014/02/DOD-Osama-Op-FOIA-Request-5-13-2011.pdf.

Judicial Watch. "Judicial Watch Sues Department of Defense for Records of Communications Relating to May 2011 FOIA Request for bin Laden Death Photos." *Judicialwatch.org*. July 24, 2014, accessed February 5, 2019. https://www.judicialwatch.org/press-room/press-releases/judicial-watch-sues-department-defense-records-communications-relating-may-2011-foia-request-bin-laden-death-photos/.

Judicial Watch. "Judicial Watch Uncovers Email Revealing Top Pentagon Leader Ordered Destruction of bin Laden Death Photos." *Judicialwatch.org*. February 10, 2014, accessed June 11, 2020. https://www.judicialwatch.org/press-releases/pentagon-destruction-of-bin-laden-death-photos/.

Karabiyik, M. Üzeyir. "Turkish Juridical Reform: It Has Achieved Much but There Is Much to Be Done." *International Justice Monitor*. 2012, accessed March 28, 2014. http://www.judicialmonitor.org/archive_summer2012/judicialreformreport.html.

Kassan, Shalom. "Extraterritorial Jurisdiction in the Ancient World." *American Journal of International Law* 29:2 (1935): 237–47.

Kayaoğlu, Turan. *Legal Imperialism: Sovereignty and Extraterritoriality in Japan, the Ottoman Empire, and China*. Cambridge, UK: Cambridge University Press, 2010.

Keinon, Herb. "Netanyahu Apologizes to Turkey over Gaza Flotilla." *The Jerusalem Post*. March 22, 2013, accessed July 17, 2018. https://www.jpost.com/International/Obama-Netanyahu-Erdoğan-speak-by-phone-307423.

———. "Sweden Looks into Israeli Actions toward Its Nationals Involved in Flotillas to Gaza." *The Jerusalem Post*. June 26, 2014, accessed September 16, 2014. http://www.jpost.com/Diplomacy-and-Politics/Sweden-looks-into-Israeli-actions-toward-its-nationals-involved-in-flotillas-to-Gaza-360737.

Kennedy, Liam. "Seeing and Believing: On Photography and the War on Terror." *Public Culture* 24:2–67 (2012): 261–81.

———. *Afterimages: Photography and US Foreign Policy*. Chicago: University of Chicago Press, 2016.

Kirschenbaum, Joshua. "Operation Opera: An Ambiguous Success." *Journal of Strategic Security* 3:4 (2010): 49–62.

Kor, Zahide Tuba, ed. *Witnesses of the Freedom Flotilla: Interviews with Passengers.* Istanbul: IHH Kitap, 2011.

Kuntsman, Adi, and Rebecca L. Stein. "Another War Zone: Social Media in the Israeli-Palestinian Conflict." *Middle East Report Online (MERIP).* September 7, 2010. http://www.merip.org/mero/interventions/another-war-zone#.UBF0yo1TSiE.email.

Kurban, Dilek, and Ceren Sözeri. *Policy Suggestions for Free and Independent Media in Turkey.* Istanbul: Turkish Economic and Social Studies Foundation [Tesev]. 2013, accessed April 22, 2020. https://www.tesev.org.tr/wp-content/uploads/report_Policy_Suggestions_For_Free_And_Independent_Media_In_Turkey.pdf.

Lambert, Paul. *Courting Publicity: Twitter and Television Cameras in Court.* West Sussex, UK: Bloomsbury Professional, 2011.

Langbroek, Philip M. "Digital Technology Leading the Way in Court Recording." *International Journal for Court Administration* 3:2 (2011): 21–30.

Lawrence, Chris. "'No Land Alternative' Prompts bin Laden Sea Burial." *CNN World.* May 3, 2011, accessed February 6, 2019. http://edition.cnn.com/2011/WORLD/asiapcf/05/02/bin.laden.burial.at.sea/index.html.

Lee, Iara, dir. *Culture of Resistance.* USA: George Gund, producer, 2010.

Lerman, Eran. "The Rapprochement Deal between Israel and Turkey: Intermediate Summary." *BESA Perspectives.* July 6, 2016, accessed July 2018. https://besacenter.org/wp-content/uploads/2016/07/Lerman-Eran-Turkey-Israel-deal-PP-348-HEBREW-6-July-2016.pdf.

Levy, Carl. "Refugees, Europe, Camps/State of Exception: 'Into the Zone,' the European Union and Extraterritorial Processing of Migrants, Refugees, and Asylum-seekers (Theories and Practice)." *Refugee Survey Quarterly* 29:1 (2010): 92–119.

Levinas, Emmanuel. *Outside the Subject.* Translated by Michael B. Smith. Redwood City, CA: Stanford University Press, 1993.

Levine, Alan. "The Status of Sovereignty in East Jerusalem and the West Bank." *New York University Journal of International Law and Politics* 5:3 (1972): 485–502.

Lewis, Aidan. "Osama bin Laden: Legality of Killing Questioned." *BBC World News.* May 12, 2011, accessed January 31, 2019. https://www.bbc.com/news/world-south-asia-13318372.

Lieblich, Eliav. "Show Us the Films: Transparency, National Security and Disclosure of Information Collected by Advanced Weapon Systems under International Law." *Israel Law Review* 45:3 (2012): 459–91.

——. "Extraterritory." Lecture at Extraterritory Project Symposium, Haifa, December 20. 2013.

Lin, Sharat G. "Gaza's Shrinking Borders: 16 Years of the Oslo Process." *Dissident Voice.* December 26, 2009, accessed March 26, 2013. http://dissidentvoice.org/2009/12/gaza_s-shrinking-borders-16-years-of-the-oslo-process.

Liu, Shih-Shun. *Extraterritoriality: Its Rise and Its Decline*. New York: Columbia University Press, 1925. Reprinted. New York: AMS Press, 1969.

Lubell, Noam. *Extraterritorial Use of Force against Non-State Actors*. Oxford: Oxford University Press, 2010.

Lucas, James R. "Props: An Overview of Demonstrative Evidence." *American Journal of Trial Advocacy* 13 (1990): 1097–139.

Luft, Gal. "The Logic of Israel's Targeted Killing." *Middle East Quarterly* 10:1 (2003).

Mackey, Robert. "Photographs of Battered Israeli Commandos Show New Side of Raid." *The Lede* (blog). *The New York Times*. June 7, 2010, accessed April 5, 2012. http://thelede.blogs.nytimes.com/2010/06/07/photographs-of-battered-israeli-commandos-show-new-side-of-raid.

Madison III, Benjamin V. "Seeing Can Be Deceiving: Photographic Evidence in a Visual Age – How Much Weight Does It Deserve?" *William and Mary Law Review* 25:4 (1984): 705–957.

Malinovic, Marko. *Extraterritorial Application of Human Rights Treaties: Law, Principles, and Policy*. Oxford: Oxford University Press. 2011.

Mason, Paul. "Lights, Camera, Justice? Cameras in the Courtroom: An Outline of the Issues." *Crime Prevention and Community Safety* 2:3 (2000): 23–34.

———. "Court on Camera: Broadcast Coverage of the Legal Proceedings." 2020, accessed August 30, 2020. https://cap-press.com/sites/pj/camera-mason.htm.

Mavi Marmara: The Inside Story. Tehran: Press TV, 2011.

May, Richard, and Marieke Wierda. "Trends in International Criminal Evidence: Nuremberg, Tokyo, The Hague, and Arusha." *Colum. J. Transnat'l L.* 37 (1998): 725–765.

Meir Amit Intelligence and Terrorism Information Center. *Overview* (blog). November 13, 2012, accessed 16 April, 2020. https://www.terrorism-info.org.il/en/20422/.

Melman, Yossi. "How Will Hamas React to Israel's Major Gaza Border Project?" *The Jerusalem Post*. June 23, 2017, accessed June 24, 2017. https://www.jpost.com/jerusalem-report/hamass-dilemma-492146.

"MGF—Millî Görüş Forum—IHH.flv." YouTube Video. 2:56 mins. May 31, 2010, accessed July 9, 2013. http://www.youtube.com/watch?v=bfFfK4CxUHM.

Migdalovitz, Carol. *Israel's Blockade of Gaza, the Mavi Marmara Incident and Its Aftermath*. US Congressional Research Service. 2010, accessed April 10, 2020. https://www.refworld.org/pdfid/4cb547b51f1.pdf.

Milanovic, Marko. *Extraterritorial Application of Human Rights Treaties*. Oxford: Oxford University Press, 2011.

Ministry of Justice Department of Information Technologies. National Judiciary Informatics System. 2015, accessed April 23, 2020. http://www.e-justice.gov.tr/General-Information.

Mnookin, Jennifer L. "The Image of Truth: Photographic Evidence and the Power of Analogy." *Yale Journal of Law & the Humanities* 10:1 (1998): 1–74.

Mommsen, Theodor. *History of Rome*. Translated by William Purdie Dickson. 1895. Republished by Project Gutenberg, 2005. https://www.gutenberg.org/cache/epub/10706/pg10706-images.html.

Morris, Benny. *Israel's Border Wars, 1949–1956: Arab Infiltration, Israeli Retaliation, and the Countdown to the Suez War*. Oxford: Oxford University Press, 1997.

———. *The Birth of the Palestinian Refugee Problem Revisited*. Vol. 18. Cambridge, UK: Cambridge University Press, 2004.

Morrison, Wayne. "Visualising Atrocity: Arendt, Evil, and the Optics of Thoughtlessness: The Scene of the Mass Crime: History, Film, and International Tribunals." Book review. *Theoretical Criminology* 18:2 (2014): 252–6.

Müller, Andreas T., and Friedrich F. Martens. "The Office of Consul and Consular Jurisdiction in the East." *The European Journal of International Law* 25:3 (2014): 871–91.

Nasi, Selin. "Turkey-Israel Deal: A Key to Long-Term Reconciliation?" *Global Political Trends Center Policy Briefs*. January 2017, accessed July 17, 2018. http://fes-org-il-wp.s3.eu-central-1.amazonaws.com/wp-content/uploads/2017/01/10110901/Turkey-Israel-Deal.pdf.

Nur, Ferry. *Mavi Marmara Menembus Gaza*. Jakarta: Kesaksian Seorang Relawan, 2010.

Open Society Justice Initiative. *Access to Judicial Information Draft Report*. March 2009, accessed September 16, 2020. https://www.right2info.org/resources/publications/publications/Access%20to%20Judicial%20Information%20Report%20R-G%203.09.DOC.

Oren, Michael B. *Six Days of War: June 1967 and the Making of the Modern Middle East*. Oxford: Oxford University Press, 2002.

Örücü, Esin. "What Is a Mixed Legal System: Exclusion or Expansion?" *Electronic Journal of Comparative Law* 12:1 (2008), accessed April 27, 2014. http://www.ejcl.org/121/art121-15.pdf.

Osterhammel, Jorgen. "Semi-Colonialism and Informal Empire in Twentieth-Century China: Towards a Framework of Analysis." In *Imperialism and After: Continuities and Discontinuities*. Edited by W. J. Mommsen. London: Allen & Unwin, 1986: 290–314.

Owen, Robert C., and Melissa Mather. "Thawing Out the Cold Record: Some Thoughts on How Videotaped Records May Affect Traditional Standards of Deference on Direct and Collateral Review." *J. App. Prac. & Process* 2 (2000): 411–434.

Özdemirci, Fahrettin. "Government Records and Records Management: Law on the Right to Information in Turkey". *Government Information Quarterly* 25:2 (2008): 303–12.

Panikkar, Kavalam Madhava. *Asia and Western Dominance: A Survey of the Vasco da Gama Epoch of Asian History, 1498–1945*. London: G. Allen & Unwin, 1953.

Panepinto, Alice M. "The Annexation of Palestine." In *Extraterritoriality of Law: History, Theory, Politics*. Edited by Daniel S. Margolies et al. London: Routledge, 2019: 200–14.

Parkinson, Brian, and Spencer C. Tucker. "Israeli Invasion of Lebanon." In *The Encyclopedia of the Arab-Israeli Conflict: A Political, Social, and Military History*. Edited by Spencer C. Tucker and Priscilla Roberts. Santa Barbara, CA: ABC-CLIO, 2008: 623–6.

Peleg, Guy. "Commando Unit Warrior Is Prosecuting: 'I Thought They Were Going to Execute Me.'" *Channel 2 News*. April 11, 2014, accessed April 16, 2014. http://www.mako.co.il/news-law/legal/Article-6cf8a45b4e15541004.htm.

Perry, Meagan. "Kevin Neish's Photos of *Mavi Marmara* Attack Published Plus Full Interview." *Rabble.Ca*. June 9, 2010, accessed August 5, 2012. http://rabble.ca/news/2010/06/do-not-publish-yet-kevin-neishs-photos-mavi-maramara-attack-published.

Perry, Smadar. "Turkish Gov't Delays Compensation Payment to *Marmara* Families." *YNET News*.com. December 6, 2017, accessed July 25, 2018. https://www.ynetnews.com/articles/0,7340,L-4974635,00.html.

Peterson, Trudy H. "Temporary Courts, Permanent Records." Woodrow Wilson Center. 2008. March 24, 2014, accessed September 17, 2020. https://www.wilsoncenter.org/publication/temporary-courts-permanent-records.

Phillips, Macon. "Osama bin Laden Dead, White House." May 2, 2011, accessed June 1, 2020. https://obamawhitehouse.archives.gov/blog/2011/05/02/osama-bin-laden-dead.

Pierini, Marc with Markus Mayr. *Freedom of the Press in Turkey*. Carnegie Europe, Carnegie Endowment for International Peace, Belgium & Open Society Foundation in Turkey. 2013, accessed February 25, 2013. http://carnegieendowment.org/files/press_freedom_turkey.pdf.

Pierpaoli Jr., Paul G. "Black September Organization." In *The Encyclopedia of the Arab-Israeli Conflict: A Political, Social, and Military History*. Edited by Spencer C. Tucker and Priscilla Roberts. Santa Barbara, CA: ABC-CLIO, 2008: 224–5.

Pinchevski, Amit, and Tamar Liebes. "Served Voices: Radio and Mediation of Trauma in the Eichmann Trial." *Public Culture* 22:2 (2010): 265–91.

Pinchevski, Amit, Tamar Liebes, and Ora Herman. "Eichmann on the Air: Radio and the Making of an Historic Trial." *Historical Journal of Film, Radio and Television* 27:1 (2007): 1–25.

Pitel, Laura. "Arrest of Turkish Judges Prompts Fears over Checks and Balances." *Financial Times*. July 17, 2016, accessed August 14, 2018. https://www.ft.com/content/79f72260-4c3c-11e6-88c5-db83e98a590a.

Porter, Glenn. "A New Theoretical Framework regarding the Application and Reliability of Photographic Evidence." *International Journal of Evidence and Proof* 15:1 (2011): 26–61.

Porter, Glenn, and Michael Kennedy. "Photographic Truth and Evidence." *Australian Journal of Forensic Sciences* 44:2 (2012): 183–92.

Quigley, Harold Scott. "Extraterritoriality in China." *American Journal of International Law* 20:1 (1926): 46–68.

Quigley, John. *The Statehood of Palestine: International Law in the Middle East Conflict.* Cambridge, UK: Cambridge University Press, 2010.

Rajah, Jothie. "Law as Record: The Death of Osama bin Laden." *No Foundations* 13 (2012): 45–69.

Ramadan, Adam. "Destroying Nahr el-Bared: Sovereignty and Urbicide in the Space of Exception." *Political Geography* 28:3 (2009): 153–163.

Raustiala, Kal. "The Geography of Justice." *Fordham Law Review* 73:6 (2005): 2501–60.

Resmi, Derneği. "Second Hearing Held in Historic Trial." The Freedom and Solidarity Association *Mavi Marmara*. 2013, accessed April 2014. http://www.mavimarmara.org/en/?p=105.

Richemond-Barak, Daphné. *Underground Warfare*. Oxford: Oxford University Press, 2017.

Robinson, Shira. *Citizen Strangers: Palestinians and the Birth of Israel's Liberal Settler State*. Redwood City, CA: Stanford University Press, 2013.

Rolnik, Guy. "Taking Stock: Behind the Smoke Screen." *Haaretz*. June 8, 2010, accessed June 17, 2020. http://www.haaretz.com/print-edition/business/taking-stock-behind-the-smoke-screen-1.294819.

Rothem, Dan. "How to Connect the West Bank and the Gaza Strip." *The Atlantic*. October 27, 2011, accessed February 20, 2020. https://www.theatlantic.com/international/archive/2011/10/how-to-connect-the-west-bank-and-gaza-strip/247475/.

Ryan, Bernard. "Extraterritorial Immigration Control: What Role for Legal Guarantees?" In *Extraterritorial Immigration Control: Legal Challenges*. Edited by Bernard Ryan and Valsamis. Leiden, The Netherlands: Brill/Nijhoff, 2010: 1–37.

Santee, David S. "More than Words: Rethinking the Role of Modern Demonstrative Evidence." *Santa Clara Law Review* 52:1 (2012): 105–44.

Santos, Boaventura de Sousa. "Beyond Abyssal Thinking: From Global Lines to Ecologies of Knowledges." *Review* 30:1 (2007): 45–89.

––––––. *The Rise of the Global Left: The World Social Forum and Beyond*. London: Zed Books, 2006.

Saxton, Libby. *Haunted Images: Film, Ethics, Testimony and the Holocaust*. London and New York: Wallflower Press, 2008.

Schmidle, Nicholas. "Getting bin Laden." *The New Yorker*. August 8, 2011, accessed February 6, 2019. https://www.thomasweibel.ch/artikel/110808_new_yorker_getting_bin_laden.pdf.

Schmitt, Carl. *Political Theology: Four Chapters on the Concept of Sovereignty*. Chicago: Chicago University Press, 2005.

Schou, Nicholas. "How the CIA Hoodwinked Hollywood." *The Atlantic*. July 14, 2014, accessed February 5, 2019. https://www.theatlantic.com/entertainment/archive/2016/07/operation-tinseltown-how-the-cia-manipulates-hollywood/491138/.

Schwartz, Joan M. "Records of Simple Truth and Precision: Photography, Archives, and the Illusion of Control." In *Archives, Documentation, and Institutions of Social Memory: Essays from the Sawyer Seminar*. Edited by Francis X. Blouin and William G. Rosenberg. Ann Arbor, MI: University of Michigan Press, 2006: 61–84.

Scott, James C. *The Art of Not Being Governed: An Anarchist History of Upland Southeast Asia*. New Haven, CT: Yale University Press, 2009.

Scott, Rachel. *The Challenge of Political Islam: Non-Muslims and the Egyptian State*. Palo Alto, CA: Stanford University Press, 2010.

Segarra, David, dir. *Feu sur le Marmara*. Venezuela, 2010.

Seibert, Thomas. "US Worries over Syria, Iran Behind Push for Israel's Apology to Turkey." *The National*. March 24, 2013. https://www.thenational.ae/world/mena/us-worries-over-syria-iran-behind-push-for-israel-s-apology-to-turkey-1.656300.

Sekula, Allan. "Body and the Archive." *October* 39 (1986): 3–64.

Sela, Rona. "The Genealogy of Colonial Plunder and Erasure: Israel's Control over Palestinian Archives." *Social Semiotics* 28:2 (2008): 201–29.

Sharman, Jon. "Turkey Halts Case over Israeli Raid on Gaza Flotilla That Killed 10 People." *The Independent*. December 9, 2016, accessed July 16, 2018. https://www.independent.co.uk/news/world/middle-east/turkey-halt-court-case-israel-mavi-marmara-raid-victims-a7466311.html.

Sharp, Jeremy M. "The Egypt-Gaza Border and Its Effect on Israeli-Egyptian Relations." Foreign Press Center. US Department of State. 2008, accessed April 10, 2020. http://www.vfp143.org/lit/Gaza/RL34346.pdf.

Shaughnessy, Tina, and Ellen Tobin. "Flags of Convenience: Freedom and Insecurity on the High Seas." *Journal of International Law & Policy* 5 (2006–7): 1–31.

Sheizaf, Noam. "IDF Spokesperson Spins *Mavi Marmara* Video for Local Political Purposes." *The Promised Land* (blog). August 23, 2010, accessed April 12, 2020. https://www.972mag.com/idf-spokesperson-spins-mavi-marmara-video-for-local-political-purposes/.

Shtern, Shai, "Victory Consciousness is More Valuable than the Outcome on the Field." *IDF* (blog). September 8, 2011, accessed March 30, 2015. http://www.idf.il/1133-13098-he/Dover.aspx.

Siegel, Jay A., and Pekka Saukko, eds. *Encyclopedia of Forensic Science*, 2nd edition. San Diego: Academic Press, 2013.

Silbey, Jessica M. "Judges as Film Critics: New Approaches to Filmic Evidence." *University of Michigan Journal of Law Reform* 37:2 (2004): 493–571.

Simon, Joel. "For Turkey, World's Leading Jailer, a Path Forward." Committee to Protect Journalists. December 11, 2012, accessed February 25, 2013. https://cpj.org/2012/12/for-turkey-worlds-leading-jailer-of-the-press-a-pa/.

Sönmez, Gülden. *Mavi Marmara* Indictment. 2012, accessed February 1, 2013. https://www.dropbox.com/sh/l0zl7g242zi1bu9/r5EMPzTa6V/STATEMENT%20OF%20GULDEN%20SONMEZ%20%28IHH%20MEMBER%20OF%20BOARD%20LAWYER%29.pdf.

Sönmez, Z. "Arrest Warrants Issued for Israeli Commanders over the Fatal Attack on *Mavi Marmara*." IHH press release. April 26, 2014, accessed June 7, 2014. http://www.ihh.org.tr/en/main/news/0/arrest-warrants-in-mavi-marmara-case/2341.

Special Court for Sierra Leone. Rules of Procedure and Evidence. 2003, accessed September 2, 2014. https://www1.umn.edu/humanrts/instree/SCSL/Rules of-proced-SCSL.pdf.

Spelman, Elizabeth. "The Legality of the Israeli Naval Blockade of the Gaza Strip." *Web Journal of Current Legal Issues*. 2013, accessed March 12, 2013. http://ojs.qub.ac.uk/index.php/webjcli/article/view/207/277.

Stahl, Adam. "The Evolution of Israeli Targeted Operations: Consequences of the Thabet Thabet Operation." *Studies in Conflict & Terrorism* 33:2 (2010): 111–33.

Stahl, Roger. *Militainment, Inc.: War, Media, and Popular Culture*. London: Routledge, 2009.

Starr, June. *Law as a Metaphor: From Islamic Courts to the Palace of Justice*. Albany, NY: State University of New York Press, 1991.

Stein, Sarah Abrevaya. *Extraterritorial Dreams: European Citizenship, Sephardi Jews, and the Ottoman Twentieth Century*. Chicago: University of Chicago Press, 2016.

Stepniak, Daniel. "Technology and Public Access to Audio-Visual Coverage and Recordings of Court Proceedings: Implications for Common Law Jurisdiction." *William and Mary Bill of Rights Journal* 12:3 (2004): 791–823.

Stoler, Ann Laura. "Colonial Archives and the Arts of Governance: On the Content in the Form." In *Refiguring the Archives*. Edited by Carolyn Hamilton et al. New York: Springer Publishing, 2002: 83–102.

Stowell, Ellery C. "Extraterritoriality—A Vanishing Institution: Part Two: Syria and Palestine." *Cumulative Digest of International Law and Relations* 3 (1934): 85–88.

Stoyanova, Vladislava. "The Principle of Non-Refoulement and the Right of Asylum-Seekers of Enter State Territory." *Interdisciplinary Journal of Human Rights Law* 3:1 (2008): 1–11.

Tank, Pinar. "Political Islam in Turkey: A State of Controlled Secularity." *Turkish Studies* 6:1 (2005): 3–19.

Tenenbaum, Karen, and Ehud Eiran. "Israeli Settlement Activity in the West Bank and Gaza: A Brief History." *Negotiation Journal* 21:2 (2005): 171–5.

Terdiman, Moshe. "Civil War in Lebanon." In *The Encyclopedia of the Arab-Israeli Conflict: A Political, Social, and Military History*. Edited by Spencer C. Tucker and Priscilla Roberts. Santa Barbara, CA: ABC-CLIO, 2008: 618–22.

Thurston, Timothy. "Law and Science of Evidence." Roy Rosenzweig Center for History and New Media. accessed June 29, 2014. http://chnm.gmu.edu/aq/photos/frames/essay01.htm.

Tilley, Virginia. *Beyond Occupation: Apartheid, Colonialism and International Law in the Occupied Palestinian Territories*. London: Pluto Press, 2012.

Today in Gaza. "IHH's Mehmet Kaya on *Mavi Marmara* Court Case." November 4, 2012, accessed April 18, 2014. http://todayingaza.wordpress.com/2012/11/04/ihhs-mehmet-kaya-on-mavi-marmara-court-case.

Turkel Commission. "IDF's Response to the Flotilla Events (Part 1 of 2)." YouTube Video, 11:39 mins. 2011, accessed August 15, 2012. http://www.youtube.com/ watch?v=Zy5SXWv8U0I.

Turkel Commission Report. *The Public Commission to Examine the Maritime Incident of May 31, 2010, Part 1.* 2010, accessed July 7, 2011. https://www.gov.il/BlobFolder/ generalpage/downloads_eng1/en/ENG_turkel_eng_a.pdf.

Turkey, Republic of. Turkish Right to Information Assessment Council. Turkish Law on the Right to Information, No. 4982. 2003, accessed April 22, 2020. https:// publicofficialsfinancialdisclosure.worldbank.org/sites/fdl/files/assets/law-library-files/Turkey_Right%20to%20Information%20Law_2004_en.pdf.

Turkey, Republic of. Second Chapter-Essence of Criminal Responsibility, Article 20. 2004. Turkish Criminal Code, Law Nr. 5327. Legislation Online. September 26, 2004, accessed April 1, 2014. http://legislationline.org/documents/action/popup/ id/6872/preview.

Turkey, Republic of. Code on Criminal Procedure, Law No. 5271. April 4, 2004, accessed April 6, 2014. http://legislationline.org/documents/action/popup/ id/8976.

Turkey, Republic of. Embassy. "Turkey and the EU." September 27, 2007, accessed February 26, 2013. https://web.archive.org/web/20070927211417/http://www. turkishembassy.org/index.php?option=com_content&task=view&id=57&Item id=235.

Turkey, Republic of. Ministry of Justice. Judicial Reforms Strategy. 2009, accessed April 28, 2014. http://www.sgb.adalet.gov.tr/yrs/Judicial%20Reform%20Strategy.pdf.

Turkey, Republic of. Turkish Criminal Procedure Code. Istanbul: Beta Publishing House, 2009, accessed April 23, 2020. https://www.legislationline.org/download/ id/4257/file/Turkey_CPC_2009_en.pdf.

Turkey, Republic of. Constitution of 1982 with Amendments through 2011. constituteproject.com. July 27, 2018, accessed July 15, 2018. https://www. constituteproject.org/constitution/Turkey_2011.pdf?lang=en.

Turkey, Republic of. Turkish National Commission of Inquiry. *Report on the Israeli Attack on the Humanitarian Aid Convoy to Gaza.* February, 2011, accessed April 9, 2020. https://reliefweb.int/sites/reliefweb.int/files/resources/Full_Report_1621.pdf.

Turkey, Republic of. Ministry of Justice. *Resmî Gazete.* September 20, 2011, accessed July 28, 2020. https://www.resmigazete.gov.tr/eskiler/2011/09/20110920-4.htm.

Turkey, Republic of. Ministry of Justice, *Resmî Gazete.* December 29, 2012, accessed July 28, 2020. https://www.barobirlik.org.tr/dosyalar/belgeler/CMKUcretTarifesi/ tarife2013.pdf.

Turkey, Republic of. Turkey Ministry of Justice Department of Information Technologies and Use of Information Technologies in the Judiciary, accessed March 3, 2014. http://www.justice.gov.tr/basiclaws/JUDICIARY_2.pdf.

"Turkey Blocks: Mapping Internet Freedom in Real Time," accessed July 15, 2018. https://turkeyblocks.org/.

Turkish Diary. "Europe's Largest Palace of Justice in Istanbul." August 1, 2011, accessed March 19, 2013. http://www.buyuyenturkiye.com/turkishdiary/haber/europes-largest-palace-of-justice-in-istanbul.

UN. UN Council. *Egyptian-Israeli Agreement on Disengagement of Forces in Pursuance of the Geneva Peace Conference.* January 18, 1974, accessed February 16, 2020. https://peacemaker.un.org/egyptisrael-disengagementforces74.

UN. UN Peacekeepers. *Separation of Forces between Israel and Syria.* May 31, 1974, accessed February 16, 2020. https://peacemaker.un.org/sites/peacemaker.un.org/files/IL%20SY_740531_Separation%20of%20Forces%20between%20Israel%20and%20Syria.pdf.

UN. UN Peacekeepers. *Framework for Peace in the Middle East Agreed at Camp David.* June 14, 1979, accessed February 16, 2020. https://peacemaker.un.org/sites/peacemaker.un.org/files/EG%20IL_780917_Framework%20for%20peace%20in%20the%20MiddleEast%20agreed%20at%20Camp%20David.pdf.

UN. *United Nations Convention on the Law of the Sea.* December 12, 1982, accessed February 20, 2020. http://www.un.org/depts/los/convention_agreements/texts/unclos/unclos_e.pdf.

UN. UN Peacemakers. *Declaration of Principles on Interim Self-Government Arrangements (Oslo Accords).* October 11, 1993, accessed February 20, 2020. https://peacemaker.un.org/sites/peacemaker.un.org/files/IL%20PS_930913_DeclarationPrinciplesnterimSelf-Government%28Oslo%20Accords%29.pdf.

UN. UN Peacemakers. *Israeli-Palestinian Interim Agreement on the West Bank and the Gaza Strip (Oslo II).* September 28, 1995, accessed February 20, 2020. https://peacemaker.un.org/israelopt-osloII95.

UN. UN Peacemakers. *Protocol Concerning the Redeployment in Hebron.* September 28, 1995, accessed February 20, 2020. https://peacemaker.un.org/israelopt-redeploymenthebron97.

UN. UN ICTY. *Report on the Audiovisual Coverage of the ICTY's Proceedings Finds that Cameras Contribute to a Proper Administration of Justice.* The Hague. April 19, 2000, accessed March 24, 2014. http://www.icty.org/sid/7869.

UN. *Security Council Report, Lebanon/Israel (UNIFIL) January 2006 Monthly Forecast.* December 22, 2005, accessed February 18, 2020. https://www.securitycouncilreport.org/monthly-forecast/2006-01/lookup_c_glkwlemtisg_b_1313235.php.

UN. *Report of the Secretary-General's Panel of Inquiry on the May 31, 2010 Flotilla Incident.* 2011, accessed April 9, 2020. https://graphics8.nytimes.com/packages/pdf/world/Palmer-Committee-Final-report.pdf.

UN. UN Human Rights Council. *Report of the International Fact-Finding Mission to Investigate Violations of International Law, Including International Humanitarian and Human Rights Law, Resulting from the Israeli Attacks on the Flotilla of Ships Carrying Humanitarian Assistance.* September 2010, accessed October 12, 2012. http://www2.ohchr.org/english/bodies/hrcouncil/docs/15session/A.HRC.15.21_en.PDF.

UN. Office for the Coordination of Humanitarian Affairs Occupied Palestinian Territory. *Barrier Update, Special Focus.* July 2011, accessed February 16, 2020. https://www.ochaopt.org/sites/default/files/ocha_opt_barrier_update_july_2011_english.pdf.

UN. General Assembly GA/11317. "General Assembly Votes Overwhelmingly to Accord Palestine 'Non-Member Observer State' Status in United Nations." November 29, 2012, accessed August 2, 2020. https://www.un.org/press/en/2012/ga11317.doc.htm.

UN. UN Development Program [UNDP]. *Istanbul Declaration on Transparency in the Judicial Process.* November 2013, accessed March 6, 2013. http://www.ge.undp.org/content/dam/turkey/docs/demgovdoc/%C4%B0stanbul%20Declaration.pdf.

UN. UN Development Program [UNDP]. *A Declaration on Judicial Transparency Endorsed by Asian Countries in Istanbul.* November 27, 2013, accessed April 18, 2020. https://www.tr.undp.org/content/turkey/en/home/presscenter/pressreleases/2013/11/27/a-declaration-on-judicial-transparency-endorsed-by-asian-countries-in-istanbul.html.

UN. UN ICTY. Courtroom Technology. 2014, accessed September 2, 2014. http://www.icty.org/sid/167.

UN. UNRW. "In Figures." 2017, accessed April 2, 2020. https://www.unrwa.org/sites/default/files/content/resources/unrwa_in_figures_2017_english.pdf.

UN. "Unanimously Adopting Resolution 2433, Security Council Extends Mandate of United Nations Force in Lebanon, Calls on Government to Increase Naval Capacity." August 30, 2018, accessed February 16, 2020. https://www.un.org/press/en/2018/sc13481.doc.htm.

UN. General Assembly. *Fifth Committee.* August 26, 2019, accessed February 16, 2020. https://digitallibrary.un.org/record/3833933?ln=en#record-files-collapse-header.

UN. UNRWA. "Where We Work." 2020, accessed September 24, 2020. https://www.unrwa.org/where-we-work.

UPI. "EU Has Juridical Concerns with Turkey." *UPI.com.* January 15, 2014, accessed April 4, 2014. http://www.upi.com/Top_News/Special/2014/01/15/EU-has-judicial-concerns-with-Turkey/UPI-34421389798136.

US. United States of America, AE195 (AAA). "Notice of Defense Motion to Compel Production of Communications between Government and Filmmakers of Zero Dark Thirty." July 31, 2013, accessed June 11, 2020. https://www.mc.mil/Portals/0/pdfs/KSM2/KSM%20II%20(AE195(AAA))_Part1.pdf.

Usher, Graham. "The Democratic Resistance: Hamas, Fatah, and the Palestinian Elections." *Journal of Palestine Studies* 35:3 (2006): 20–36.

Uzun, Alper. "Evidence by Documentation and Its Exceptions under the Code of Civil Procedure." *Erdem & Erdem.* September 2013, accessed September 16, 2020. http://www.erdem-erdem.av.tr/publications/law-post/evidence-by-documentation-and-its-exceptions-under-the-code-of-civil-procedure/.

Van Bynkershoek, Cornelius. *Treatise on the Law of War.* Clark, NJ: The Law Book Exchange, 2008.

Van Dyck, Edward. *Capitulations of the Ottoman Empire since the Year 1150: Part 1.* Washington DC: Government Printing Office, 1881.

Varble, Derek. *The Suez Crisis.* New York: The Rosen Publishing Group, 2008.

Versan, Vakur. "Kemalist Reform of the Turkish Empire and Its Impact." In *Atatürk and the Modernization of Turkey.* Edited by Jacob M. Landau. London: Routledge, 1984: 247–50.

Veterans News Now. "Israel Must Be Held Accountable." March 28, 2014, accessed April 20, 2014. http://www.veteransnewsnow.com/2014/03/28/israel-must-be-held-accountable.

Von Martens, Georg F. *The Law of Nations: Being the Science of National Law, Covenants, Power, etc. Founded Upon the Treaties and Customs of Modern Nations in Europe.* Translated by William Cobbett. 4th ed. London: William Cobbett, 1829.

Walbank, Michael B. *Athenian Proxenies of the Fifth Century B.C.* Toronto: Samuel Stevens, 1978.

Walker, Wyndham L. "Territorial Waters: The Cannon Shot Rule." *Brit. YB Int'l L.* 22 (1945): 210.

Weiss, Philip. "UN: Two Men Killed on *Mavi Marmara* were Holding Cameras when They Were Shot." *Mondoweiss.* September 25, 2010, accessed April 6, 2020. https://mondoweiss.net/2010/09/un-two-men-killed-on-mavi-marmara-were-holding-cameras-when-they-were-shot/.

Weizman, Eyal. *Hollow Land: Israel's Architecture of Occupation.* Brooklyn: Verso Books, 2012.

Weizman, Eyal, Ines Geisler, and Anslem Franke. "Islands': The Geography of Extraterritoriality." 2003. Reprinted in *Extraterritorialities in Occupied Worlds.* Edited by Maayan Amir and Ruti Sela. Santa Barbara, CA: Punctum Books, 2016: 117–122.

Wigmore, John Henry. *Supplement to Treatise on the Anglo-American System of Evidence in Trials at Common Law.* Boston: Little, Brown & Company, 1915.

Williams, Chris A. "Police Surveillance and the Emergence of CCTV in the 1960s." *Crime Prevention and Community Safety* 5:3 (2003): 27–37.

Yaakov, Yifa. "Netanyahu: Syrian Chaos Necessitated My Apology to Turkey." *The Times of Israel.* March 23, 2013, accessed July 17, 2018. https://www.timesofisrael.com/netanyahu-syria-major-factor-in-turkey-normalization-decision/.

Yanarocak, Hay Eytan Cohen. "Turkish—Israeli Reconciliation: The End of 'Precious Loneliness?'" The Moshe Dayan Center. Tel Aviv University. June 26, 2016, accessed September 16, 2020. https://dayan.org/content/turkish-israeli-reconciliation-end-precious-loneliness.

———. "Turkey's Long Month: Agreements to Normalize Relations, Terror, and a Failed Coup." *Turkeyscope* 4:7 (2016), accessed September 16, 2020. https://dayan.org/content/turkeys-long-month-agreements-normalize-relations-terror-and-failed-coup.

Yilmaz, Ihsan. "State, Law, Civil Society and Islam in Contemporary Turkey." *The Muslim World* 95:3 (2005): 385–411.

YNET. "Turkish Court Rejects *Marmara* Victim's Family's Compensation Plea." *YNET News.* December 25, 2013, accessed September 16, 2014. http://www.ynetnews.com/articles/0,7340,L-4469745,00.html.

Zertal, Idith, and Akiva Eldar. *Lords of the Land: The War over Israel's Settlements in the Occupied* Territories, *1967–2007.* Or Yehuda, Israel: Kinneret, Zmora-Bitan, Dvir, 2004.

Zion, Ilan. "Israel Digs Deep to Thwart Tunnel Threat from Gaza Strip." *AP.* January 18, 2018, accessed January 24, 2018. https://apnews.com/322f1f35210d47bfa78647fa5f4a226d.

Index

www.ingramcontent.com/pod-product-compliance
Lightning Source LLC
Chambersburg PA
CBHW050439280326
41932CB00013BA/2176